Raising Timber

Joy McCalister

S & H Publishing, Inc.
P. O. Box 456
Purcellville, VA 20134
www.sandhpublishing.com

Publisher's Note: This is a work of fiction. Names, characters, places, and incidents are a product of the author's imagination. Locales and public names are sometimes used for atmospheric purposes. Any resemblance to actual people, living or dead, or to businesses, companies, events, institutions, or locales is completely coincidental.

Ordering Information:
Quantity discounts are available. For details, contact the "Special Sales Department" at the address above or email sales@sandhpublishing.com.

Raising Timber/Joy McCalister
ISBN 978-1-63320-040-1 Print Edition
ISBN 978-1-63320-041-8 Ebook Edition

The Beginning

THE BOY, TIMBER

Mothers always want to tell the story. And they usually get to, just because they say so. But the boy's story is not the same as his mother's. He was born a kitten and was once an Indian. He might have been a fireman, too, but he wasn't sure anymore. He was thrown away because he had a broken face. Once, when he was bigger, and thunder and lightning shook the cabin so that the windows rattled like angry pots and pans, the boy crawled up the ladder to his parents' loft. He wasn't afraid in the way his mother thought as she tucked him back in his own blankets, safe and sound. The next morning, she promised, the sky would be clear blue. But he wasn't scared of the storm, he was simply watching and waiting. What would it bring, this power unleashed? What would it bring to the world?

LAINEY

A cold drizzle fell the day I first held my son. It had the feel of one of those Rocky Mountain late spring storms that would end in a world coated with ice. Beautiful but terrifying—a prophecy of motherhood. We filed behind the case worker into a small cubicle. The baby was facing the window and the sleety mess beyond. Then he turned toward us, his tiny chin and recently sutured lips making the slightest movement toward the window, as if he were pointing, Navajo-style, to the view. This is our son Timber, I thought. My husband squeezed my hand.

Speaking to the foster mom, on whose lap the baby sat, the caseworker said, "Margaret, I'd like you to meet Cristian and Elaine Clayson."

"Elena, but Lainey is best," I corrected. Timber's foster mom, an elderly woman with gray-streaked hair in an old-fashioned bun, had dressed the one-year-old like an infant, in a long-legged onesie with a hand-knitted ducky sweater. Timber looked at us sideways as we took in his gangly arms and legs and spray of shiny black hair. His breath moved ragged through his open mouth. Obscene stitches poked out beneath his nose and the skin looked bruised and sore where his cleft lip had recently been joined.

"Come here and let's see you, you goofy little thing," Cristian joked as he strode across the space and swept the baby from the old woman's lap. The case worker dropped her folder. Cristian was going to blow this, I thought. Goofy? What was he thinking?

"Careful of the stitches," snapped the case worker, but Cristian was already cradling the back of Timber's neck and gently tracing the scabs along his surgery scars. The baby's eyes were riveted on Cristian's. I stood rooted, fascinated. This was the moment. If I were a normal woman I would heave and push and they'd put a slimy baby in my arms and I'd love it. Forever.

But Timber wasn't some tiny newborn. He was long and lanky, and he really did look goofy with black X's over his mouth and three crooked teeth where two should be. His eyes shone black as he turned to stare deep inside me. I wanted to kiss his cheek just to taste the color of his skin.

Beside me, the case worker was talking nervously about the surgery scheduled for the following month, and the probable need for at least two more cosmetic surgeries to remove and repair the remaining evidence of his birth defect. "They think the hearing in his left ear may be compromised," she was saying, "but until he's a little older nothing is certain." We'd heard all of this before, of course, had studied pictures of Timber in the department's "available for adoption" album for months now, waiting for this moment.

"Here you go," someone said, and then I was holding my son. His hand came up around my neck and his fingers opened and closed on my hair and he laid his head against my chest and, I swear, he sighed. Without realizing it I had turned my back on everyone in the room, and we stood there, Timber and I, holding each other in front of that depressingly drizzly windowpane. Something washed over me, and the scars of my son and myself were forever joined and made beautiful—I was not just any mother but this precious boy's mother. My heart cracked open with the effort of delivery and I wept.

Cristian gathered up Timber's diapers and clothing and discussed a transition schedule for ultimate bonding. Then we left the room, the building, the city, and the foster mom our son had known almost since birth. As Cristian wove his way carefully up the slick mountain canyon road, the radio broke into our peace with more details of a deadly shooting at the Air Force Academy. We'd heard first reports just as we arrived at the county building. I felt selfish but clicked the radio off anyway. This was our first day as a family, and I refused to share it with someone else's tragedy. There were plenty of sad stories to go around; we had our own. What we were looking for now was salvation. Timber was here to make us whole, a real family. Sloppy wet flakes accompanied us all the way home to the little cabin below the cliff.

Chapter One

"Mommy. Guess what I see? Is a bird what's all dry up!" My son Timber bursts through the front door with his joyous news. Midway across the room he halts for a second, shaking his hands while muddy slush drips on the aspen-colored carpet, waiting for his brain to make sense of my screamed "Take off your filthy boots!" Timber's connections are a little slow sometimes, especially when he's putting thoughts into words, or in this case, words into action. His speech seems to be lagging further and further behind his peers—apparently another little genetic gift to accompany his now invisible cleft lip. Timber cocks his head and gives me a sideways grin.

It is too late for the boot warning, but I've recovered enough for a lecture. I am the one, after all, who always has to clean everything up. The least these males could do is acknowledge their sins. "Timber James Clayson, look at that mess. You just tracked mud everywhere and you're still dripping."

"Uh," he says, looking down, "Whose dog dripper-slobbered?"

The boots' tread shows distinct patterns of zigs and zags, which Timber says look just like car tracks. He smiles.

"Mud drubble no everywhere, Mommy, I no go in bathroom." Or up the ladder to my loft, I think, glancing across our one-room cabin.

The kitchen is crammed along the back wall, marked off from the living space by the back of our old leather couch butted up against a homemade butcher-block topped island bar that serves as our dining table. Timber's "room" is a fold-down Murphy bed and red-painted dresser and bookshelf on the side opposite the walled-off bathroom.

I continue to point, one hand on my hip. "Timber, say, 'I didn't go into the bathroom.' And at least go stand on the tile at the door. It's really hard to get this muck out of the carpet."

"Did go dribble muck?" Head tilted, eyebrows raised. I should be unable to resist his charms. "Timber. Now. Get off the carpet." Two long strides put me at his side.

"Ahh—'cause I stupid. You no love me."

Just barely six years old, and he has my buttons completely named and numbered. I am carrying his wriggling form back to the door when he shoots out that last comment, and I want to throw him the rest of the way. Or throw myself. He's been playing the "stupid" card for a few months now, and it always has the desired effect. I forget the issue at hand and spend several fruitless minutes trying to convince him of his innate brilliancy. This you-don't-love-me thing is new. It is a big, shiny, red disaster button in the middle of my heart and it hurts.

"Timber," I cry. I don't even know how to begin to address the issue. Let's just pretend it didn't happen. True to form, five minutes later, with his dirty boots off and a cup of his grandma's Mexican hot chocolate in hand, he is happily chattering about the animal tracks he'd been following in the sloggy yard.

I tell him he probably has Native American ancestors and they probably gave him the genes for that. He's confused. Didn't we buy these hand-me-down Levis at the thrift store?

We don't actually know if Timber is Native American, Latino, or what, although with straight jet-black hair, eyes so dark you can't see pupils, and what I call "cinnamon bear" skin, Timber looks Indian. He was abandoned on the steps of a fire station in southern Colorado a couple hour's drive from several different reservations and an armful of scattered towns. There's a law that makes it illegal for the authorities to prosecute mothers who take their babies to police or fire stations, but the idea is that the mom goes inside and provides a little basic information and makes sure the child is taken in. Timber's birth mother didn't do that. She did, however, wrap the three-day-old infant in a fashionable and expensive Tall Timber ski jacket and plant a lipstick kiss on his forehead.

I know this, as does everyone in Colorado who saw his image on the nightly news that day. Here was a tiny brown baby with a soft tuft of straight black hair sticking up in a Mohawk and that haunting space above his tongue, mewling like a kitten while a firefighter filmed a buddy picking him up out of the box. They'd been up the street trying to catch what had looked to them like a funnel cloud and never saw the woman or girl on the station steps. So maybe she was watching carefully the whole time. I tell Timber she was. I'm already crafting a mythical history of sorts, little details that can grow in his memory to fill in the hole of who he is. The not-quite-a-tornado is a big part of the story I'm formulating. Surely the mother knew he'd be safe in the station. Someone wanted this baby to make it.

We didn't meet Timber until a year after that; five years ago last week, in fact. We had to go through the foster/adopt program and the long process of qualification just for Timber. We knew the second we saw the news footage, that we had to have that child. Even though he was abandoned, it took months for him to become free for adoption. We weren't the only contenders, either, but our ethnicity actually played in our favor for once. My mother is Mexican and my father is a typical American mutt. My man, Cristian, boasts Louisiana-Cajun skin glistening with grayish undertones in what I call Bayou Mud. Anyway, we're about as "mixed" as you get up here in the mountains, an ideal choice for a baby whose genetic makeup could include anything. Timber was first placed in a Navajo foster home, where he remained until we got him. The adoption was finalized months later.

Timber looks at his reflection in the big window beside the table. Beyond, the sky is darkening and beginning to produce something like snow. Springtime in the Rockies. He looks at me sweetly. "Sorry, Mommy. Sorry for say stupid. And you no love me."

"Oh, Timber," I cry, standing behind his chair and cradling his head against my chest. How did I ever think I could handle this mother thing? "It hurt so badly, honey. Please don't do it again. I do love you."

"I love you too, Mommy..." A pause; I hold my breath...

"Drubble-flubber."

If he keeps this up he's going to give himself that disease where people can't stop screaming cuss words—Tourette's Syndrome, or something.

We hear the sound of stones crunching in the dirt driveway, amplified in the cold. Cristian. After all these years together, his approach still makes my heart flip. Even when I'm mad or bored, that man moves me.

Like his son, he bursts through the door without removing his trademark cowboy boots. He dips his head forward in a kind of mock bow, removing his other trademark, a black Stetson. Only ten years out of the bayou, and the chameleon acts like a lifelong mountain man. Sometimes I think it's a character flaw of his—adapting too quickly. It makes me nervous. I wonder if I'll ever know who he is, really and truly, beneath the act. I know the roots, of course.

I blame his sweet but flaky mother's not so stable childrearing. I never met her but heard all about her from her daughter Vanji. Cristian's gorgeous little sister is my best friend. We were assigned as roommates our freshman year at Colorado University in Boulder, and I soon learned about Evanjaleen and Cristian's obscenely overweight mother, Honey. One late night, studying for one of those 'know yourself by digging up the ugly past' kind of Psych 101 assignments, Vanji and I swapped stories over a huge bowl of Halloween-colored M&Ms. Day-After Clearance at Walgreens. Vanji told me about the parade of losers her mother had taken in throughout the years as she grew larger and larger. Had Honey prostituted herself, I wondered? But Vanji said no. Sadly, she'd believed the fast-talking "gospel" men who knocked her up and occasionally sent money. Her kids' names were badges of honor.

Vanji is good at voices, and though I never met Honey I could picture her, swinging jowls and all, as Vanji intoned, "Don't answer to Chris, baby, you ain't no Saint Christopher. You is Christ-SHUN, chile' of Jesus."

The power had stopped with Evanjaleen, who declared herself Vanji as soon as she could talk and set the spelling as soon as she could write. I don't even know who tagged me Lainey instead of Elena, which shows how much more self-aware Vanji is than I am. Vanji was seventeen when their mother died, and had already been running things for years while Honey lay huge and sick on a sagging plaid couch. When Cristian called home from a grueling schedule of kitchen slavery disguised as culinary internships, Vanji and Honey lied about how great things were. And despite working and cleaning and feeding herself and her mother, Vanji made extraordinary grades.

Cristian thinks it was probably some kind of stomach cancer, but Honey, stubborn as my own father, never consented to see a doctor. By the time she died she couldn't have left the couch if she had wanted to. She was a stinking whale of a woman using catheters and tubes that her daughter had to clean. Vanji has issues. Vanji, whose traveling church-soloist father was pasty white, has silky skin the color of café con leche and long brown hair with loopy curls when she relaxes it. She wears her color like a sweater, draped casually over her shoulder. She can slip it on or off immediately, imperceptibly, as a situation warrants. She's as thin as Honey was obese, and Cristian and I worry about eating disorders. Honey called her children "miracle blessings" and they are, to me. Ironically, it gives me hope for Timber. Maybe he'll make it despite my mistakes.

Vanji is madly, hopelessly in love with her nephew and thinks our choice to adopt him was the noblest thing ever done in the history of mankind. Cristian is her lighthouse, her pseudo-parent. I'm her sounding board and confessor. We worry that she'll never let anyone but the three of us into her life.

Vanji and I had already become the deepest friends either of us had known before I met her handsome brother. I dreamed about him for a year before the idea of dating seemed more than the remotest wish on the horizon. Then we dated throughout my junior and senior years and almost moved in together before finally getting legal. Vanji is the one who convinced me to keep rooming with her and then sort of steered us down the aisle.

I glare as Cristian begins to take another step across the cabin in that dirty cowboy boot. "Stop!" screams Timber. "Mommy don't want no dribble on the clean."

"Clean?" asks Cristian, raising an eyebrow and looking at Timber's tracks. It makes me furious. I am too mad too fast. But he notes and stops. Probably the steam coming out of my ears gives him a clue.

"I'm sorry, Lain" he says, picking up a little brush and knocking some of the dirt into a dustpan as he comes over in stocking feet. His socks have holes.

"You should throw those out," I say, softening. The exposed toes wiggle up and down.

"You should give them a massage. I've been standing and moving on these puppies since 4:30 this morning. You have no idea how cold and hard that cement floor can be, Lainey."

Cristian's boss, Travis, is too cheap to put in new rubber mats, and the old ones disintegrated into chunks of greasy slime a couple of months ago. Even after one of the teenage waiters fell and badly cut her lip, all he'd consent to do was throw out the old mats. Foot and leg problems are common complaints of aging chefs. I don't want Cristian to become crippled by his career. It's ludicrous really. It's not like he's a sports star who's making enough to live off once the old knee goes out or something. He's a cook, for crying out loud.

9

"Threaten the idiot, Cristian. The only reason anyone eats in that greasy spoon is because you are there. Travis knows it. Come on, you know China Flower would love to have you."

"Who a Indiot, Mom? Is him like me?"

"No, not 'Indian,' 'idiot.' And don't repeat that." I give Cristian a cup of chocolate and plop beside him on the cracked leather couch with a cup of my own. Timber swivels back around to the table, repeating softly: idiot, idiot.

"You did it now, Lainey." Cristian throws his leg across my lap. His calf muscles are tight, balled up. Those stupid cowboy boots don't help, but I don't dare go there. There's something fragile about my Cajun-mountain-cowboy chef and I'm not out for a fight. I'm on his side.

The storm outside has turned from almost snow back to rain, and thunder begins to rumble as large drops pelt the tin roof far above our heads. The syncopated rhythm of the rain indicates that Cristian made it home just in time. I rub the greasy, stinky sock, sliding my fingers gently over the exposed toes. Yuck. Cristian moans a little and leans back suggestively so I stop. Timber is right behind us, for crying out loud. I make a move to get up and wash my hands, when Cristian puts his hand on my arm to stop me.

"Lainey, there's something I want to talk about. You know the old Whippoorwill?" Of course I do; it's the abandoned restaurant/lodge along the highway. A kitchen fire some twenty years ago shut things down, and the owner never reopened. People have been trying to buy the property for years, but the owner lives in California and isn't interested. Or at least that's the rumor.

"Turns out it's part of the Thorndove estate, and Billy's dad is looking to offload. You know how Billy wants to set up the jeep tours thing? His dad promised him start-up money if they sell the Whip. They've kept quiet all this time while people wondered about the place, but it was the grandfather's all along. Didn't want anyone to know how much property he owned, I think. It's a lot more than

I knew about anyway." Cristian leans onto me and rests his head on my lap. He looks up like a little nursing baby and says, "Billy came to talk to me today, Lainey. He wants us to think about it. Our credit is good and Bill Senior will even co-sign if needed. But…it's huge, Lainey. It would take you and me both, full-time plus, and it might be a couple years before it turns into real money. We can meet, there, this Thursday, if you want…"

Cristian stops and closes his eyes. A restaurant of our own. Cristian is a great chef, but he's always worked for jerks, like his present boss, Travis, the Lone-Star wonder boy. Travis tells him to use less of the good stuff on his favorite dishes, squelches his creativity, and drowns the kitchen in clouds of cigarette smoke, so that delicate flavors are destroyed before they even reach the customers' palates. Cristian's cooking brings people from miles away, but an increase in restaurant revenue has never yet translated into a raise.

I look around our cabin at the cozy furnishings. I'm content, really, even though a separate bedroom, with a locking door, would be really nice. We could give Timber the loft. Other than that, there's no big thing I've been wanting that we can't afford. The Liberty is still in good shape with the lease paid off last year, and Timber takes the bus to the public school down the road. We talk off and on of replacing the ancient Tercel that Cristian takes when our schedules don't mesh, but it's a reliable rusted tank that will never completely die. So what if our economic stability means mortgage debt and no real assets?

"It's a good time to take a risk," I say, my mind already made up. Like a child who just made his birthday wish, Cristian opens his eyes.

"I want stainless steel," he laughs, "Fridge, freezer, stoves—the whole shebang."

"No—too cold and too expensive. What about retro enamel? Harvest orange, avocado, that weird brown stuff and 50s red. Mix and match the old stuff; garage sales, flea markets. If the kitchen were open to view, the whole thing could be like a showroom…"

"Antique-chic. Yes. That's it." Cristian leaps from the couch tossing a pillow in my direction. In the kitchen he spins Timber's barstool around and locks into his gaze. "Want to start a restaurant, kid?" Timber thinks. He reaches onto an imaginary plate and takes up an imaginary strand of spaghetti, lifting it carefully to his father's lips. Cristian's eyes cross and he sticks his tongue out.

"Okay, Daddy. But I getta open the 'frigerator if I gonna be cook, okay?" He's banned because of a lack of shutting; opening is no problem for him. Timber's head is cocked again, waiting for his dad's response.

Cristian tips Timber's chin up and smiles into his eyes. "Got it. Now go open that refrigerator and get me three eggs. You're cooking tonight. We're having poblano crepes."

There's a notebook on the floor, and I look around for a writing utensil. Three eggs don't balance well one on top of the other, but I am barely aware of the clean-up going on in front of me as I begin scratching ideas at the kitchen counter. Cristian is calm and doesn't even react to Timber's "broke yolk smoky folk" singsong.

We've got to see the inside of the Whippoorwill. How can I begin thinking about the layout when I don't even know the infrastructure? And yet I have a million ideas.

"Cristian. What's the theme? I mean, are you going Cajun or cowboy or French...?"

"Baby," he says in a John Wayne voice, "Tonight I'm going Mexican-American, sweet and spicy."

Chapter Two

Rivulets streak the car windows while I wait in the kindergarten carpool pick-up line. Winter's snow has disappeared even beneath the densest trees after three days of rain. I'm not especially cold, but being wet doesn't put me in a great frame of mind. Life hangs suspended and unreal, as even the excitement of the potential restaurant is in a waiting stage until tomorrow's meeting with Billy and his father.

Blah. My body, in a premenstrual ache, echoes the dreariness. Teachers in rain slickers and black umbrellas run back and forth from the temp building to the next waiting car with tiny kids whose rubber boots come up to their armpits. My bootless son has squeezed past the aide in the doorway and hangs backward under the run-off of the roof gutter, mouth open, eyes shut. He's going to drown himself. If I don't kill him first. I pull the grocery bag with an extra outfit from under the passenger seat and toss it back next to where Timber will sit beside his floppy, stuffed alter-ego, Mad Rabbit. Or maybe today it's Happy Rabbit. Nah, more like Drowned-Rat Rabbit.

It doesn't rain often in Bailey. We have more than 300 days of sunshine, and when it does rain it is almost always a short shower. None of that monsoon hurricane stuff Cristian grew up with. But we do get thunderstorms, great bursting crashes of pure electricity that thrill and terrify. Growing up in Harris Park, deep into the no-man's land of the higher mountains, I would stand at the window and watch the storms. My big sister and three little brothers would beg me to shut the curtains, and I would oblige, my own body squeezed against the pane, praying for a bolt to crash into the neigh-

13

bor's ugly ponderosa. Without the tree, I reasoned, I could see farther down the valley of cardboard-cutout blue mountains.

The teacher brings Timber, sweetly shepherding him in front of her all the way to the car. I'd be yanking him along, like I did when I dropped him off, late since he missed the bus this morning. Timber's teacher always does the right thing. She says things the way child psychologists tell normal people to talk. Nothing is ever negative, and the child is so won over by the sheer reason of what you say that you don't even have to raise your voice. She makes me sick, actually. It's not her fault, of course; it's mine. I am sick over the guilt of my failures as a mother, which mount up hourly along with all my other imperfections, and sometimes I think I might drown in it all. Should I try the rainspout?

We were out of milk this morning because I didn't go shopping yesterday. Cristian choked when I suggested he use powdered milk, and Timber pounded his bowl yelling "Horsey oats. Horsey oats." Of course, we didn't have any packets, either, so I tried to cook some the old fashioned way, on the stove with brown sugar. My son did not approve. Mushy gross, he said, not horsey oats. At least it rhymed. He was able to keep that chant going for four minutes straight. I timed it. One of my biggest failures in life is trying to cook three meals a day. Even when I think I do an okay job, I'm aware that the guys are merely choking it down because they're hungry. What was I thinking, marrying a chef? When he cooks it's memorable. I shower him with well-deserved compliments. Thing is, he cooks all day for other people and feeding the Clayson clan, well, at least Timber and me, has become my responsibility.

"Thank you," I say to the teacher, taking the paper from her hand. It's a form that must be filled out and returned tomorrow. The way things are going, I'll probably forget that, too. Or screw it up. I have been trying to sew all afternoon. My bedroom window's curtain ripped, and I thought I'd just borrow my mother's old Singer and sew a straight line and have a new hem. First mistake, I folded it up backwards. Wrong-side up. Stupid. And as if that weren't enough, when I tried to rip the seam the whole thing ripped off. Sun-rotted, I guess. So I finally attached some really ugly fringe to the bottom, to make it long enough to cover the window. But it isn't. And it's crooked. If we had internet like the rest of the world I could post an award-winning Pinterest Fail. I can do nothing right.

"Today we maked masks, and mine most stupid. I no can do nothing and Brian and Taylor laugh at me and call me baby. I hate school and I never go back. Never."

"'Today we made masks,' Timber, and sometimes we have to do stuff we don't like. Know what?" I glance in the rear view mirror but he's banging his forehead against the window and doesn't see me. "Today I have messed up everything I've tried to do."

"Nah, you is a growed up and you know all the things. 'Cept oatmeal. Oatmeal you maked gross. Mushy mashy gross. And Rabbit is hungry still." He accentuates hungry with a hard kick to my seat back.

I grit my teeth. I hate it when he kicks my car seat. "I am a grownup, Timber. And, no, I don't know everything. So let's go to Sonic and eat and then get groceries."

"No, I wanna go Crow Barre and see Daddy. Daddy make me cheesy macaronis." Timber is staring at me now, at my reflection in the rain-smeared window. In the rearview mirror his dark eyes are shining coals. Is it another failure that I don't want to go to Cristian's restaurant and see the surprised expression? As if I couldn't come up with anything to pass the time and had to drag our son to bother him at work. Okay, I know he wouldn't really think that, but his boss would. Travis is always looking for an excuse to make an ugly comment.

"Sorry, can't do that today, because we have to get groceries. You want milk and oatmeal packs, right? And some carrots for a snack at school tomorrow?" And new curtains, I think. But today isn't the time for a Denver run. Maybe I'll ask Cristian about that later. He's the one who does the budget now, after I messed up a couple car payments our first year of marriage. He handles the money, vacuums and irons because I am bad at all that, and of course, does the good cooking. What do I do? Burn oatmeal and destroy curtains.

THE BOY

If his mother didn't stop yelling at him the boy was going to break something. Maybe Rabbit, although he knew he would be sorry if he actually hurt his favorite friend. Everyone always yelled at the boy. "I'm not yelling," they would yell, "my voice is quiet…" But they would have an angry face which meant they were yelling. The world was too loud, usually. Too loud and too bright. All the boy wanted right now was to feel warm, like a little baby. Quiet and calm and soft. He held Rabbit that way for a second, but he didn't want his mother to see and forget he was angry.

The boy kind of liked the rain even though it wasn't warm, and he let himself feel just a little happy about the gray sky blocking the sunshine that sometimes hurt his eyes. Anyway, he really did like the water pouring over his face and onto his head, which was itching because this morning he put some of his daddy's whisker stuff on just to see, which no one knew about except himself. It was his very own secret, like the dead bird that he had just hidden under the rock on the coldish side of the house so that he could pull it out to look at when they were not watching.

Everyone hated the boy. It was true. The boy was stupid and ugly, because he had a little ziggy line under his nose. Also he couldn't always tell what words were coming into his head unless he had the right ear looking at them because not much sound came into the one that felt always squishy. This was another secret, though, that the boy didn't share with anyone. No one else knew about his squishy ear, and he could play his own game, sometimes, where he would plug the other one and be in a place where no one was yelling at him. Except usually they yelled more until finally someone was looking in his face and holding his hands, and he had to let the words go slipping down into both ears.

The boy glanced sideways at the blurry window version of his mother but she wasn't paying attention. He stuck his lip out farther and pushed his eyebrows together like a rap star. She still didn't notice. She was mad at the boy, so she was ignoring him. He was mad too so he kicked the seat again. She didn't yell out loud with her mouth and tongue but her fingers yelled, white and stretched on the steering wheel like they were squeezing the boy's arm. Or maybe his neck.

Today was another Worst Day of His Life. Everything started when he woke up and she made him put a glob of slime in his mouth and she called it oatmeal but it was definitely NOT horsey oats like it should be and he gagged and spit it and some got all the way onto the refrigerator and he could not Get Up and Wipe it Off because he was so tired and hungry. His arm still hurt from the yanking pushing here's the rag that he dropped limp and didn't even do it.

Happy Rabbit was how he felt when it didn't matter what word was the right one or whether you made a lot of noise when you stepped on something that crunched. Like walking through the forest with his father. That was a good time. But wearing the scratchy sweater because the temp room was cold, they said, and getting in trouble for stepping on a Styrofoam cup, even though stepping on Styrofoam cups made the best sound, and having that dandelion-haired girl stick her tongue out when you accidentally knocked over her bottle of glue—these were parts of a Worst Day Ever.

LAINEY

Timber bangs his head on the window repeating something like "macaronis." I feel so low I want to bang my head too. I turn on the radio. It's set to a church station, because that's the only thing I've found without cussing these days and so far Timber hasn't learned that lovely skill.

It's not even music. It's some woman talking, and just as I reach to shut it off she says, "I can do nothing. I burn water, yet still I am fat. I yell at my kids but they still do not behave. Does anyone hear what I am saying?" Canned laughter indicates no. "So how come the world keeps telling me to build up my self-confidence and learn to say 'no' and treat myself like numero uno? I mean, get real. I'm a royal loser."

Timber has stopped banging and listens, like me. He holds Hungry Rabbit by the ears, which he has twisted together. Sore Rabbit, I think.

"Roller Rabbit." declares Timber. "Loser me, loser you."

"Maybe that's the key, Sister. 'Royal.' As daughters of the king we are royal and we are losers. Whosoever desires to keep her life must lose it. God doesn't help she who helps herself, darling, God helps she who hits rock bottom and cries out for help from the slimy pit. If you've got it all together I guess you don't need help anyway. Jesus said that he did not come to save the healthy but the sick. I am not afraid to admit it. I need help. I'm sick." More canned laughter.

"She sick." Timber gags and then, looking up, unfastens his seatbelt.

"She is sick, Timber. Don't undo that until we stop. How long do I have to keep telling you?" Static indicates that I've lost the radio station, so I just push the dial off while we wind up the drive and into the Safeway parking lot. Now I'm not some fanatical like the radio woman, but I guess I do, basically, believe that someone out there is in charge. So, God, where are you? Any chance I could get a little help?

I put the jeep in park and realize that Timber is finally struggling to pull on his dry shirt now, just when I am ready to go in. It's not as though he couldn't have done that during the twenty-minute drive. Take a breath. I step out into the silvery after-rain of a clearing sky. The keys fall from my hand and I lean over…

… but in that instant a light pole in front of me grabs my attention. My neck snaps up like a magnet flipping to its polarized side. And…POW.

Chapter Three

THE BOY

The boy was right about the Worst Day Ever. He knew he was, because his mother had her mouth corners turned down in that yelling way. Instead of asking about all the very bad things that had happened to the boy, she had sighed and told him to shut up by ignoring him and telling her own dumb story and listening to the radio. He was completely wet and frozen and then he saw the folded extra shirt at the other end of the bench seat. He slapped it open just to be sure she hadn't brought that long sleeve green shirt he hated but it was the dinosaur one. The wet shirt stuck to his skin and it was hard to peel it off. The boy wanted to cry but he didn't want her to say Don't Be a Baby so he fussed and twisted and kicked until it finally came off. The dry dinosaur shirt, which was not his favorite and he would only wear until he got home and could get a different one, went over his head easy because it was stretched out in the armpits on account of him pulling his knees up high inside some-times. The boy's head popped out the top and he glanced at his mother again with a huge sigh of his own, wondering if she noticed his effort.

But his mother was not frowning now. She was looking up and so was the boy, and he saw the big light on the top of the tall pole in front of their car explode. It just blew up. There was a sound so loud you couldn't even hear it. Suddenly, for absolutely no reason, pieces of glass flew out in a billion directions and then fell like snow, like slow motion in a movie that the boy wasn't supposed to see and got yelled at for sneaking out behind

20

the couch just because he fell asleep and forgot to go back to bed before they noticed. Beautiful little snowflakes of glass rained softly down and then the boy looked at her again and she was falling, also in slow motion. The pieces of light flew in and surrounded her body in a kind of halo. The light was special. It was full of super powers. The boy knew this because he had seen comic book pictures of super powers, and this was exactly the same. The boy wanted to reach out and grab some for himself but he was too scared. He worried the lights might just fly away or make his mother disappear into the silver sky without him but she stayed in one place, frozen with her face turned up into the glittering lights. After a long time the boy noticed that her hair was sticking out straight all over and something like a scream was also falling, gently, through the air. He reached his hand to his open mouth and covered it, but not before a tiny spark of power fluttered inside.

LAINEY

White. Something brilliant. Hot and cold. The silver sky is connected to the pole. Pieces of molded glass fall. I'm frozen; can't... my fingers are stuck in the act of curling around my keys. Everything implodes in a release of earth-bound light. White. Cold. Silence.

"Mommy," Timber is out of the car now, and he's crying. Eyes huge. I can't breathe. Something's wrong with my chest. Can't...I'm choking. I'm seven again, fallen from my bike, and the wind is knocked out of me. I have to inhale or die. Breathe, breathe now. Gasp. It hurts. Air burns my lungs and I'm saved. Someone is sobbing. Did the car door get shut on me? Car alarms sound all around. Or is it me? It is—I am crying, weeping uncontrollably, even though

I think I am okay. I can't breathe right. And my heart is jumping all over. That's the weight I feel, it's my heartbeat that won't sit still.

"Get her somewhere dry: the car. Lay her in the backseat." I'm here. They talk over my head like I'm some kind of coma patient. But words don't form.

"Okay, she's breathing now, let's get her up."

"Yeah, they've been called." Hands under my arms, lifting me. I straighten up and someone says just relax. An old lady is patting my head, very motherly. I've seen her before, in a grocery line, maybe. A guy in a Broncos cap is holding my shopping list and it looks a little soggy.

"Is this what you were after?" he asks. I blink. "I'll be right back, Celia," he says to the white-haired woman who is now gently massaging my shoulder. She nods, "Better not get perishables. Who knows when she'll get home." A whining comes into focus. Siren. "Celia" laughs.

"Must be someone young behind the wheel, because the rescue station is just on the other side of the highway. It's got to be someone still excited about using a siren."

A moment later an ambulance slides in the space beside us, crunching a piece of the broken globe.

"Thomping ethplodeth," I lisp, baby-talking. My tongue is thick and my mind is mush. The old lady hushes me and calls to the ambulance guy.

"Hey, kiddo." Celia must know everyone.

A lanky kid who doesn't look old enough to drive, let alone drive an ambulance, jumps out with a CB stuck to his face and barely constrained glee. Great. It's the rent-a-cop version of mountain care. The kind of guy who begged for a scanner on his 13th birthday. But despite the obvious thrill he gets from a "real emergency situation," the kid seems to know what he's doing. He checks my heart rate, listens to my still-burning lungs, and writes in a small notebook. He observes my eyes, looks at the key-shaped burn on my right palm, and asks a bunch of questions I can't answer. He wants to know if "1TheMan" on the top of my contact list of my cell phone, which he holds in his hand, is someone who should be called. I nod yes and someone takes the phone away. "No coverage," and the phone is put back on the seat beside me.

"You're really lucky, you know. Lots of people die from light= ning strikes. Once when I was in school, this guy was four=wheeling, and dude, he was hit straight-on. Burned a circle into the back of his head where the bolt got him. Blew his nose ring into the hood of the Landcruiser. They found this glob of molten metal imbedded there, did tests. Wal-lah—silver. Dude even lived through it. Changed his life. My brother said he never touched another…"

"Timber." My voice is back, but where's my son? This EMT poster boy is trying to push me back down, but the old lady named Celia understands. "I'll find him, honey. Your little boy, right?"

"Timber? That's a crazy name. My aunt, she named her dog Kat. With a K, right? But who knows there's a K when you just hear the word? There she was, yelling out the door every day, 'Cat, come in,' and people all shaking their heads because, you know, cats don't come when you call."

Celia doesn't hear the driver, because she's at the back of the ambulance and sure enough, she has my son. Why would he think he could just climb into an ambulance? Later, I'll kill him. The ambu= lance is parked sideways, and the side is solid. I stare at the white metal sheeting. I cannot hear them or see anything anymore, but I just know they are there and that everything is fine. It's like a blanket over my shoulders and the whisper of a father: it's okay. At the same time the voice of the over-eager first responder kind of dissolves into silence.

The lanky kid shines a light in my eyes again and I blink him away. Finally I realize he is repeating something about who is the president. I answer with a political joke and he laughs. "Well, me neither, but here we are." I have dialed Cristian's number and am trying to explain to him what happened but can't get the words out straight. I hand the phone over and hear that the incident knocked the heck out of her but she's gonna be fine, Sir, and that I should be good to drive home. The phone goes back to my ear and I choke out a yes, of course and I love you too before hitting the right button.

"Here he is," says Celia from just over the young man's shoulder. Timber is holding her hand and kind of flopping against her leg. It's too bad he's so shy. He'd be a kidnapper's dream, until they got tired of his constant chatter. Celia looks at me curiously. Everything appears outlined. High definition reality. Must be a side-effect from the buzz of the jolt or something.

"Timber?" says the EMT. "Is that really your name?" Timber grins, bobbing his head up and down.

"Cool. I bet people always cover their heads when your parents call you to dinner, huh? I mean, TIM-BER. Like a tree falling, get it?" Timber is just barely six, but I bet he's heard it a hundred times already.

Still, he laughs and straightens his arms, and to everyone's dismay, falls like a tree, straight backward, to the dirty pavement. His head hits hard. The crack resounds like a rifle shot across the parking lot and passersby gasp.

The EMT flies from my side to check Timber's level of consciousness. My son's eyes flutter open and his black pupils move frantically until he finds my face. I reach down to touch his fingers as they reach for me. A wave of dizziness passes as I plop beside him to touch his cheek with my burned hand while the young technician checks his pulse and gingerly touches his neck from the other side. Consequence? When will he think before he acts?

"You're okay, Timmy," I coo. "We are both okay." His black eyes blink and he pushes to sit up beside me, despite the tech's warnings and pleas. Finally he gives up and lets Timber snuggle into my lap.

"He'll probably do that again sometime," I admit. "He has trouble learning from his mistakes." Celia walks around to lean on the car above us. I pat my son's back while the EMT asks more questions and scribbles furiously in his notebook. I have to sign what feels like dozens of forms refusing additional treatment and/or transport to a medical facility. He keeps apologizing, saying he didn't know. Well, duh. Who would? It's strange, sitting in this wet parking lot with people walking by rubbernecking while ambulance lights dance over their shiny cars. What is weirder, my getting struck by lightning or my son intentionally whacking his head on the ground?

Five years of doubts wash over me as I caress the back of my son's neck. I'm not a professional. I'm just an ordinary woman, so why did I ever think I could take on this kid? Am I just making things worse for him? We make eye contact, and I see love and fear and concern mirrored back at me. Deep down, beneath my own fear, I know he's okay.

"Can you fly?" he whispers. It's so quiet I'm unsure of what I heard. Before I can ask him to repeat. he has slid away, eyes on the shiny pieces of glass which stick to his shirtsleeves. I rise slowly and extend a hand to help him the rest of the way up. He refuses, pushing himself up to his knees and then scrambling to stand.

"You must be a wonderful mother." Celia speaks softly, also almost whispering. As she looks out across the parking lot I notice the many crinkles and laugh lines which fill her face. There is something sweet and comfortable in her presence. Timber moves back to me, burrowing into my sweater sleeve as the driver closes up the back of the ambulance.

Timber sniffs, pulling on my sore hand as I try to talk to Celia. "Mommy say no Crow Barre, we come here for to get groceries and hotdogs. But I don't get no hotdog and everything go ka-bang."

"It isn't charity, it is neighbors loving each other. Just relax and accept it." Words accompanying a bag of chili dogs from Sonic and

25

a grocery bag handed over by a man in a baseball cap. He smiles as he drives away.

Timber has eaten an entire hotdog without throwing up and is walking and talking, so after checking his vitals one more time the medic finally climbs back into his ambulance. Timber has folded his hotdog paper inside out and is licking the catsup. He waves at the ambulance through an open window. Thick-skulled, calls the driver. No joke, I think.

Chapter Four

THE BOY

From the back seat the boy watched his mother say goodbye to Celia. Celia wasn't Missus Celia to the boy and just Celia to adults but really truly Celia even to the boy. Celia said so herself when she showed him inside the ambulance truck with a sit-up bed for hurt people. She knew many things and would tell them to the boy if only he knew what to ask. Probably his mother knew the right questions, and maybe the boy would find out things by remembering to be quiet and listen.

Lainey. I'm Lainey Clayson. said the boy's mother, her whole long name to Celia. Celia talking back to her said her friend Elaine was also a Lainey. That funny thing, to be a Lainey, made the boy giggle a little. But his mother said then something new that the boy did not know, that she herself was supposed to be Elena, in her real self, and she said the word Elena like Grandma did, like her tongue was dancing inside a smile. Like it was a Mexico word almost. And then Celia put that Elena word with Grandpa Morse and said, Oh. You are Elena Morse, aren't you? Which was silliest of all since his mother had already just said as clear as day that she was a Lainey Clayson.

And the boy marveled while the women got happy eyes and talked things old gone by that they once knew and how time is fast going but while they were talking on and on he watched the numbers on the dashboard of the Liberty and saw one change from the up-down line into a swan number and then he waited and waited and waited. There was no fast to the time, that was for sure. Slow, slow, nothing, and then finally one day he realized that the number was a new one, the thing like a half a snowman going on walking down the way. And still they talked. But the boy forgot the clock when he looked at his sleeve and saw some magic dust there still. He remembered and looked out the window and saw the glass and accidentally yawned, big and loud, but then thought of the flickering lights and put his hand quick over that open mouth. Oh, said Celia again. That boy must need to get home and rest—but not to sleep, because of the bump, not just yet. They would have breakfast together at the father's restaurant, they said, but it wasn't going to be with the boy because he was always going to school which he hated.

The boy and his mother would have got to ride all the way to the city in the ambulance except that they were not hurt like smashed in a car accident or fallen off an airplane but only ordinary bandage on the forehead hurt. It would have been fun to ride in the ambulance and the boy was sorry that he was not worse hurt, and maybe even a little sorry that his mother wasn't either, even though all that glass fell inside her.

"Buckle up." she said, and he did it right away pronto, because he suspected that she was about to launch the rocket into hyper drive. Magic sparks still floated by and when he leaned to look out the window he could see universes streaking past like in a video game. His mother was laughing and the boy was scared. Maybe she would think it was funny to do something dangerous, and the boy didn't get as much super-power dust as she did, and anyway he didn't know how to use super powers. He realized with a shudder that he might not be strong enough to survive.

For instance, what if she dove underwater for a long time? The boy would certainly drown. He held one hand across his lap, close enough to grab his nose and hold his breath if necessary. Unless he now had underwater fish breathers. How would you know? He touched his neck where gills would probably be and held his breath, practicing. But the rocket ship flew smoothly through the atmosphere. When the boy began to relax he realized that his head was hurting again from where it hit the ground when he was timber-a-tree-falling. He thought about whimpering but before he could make a sound Flash Mom said: Is your head hurting, little man?

She could read his mind. Or, maybe he could speak without words and make her understand. He screwed his eyes tight and tried to think about nothing. Instead it made his head hurt again and he thought, ouch. He saw Flash Mom looking at him with the rearview mirror and he could see red pain. The ship was pulling up right outside their cabin and she was talking about ibuprofens and thinking twice before doing that again and the boy was ashamed to have hit his head since he was now a super-hero, mind-speaker and traverse-er of light and galaxies. He lay down inside, on the couch without complaint, and took a secret short nap and dreamed of light.

When his father got home the boy watched carefully, but he didn't think that his father could see his new power. The father was mostly worried about his wife. Lainey was how he called her, since he didn't know her real name either. The boy was sad, but also a little proud, to think that maybe the magic was invisible except to himself.

LAINEY

The dream is fading so fast I can't hang onto the sense of it. I am still scared, though. Panic boils up until I realize Cristian is beside me, speaking sharply and shaking me a little. Blink against his words. Focus on his face, framed in a moon halo against a gray wall.

"Are you finally awake now? What's the matter? What were you dreaming about?" I stare at him. How should I know? He woke me up too quickly to remember. My heart is racing.

"Your heart is racing. I think you better sit up, Lainey." Cristian's hand is on my neck. Like he is trying to read my pulse. The thick wool blankets are hot and I push them to Cristian's side of the bed.

"What do you know about taking a pulse, silly? I'm okay. It's just an aftereffect of the shock. The ambulance guy said it might happen off and on for a week or so." My hand is throbbing, though, beneath the key shaped scab which is itself kind of numb. A sudden reddening on the wall opposite the window announces the sun's appearance above the eastern horizon. A new day dawns.

"Lainey. You are incredible. Who gets hit by lightning? My wife."

"You always knew I had an electric personality."

"Yep. Well, we need to get Timber up and off to school so we can get to our meeting with Billy and his dad. Do you want the first shower? I'll smack the kid around today." He leans toward the banister and yells, "Timber. Time to get up, buddy."

A muffled, bubbly voice answers, "Why, Daddy? 'Cause I'm already up."

It won't be the first shower. Timber is in the bathroom, from the sounds of things, pouring cupfuls of water from the sink over his head and down his back and onto the floor, while jumping in and out of the tub. Now there's probably not any hot water left for me. He's singing the Rain, Rain, Go Away song, but it fades fast when I open the door and yell at his soggy silhouette behind the half-open curtain. It's half-open, I see, because he has been yanking down on it again and has ripped three more holes from their hooks.

"You just trashed the bathroom, Timber. There is water everywhere." I kick his saturated inside-out pajama bottoms with whitie-tighties still connected. "You make me so mad. You want to buy a new shower curtain? A new floor? Don't you think Dad and I would like some hot water too?"

"You hate me! I didn't break nothing. You just mean old mommy."

Timber pulls the curtain open again with the water still running, spraying me and getting even more water on the floor. I push him sideways roughly and turn off the faucet. I don't care that he's covered in suds. I don't care if I pushed him too hard. He is six, not two. Too big to shower with Mommy. I keep telling Cristian he has to do it. Shower with him, give him lessons. Here is how you shampoo your hair. This is when you know it's rinsed. Don't touch Mommy's Nair.

Timber is naked, soapy, and blubbering. I'm shaking. Hot tears break out of their ducts. "You make me so crazy," I scream, in a duet with his whiny chant.

"You hate me. You hate me. You hate me."

Cristian leans into the wardrobe, pulling out the shirt he's going to iron. I've wiped my face before he turns back to see me climbing carefully up the ladder. As if he couldn't hear. As if I didn't need him. As if it wasn't his fault in the first place; I have told him to teach that boy how to bathe.

Finally he looks at my glowering face.

"Lainey, I didn't know he was up already. Neither did you. It is not my fault, is it? Anyway, at least he's actually doing something for himself, without being told, right? I'll get him out of there and dressed and stuff, and you just take your own turn, okay." He pauses, realizing that maybe it's more than a little splash that's bugging me. "Or is it too trashed? What did he break this time?"

I don't want to speak and I certainly don't want to accept his half-assed apology or offer my own, but darn that guilt. It tastes like salty coffee between my clenched molars. Cristian wraps his arms around my stiff and angry body, and that's it. I yield and cry. I'm so bad, I tell him. I can't do this. I don't know how to do this. Why is our son such a baby? Why can't he just say sorry and move on instead of making things worse? Cristian holds me without answering. He doesn't have an answer.

"Not to ignore the situation, Lainey, but we have to get moving. Timber's bus will come and we have the meeting."

I make no comment; don't even kiss my baby good morning when I pass him at the foot of the ladder. He is still soaking wet, with sudsy bubbles over his hair and back. He is still screaming about me being a regular old meanie. He should show me, he threatens. Then I would be nice. I shut the door in his face and push in the latch button. The blue fish cup lies broken sideways in the sink where he cracked it. What a shame. He loved that cup. I hang my nightgown on a hook and step very carefully into the stall. No need to give the water time to warm up.

The still-warm spray eases some of the anger from my bones. Timber's cries fade out, probably soothed by his father as he wipes off the soap. And suddenly I am awake, alive as never before, to the tiny pulsation of each individual drop of water. The soft colors of morning sunshine fragmenting through the glass block window next to me are more clear and distinct than I have ever noticed. Once upon a life before Timber, Vanji and I tried some web design work, and I can identify each ray of color by its RGB number today. It's as though light is separating and fusing before my eyes. I can even calculate the angle of the beam which is reflecting off the decomposed granite cliff side behind the window, and how far it's traveled from the sun. I am a genius.

This clear, all these details of the morning around me, yet I can't figure out how to keep from screaming at my son. If I were his real mother would I be better at keeping my cool? Would he obey me better if I had a genetic claim on him? And something is suddenly clearer to me than even these colors and sensations of the morning: Timber's "real" mom left him. I would never, ever, abandon my boy. As angry as I can get I would never get that angry. He could do the worst things in the world and I would forgive him. We all have our faults and failures, but we belong together. He is as much my son as if he had been squeezed from my DNA.

The water is cooling even faster than my blood, and I haven't shampooed yet. Lather, quickly, and rinse. My scalp tingles. My nails bend slightly as I run them through the roots, a small tear in the right pointer snagging on a strand. I really ought to force myself to eat Jell-O.

The towel is soft. Droplets mixed with my tears soak into the terry cloth away from my skin with a little pop. The slightest residue of minerals forms minuscule outlines of those drops all over my body, until I rub them out with the towel. I look at my skin and see beneath the hair, into the weird layers of cells and on down. I glance up through the ceiling tiles, into insulation, water pipes, and on up past the floorboards of my bedroom loft. Sky. Clear blue sky above.

Over in the kitchen I imagine Cristian's blistered feet splayed in front of the stove as he cracks eggs while Timber crouches beside him, whimpering now about putting on his shoes.

Shut my eyes. Open them. Was the strike some kind of miracle? Curse? Supernatural answer to my prayer for help? I seem to know everything today. I am abnormally over-aware. Conscious of every detail. Except how to be a better mother. How to discipline better, maybe, keep my cool; or love bigger. One would think this a more useful gift from the lightning bolt. A quick zap of extra love.

"Lainey, where is Timber's backpack? We've got four minutes to get to the bus stop."

Cristian stands framed in the bathroom doorway, sleeves pushed up to reveal muscular black forearms. Backpack?

"It's in the Liberty, I think. I don't remember bringing it in. Sorry."

"Let's hope he didn't have homework."

"Cristian, for crying out loud. He's in kindergarten; who cares? Oh, but I had a form…I forgot it. I'll fill it out for tomorrow, okay?" Cristian is shaking his head. He might as well just say, besides being a hothead you're an airhead who forgets everything important. Another little sister type. I stomp upstairs to get dressed so that he doesn't stand around tapping his feet for our morning meeting.

The warped and oxidized mirror above my dresser doesn't believe in flattery. I wish its distortion was vertical, but instead it stretches my chubby cheeks even wider. A ponytail is probably a good choice, since there won't be time to dry my hair, but it looks so severe.

"I hope it doesn't rain again today," I mumble to my reflection, but already I know it will be a brilliant, sunny day. I read it in the rays of light. The only clean option I find in my closet other than a sweatshirt and jeans is a grey short-sleeved turtleneck. It goes with some nicer black pants, but I haven't tried them on in at least a year. Yuck. A roll of flab perches right on top of the waistband. The sad thing is I can't even blame Timber for my "baby" fat. Unless you count stress eating. But the sweater is long and hangs down over my belly and even my butt. I perch on the edge of the bed to make sure it works sitting. Good enough.

I'm finishing off with mascara when Cristian pokes his head up the ladder. I toss the makeup back into an old shoebox and join him downstairs.

"I like it. You look really professional." He wraps his arms around my shoulders and kisses the back of my neck. No need to show him the belly roll.

Cristian holds me for longer than usual. An apology. I relax against him, soaking in his strength. My apology. I whisper it out loud. "I am sorry." We are every bit as inconsistent as Timber. He left the house with a coveted Pop Tart which made him more or less happy and now we are more or less happy. Suddenly a peace wells up. Huge. Larger than my anger, the good feeling floods the whole cabin. Just say sorry, I say to my son, twenty times a day. About time to listen, I guess. Despite myself I love this man. I love that boy.

"Should I do the tie thing?" he asks. He's got two; one is a tacky singing Santa and the other is bluish. His button-up chambray shirt is lavender.

"No, Babe. You look fine. Are you nervous?" Surprisingly, I am not. It's as if I already know the outcome. It is favorable. I do know the outcome. The air is charged with a kind of kinetic goodness. It's been a long time since I was so sure that everything really will be okay. Maybe since Timber was tiny. Maybe since they said he wouldn't be just like everyone else and we were glad for that.

"Off to the races," he quips, holding wide the front door. A jay caws angrily and the smell of tractor trailer brakes mingles with the pines. A good day. It can be a good day still.

Chapter Five

THE BOY

It was hard to make the big yellow bus slow down, but the boy did it by concentrating with all his force. The bus screeched its brakes and slowed while the boy and his father flew down the driveway toward the pull-over spot on the highway where the bus would wait thirty-seconds-no-more for riders. Riders at this stop meant only the boy, except for one time before Christmas when two sisters from another route missed their own yellow bus and their mother pulled into the boy's driveway to wait for a chance to get to school on the boy's bus instead.

But the driver didn't know about the boy's powers and must have thought it odd to watch her bus slow down under her feet while the boy and his father panted up to the stopping place.

"Behave." said the father, which was not the "be good" that the mother always said but was mostly the same thing which meant that they thought he was too bad to know not to be bad. The boy stood at the top of the bus's steep stairs and looked down the aisle at every seat full and no one moving or noticing or saying sit here it is okay. The driver yelled Sit Down So We Can Go and the boy wanted to turn and run, back down the stairs and into the father's arms but could not. He couldn't even think how to super-power his question: where? into the driver's private mind and a third grader laughed when the boy sat across the aisle beside the third grader's friend who had to scoot over and sort of picked up his backpack so that there was almost room for the boy's small bottom perched at the corner of the bench. When the bus lurched the boy slipped off and hit his head on the hard bar of the seat in front and even super powers couldn't keep his eyes from running out all over.

The boy remembered the falling lights, so beautiful. But the sunlight polka-dotting and spinning through the pine trees and into the yellow bus was a different light. Maybe a tiny bit of super powers came from the lightning, but it wasn't enough. He heard that boy laughing again, and even though the one beside him said sorry and here let me move over, he knew, the thrown-away boy knew, that he would never change. He wasn't super after all; he was stupid.

LAINEY

This is way stronger than déjà vu. I walk through the next hour watching words pour out of lips with some kind of second sight. We park in back of the old Whippoorwill lodge, so that the meeting is not obvious to the overly interested public. We greet one another and then Bill Senior removes a large padlock and we enter the abandoned Lincoln log-style restaurant's office. Cold air slaps our faces and trickles down our backs. We leave the heavy door propped open because even the thin spring air is warmer than the air inside. Bill wipes some dust off a bent-up folding chair and offers it to me while taking its twin for himself. The other two men perch on the edge of a sagging couch that is not quite good enough for the dumpster. It's agreed to talk first about the financial possibilities and then, if we're still interested, to check out the place. I feel my own laughter, or comments, or uh-huhs and nods move up through my body and out, as if I'm trapped in a puppet.

Billy Junior is dressed as always, like a lumberjack who's been left out in the elements a little too long. His padded flannel coat has so many holes you see almost as much of the green plaid of his shirt as the red and black buffalo plaid of the coat. He shaved a little for the occasion, because his neck is red and scratched along the edge of his thick yellowish beard. Billy and I have known each other since our first day of grade school and were off-and-on friends, depending on the year and whether girls and boys could be friends or not. He fell in love with soft-spoken brown-haired Julie on the first day of eighth grade when her family moved up from the city, and they married right out of high school. She's finally about to give birth to their first potential William, and Billy's pride and nervousness are evident in every glance of his glittering eyes. Whenever dollar amounts are mentioned Billy lowers his head apologetically. He really hates asking his friends for interest. I love this guy.

Bill Senior has the look of a Western Colorado senator. He has, in fact, served politically but just as a county commissioner, back when Billy and I were in high school. Park County is full of trans-planted Midwesterners, Californians, Texans, and us few weirdos who were born here, each of whom thinks he's some kind of vigi-lante cowboy. Not a good place to try and tell anyone not to dig a well, or how to landscape for fire protection. Not a good place to be an honest county commissioner. Despite an ugly recall Bill main-tained his dignity, and you can't help but respect him. In contrast to his son, Bill sports a well-made blazer, black cowboy hat and boots about a billion dollars better than Cristian's, and a turquoise nugget bolo tie.

Bill's father, the William Jay Thorndove Number One, died last year. He lived secluded and alone, surrounded by the mountains he loved in the midst of a great property which is now under the care of Bill Number Two. Before today I knew little about him. Billy tells us that his granddad was Ute, but shortened Jaybird to Jay and gave himself the "William" during his brainwashing boarding school years. He proceeded to make a fortune in real estate, quietly buying low and selling high. Bill, in whom the Ute is obvious now that we know, just recently learned these secrets while sorting through his father's documents after his death.

While I'm watching the show before me, my heart breaks for the old man who was ashamed of his own skin. I am afraid for Timber and worry again about Cristian, who once confided that if his flesh were lighter, like his sister Vanji, he might have tried to "pass" as Mediterranean. Now that the Thorndoves know the details about their Indian heritage they are even happier to do business with our family, they say, since we're about the only people of any color around here.

Just as "The Bills" rise to shake Cristian's hand, a light breaks through a broken and plastic tarp- covered window, illuminating dust mites and providing a heavenly glow to the ceremony. The whole seen- it-before feeling disappears. Finally. I'm back to normal. Back in my skin and stuck in the here and now. I shiver inadvertently. Ah--choo...

"Sorry," says Bill Senior, noticing. "I should have thought to fire up the woodstove or something. It's a little chilly." He begins to remove his jacket, to hang over my shoulders.

"No, I'm fine, really. It was just the dust. See, I have my cloak here." I slip it on, with Cristian's help. He's embarrassed that another man was more chivalrous and attentive to my needs. Hopefully he'll try and make it up to me.

"Okay. Now we know we could work a deal if you're still inter-ested after we go check out the dump. Remember, we're talking ten years' worth of mouse turds." Billy swings open the inner door and we all step through into the darkness of a boarded-up dining room.

Bill flips on a powerful lantern and shines it slowly around the room. The light climbs over hand- hewn rustic tables and benches. I am thankful to note a dry, dusty smell rather than must and mold. "It was actually a main ranch house for this valley, originally. There was another building, a bunkhouse, out back above that sinkhole that used to be a little pond. It burned years ago. The pond didn't burn; the bunkhouse did. Don't think Billy was even born. Brenda Ann was around, because I took her fishing. Little bit of a thing, Brenda Ann. Stocked with trout. The pond, that is." I giggle, not at the thought of a pond burning, or a child being stocked with trout, but of Billy's sister, about four years older than us, ever being a little bit of a thing. Got a touch of the lumberjack just like her brother. She's been Big Brenda as long as I can remember.

Cristian is looking at the long tables flanked by benches. He walks up and down, running his hand thoughtfully along the hand-hewn edges.

"That's probably one of the major problems," says Bill. "Not many restaurants around with big old family-style tables. Probably have to contract to chop 'em down, or figure in the cost of new furnishings."

Wires hang down from the ceiling in one spot and below them is what looks like a pile of bones, while the other five antler chandeliers are intact, though filthy with greasy cobwebs. Amazingly there is no sign of looters or squatters. Other than a squirrel who scurries into the rafters.

"I don't know what you're thinking, style-wise," continues Bill, "but you definitely got an antique, and by antique I mean antiquated, mountain lodge here now. If you want to modernize, there'll be a lot more remodeling expense, so when you draw up a plan make sure and figure it all in."

"Let them look, Dad. How can they have any ideas yet? Let them get a feel for what's even here." Billy pushes against swinging bar doors and we enter the kitchen behind him. He heaves and pushes, and between himself and Cristian they remove a large sheet of plywood that was propped on a bank of deep enamel sinks under a big window. Immediately the light pours into the room and it actually warms me. The pungent smell of cinnamon and cloves tickles my nostrils. I wonder how it could have lasted through the years, but then I feel and hear the crack of a broken spice bottle beneath my clog.

"Careful, don't get cut," advises Cristian. Duh. He brushes the glass aside with his boot to protect me. He grabs the fingers of my right hand, the only part not wrapped awkwardly in gauze, and whispers, "Well?" He's pointing at a giant gorgeous red enamel stove. He reaches behind and clinks the white sink. "Old enamel, didn't you say?" The other end of the kitchen corridor is a walk-in cooler. Its door is also enameled but in a pale peachy color.

"Seems to me," interjects Bill, "we need to get some service restored, electric anyway, so we can find out what the state of these appliances actually is. Whether you choose to manage, or buy outright, or do a land contract, we can't really go forward until we know the costs involved. Make up a plan; dream big and dream small, and we'll find what works for everyone involved."

Billy steps out of the cooler and the door seems to seal well behind him. "What else do you want to check now? Should we just give you a little time? Yeah, I think so. Brr. Come on, Dad. Let's wait for them out back where it's warmer."

Bill grins. "This is the one who should be in politics, I keep telling him. My boy knows how to read people. He's right. We'll leave you two alone for a bit. Cristian, Lainey." He nods and follows Billy out, his boot crushing another cinnamon stick. The aroma cuts straight through the dust. I sneeze again. Cristian is moving through the kitchen in imaginary circles. He's a gourmet chef and swears by ritual. I can see a problem already. When he's moving, spinning, no one can get in the path. But this layout puts everyone there. Waiters wait impatiently for their orders right in front of the stove where the chef is working. The prep counter seems too close to splash-back from dirty dishwater. There's a large dirty open space between the oven and the far wall, and it looks like this was where the fire that closed the restaurant started and stopped.

It was a small fire, but it began with an explosion that almost killed the cook. I explain this to Cristian while we examine the damage. It appears that another, smaller stove must have been removed from the space after it blew. A gas line had plugged or something, as I remember. The wall is bad. We leave the kitchen and step around stacked metal chairs, which don't match the heavy wood of the tables and benches, to look at the other side of the wall. The fire damage is clear. Aged green-on-cream bucolic wallpaper is burned away in spots and peeled back in others, revealing the two-by-fours beneath. Instead of pink insulation the wall looks as though it had been stuffed with wadded newspapers.

"Lucky the whole place didn't just explode like kindling," Cristian marvels. "This place is as bad as the hole I grew up in." He runs his hand along an exposed joist.

"Actually I'm surprised how little is burned. When I was a kid and the place shut down, the rumor was that everything inside was destroyed. I used to think there was a ghost of the charred remains of the dead cook, until my dad told me that no one died. He was on the volunteer rescue that year so he knew some of the details. He got on my case after he overheard me telling my little brothers to watch as we drove past because sometimes you could see the stump-arm ghost moving through the trees up there."

Cristian laughs. He grabs my wrists and bumps me to his chest, staring in my eyes. "You're so mean. I'd never have said something so scary to Vanji."

"Course not. She would be the one saying it to you. She's mean, just like me." I am mean, I think, shouting at our son. Why'd it make me so angry, anyway? Now that time has passed it seems like such a little thing, his unauthorized shower. After all, like Cristian said, he was actually trying to do something for himself for a change.

"Well, you do always tell me these scary stories and I never know which ones to believe." He pecks my lips then lets me go. Catch and release. Bailey is a beautiful place, but there are way too many ghosts in my memory. The stories I tell Cristian are usually true. Horrific car crashes. Natural disasters. Unusual cancers and diseases. A red spot on a hillside.

A different ghost comes to mind, but it is a simple memory. A series of memories: a younger me, locked out of the bathroom and desperate. An older sister who mocks me through the door: "I'm telling Mom, I'm gonna pee my pants," Running to meet the bus, hair uncombed and dripping wet in the cold, trying to catch up to a fashion plate sister. No wonder I was ticked this morning. It's as though an electric buzz has helped me remember. How many times did Angela do that to me? All through junior high, I think. It's not about Timber, it's about me. Poor little middle child Lainey.

Cristian puts his hand behind my neck and I feel a quick pressure as he pulls me close again and his lips fold over mine. My bandaged hand perches upon his left bicep.

"I want it," he whispers.

"Right here? Right now?"

"Yep. I want you, and I want this." Cold air bites my cheek as he pushes me out to arm's length. His eyes are black magnets, pulling me back in. His voice drips with earnestness. "Lainey. I can do this. *We* can do this. You are the artistic director. I'm the chef. Can't you see it?"

I can see it. I love the oldness. I love the impractical tables and uncomfortable benches. I love the antique stove and chipped up three-bay sink. Hanging onto each other like teenagers we move back into the kitchen. But there's so much at stake. We can fail. Lose everything so easily: money, reputation, stability. Timber likes continuity of schedule. He likes it when we try to keep things as regular as possible. Will he freak? Regress to diapers or kicking fits?

"Bust the wall out." Cristian raises his left eyebrow and squints with his right eye.

"Huh?"

"Bust the wall out. Look, then make a separation between prep room and a cook room. Or, we move the stove down here and put a serving counter through the burned wall. With a door at the cooler end, for the salad girl. Lainey, are we having a salad bar? I hate salad bars. Hey, what am I serving?"

This is fun. It's the most fun we've had since Timber was tiny and we used to lick Cheerios and stick them on his face. His eyes would cross if you got one on his nose. I am laughing and I feel good and I can almost forget about getting zapped by lightning. Anyway, something seems to have already helped my attitude about Timber today. If electricity helps I'll take it. I could use any kind of help I can get.

It's just about time to get Timber from school, so we take out the camera and run around snapping a lot of pictures and then go out into the thin sunlight to thank the Bills for their time. Bill Senior gives us a full month to think about things before presenting a plan. No one else will get a chance in the meantime. He's in no hurry, he says, but I know that Billy is waiting for a little start-up money for his own new venture. Start-up money. Where will ours come from?

"One last thing," says Bill, as I'm squeezing the door handle of the Liberty, "You have to have a new name. I just read in the paper that Johnson's Junction Inn is changing to Whippoorwill Woods. Being only about fifteen miles away it could be confusing. Plus, I never was a 'Will' but still…little too close to Bill. I never liked the idea of getting whipped." He smacks the side of the jeep, presumably as an all-clear.

Billy stretches his back and walks towards his truck. "Julie's waiting for lunch. Told her I'd be home."

Cristian calls, "Hey, Billy, when is she due?"

"Two weeks. But it could be any day. I got my cell phone on all the time now, even if there's no coverage."

I smile, as I slide into our Liberty. "I'm sure everything will be okay. Pass along my love and tell Julie if she needs anything, call me." Not that she would. Julie is the one who is always taking food to someone. If anyone is sick or hurt or out of work or maybe just too skinny, Julie goes popping over with a casserole. Nice looking, too. The kind of food that's actually worthy of Pinterest. She brought us about a week's worth when we first got Timber and another batch a year later when the adoption was finalized.

I pull my sweater down over my muffin top as the door shuts. Probably a good thing I never could get pregnant. Imagine the shape of me plus baby fat. Sick. Cristian grabs me unsuspecting and plants his lips on mine, again.

"Oh, yeah," he says, "this is good." He slides the shift stick into drive and we pull out from behind the restaurant. We have to wait for a couple cars to merge onto the highway, and someone honks and waves. The car is red, but I don't know who it is. Cristian always knows people by what they drive, but I'm clueless about makes and models, even when I've ridden in them. Cristian's too preoccupied today to notice the honk. He's probably visualizing our future sign: Clayson's Crawdads & Catfish.

Sure.

Chapter Six

There's a red car in the Crow Barre lot. Celia is already here, even though I am about ten minutes early. She's still adjusting a rain jacket on the back of her seat and smoothing her clothes as though she has just sat down. The back of her head is an attractive mixture of gray and white in what my father always calls "those kinky poodle perms."

Celia's curls are the opposite of my mom's straight and shiny hair. Mom has gone white in thick streaks, the way some women pay for highlights, and I think she may be the only female I know who is very much contented by her looks. It's one of those things that infuriate me about the woman. She carries herself with this regal dignity and has a really vain self-image. Think, Mexican Cruella DeVille. She is no stereotypical brow-beaten immigrant maid. I guess it's why Angela is the favored child. She, too, believes she is a princess. I might as well be the ugly stepsister. My skin is dull; my hair has no sheen.

I remember hearing Dad once telling his buddy, "This one has too much of me. She's the smart one." He laughed and turned the conversation. I don't know, maybe that should have been enough for a nine-year-old, to be the smart one. But it wasn't. I still hate mirrors and anyway, I soon learned that academic performance didn't get me attention either and I just learned to live without. And then one day, Cristian entered my life. Tall(ish), dark, and handsome met short, squat me and called me pretty.

"Lainey, snap out of it." I jump at Cristian's touch.

"I've been right in front of you," he laughs. "You're kind of dazing out again, aren't you? Celia says you're meeting her for breakfast." We've reached the table now and Celia begins to rise up.

She leans in awkwardly to give me a little hug. I don't know what to do and our heads bump. She laughs. "Sorry. I keep forgetting that we don't greet huggy-kissy here. It's just that you have such a beautiful coloration, Lainey, that I almost feel like I'm back in Panama."

Huh?

"Greetings. I mean, I spent seventeen years in Panama, and there we greet with the kiss-kiss hug."

Cristian speaks while pushing my chair in for me. "You were in Panama? Did you just move back?"

"Goodness, no. I guess it's been almost a year and a half. It's just that things get so ingrained..."
Celia settles back into her chair, readjusting her jacket as she does so.

The pieces finally are falling into place. "No wonder I haven't seen you around enough to remember who you are. I thought I must be crazy not to have seen you since childhood—my childhood—because I was only gone for a bit in college and then we moved back here. Me and my husband."

Cristian flips our white porcelain coffee mugs and we both smile and nod. He goes for the pot and I continue, "So why in the world did you live in Panama? What was it like?"

"Oh, goodness, Lainey. Now, you're lucky that I've been back in Bailey for a while. When I first returned I would have tried to answer you. Three or four hours later I would have noticed you again, asleep in your soup. Let's suffice it to say that Panama is an amazing land, full of contrasts, color, and flavor, and I miss it dreadfully. And yet, I am also somehow glad to be able to relegate those seventeen years to the decorations on my cabin walls. I do maintain correspondence with a few dear friends, of course, but I am glad to finally be home."

Cristian pours the coffee himself because he is listening in. He's added a small dollop of pure cream to mine (not on the menu or expense forms), and the liquid in the mug matches his fingers curled around the handle. Cristian has been begging for a fancy espresso-cappuccino system but Travis won't budge. Still, by experimenting and ridiculous standards of cleaning the existing coffee pot, Cristian manages to extract a really good cup of joe.

I didn't tell him I was meeting Celia, simply because I forgot last night and he left before I woke up today.

"Cristian," I say. "Celia helped me out after the lightning...thing. She took care of Timber while I was out of it. And guess what? She's a local, too, and I actually used to go to this kids' club thing at her church when I was little."

"Oh, really?" Cristian arches his brow. He already knows about the kids' club, because that was my saving grace when he proposed with one condition, that being that I could prove to him (despite the fact we'd been sleeping together for months and had never set foot near a church together—still haven't, in fact) that I had asked Jesus to save my soul. Seems even with full-throttle bedroom backsliding, he'd once made a very solemn oath to his mother and intended to honor it by marrying into the religion his name represents. Cristian believed, he said. He just didn't need the hypocrisy of church people.

Now he looks like he's going to ask for a text of my conversion prayer or something.

"Cristian," I whisper. "I think Travis' car is pulling up in back." It's mean of me to acknowledge how intimidated he is of his boss, especially just because I want him to leave Celia and me alone to talk. I immediately regret my words. There's a hurt and betrayal in his eyes. I've wounded him in front of Celia.

She speaks. "You know, I'm ready to order, folks. Cristian, have you whipped up some of those breakfast chiliquiles today? I'd love a plate. Lainey, if you need more time you can take all you want."

"I would like the same," I say, trying to say sorry with my own eyes. Cristian won't meet them.

Travis is a jerk, but a smart one. He takes ongoing surveys about his menu and has Cristian make a new plate each week for a trial. If it's a hit, the least-ordered food of the week before rotates off. People come in on Mondays just to try the new dish and get in on the voting. Chilaquiles were a write-in suggestion from my father, since Mom stopped cooking big meals when the last brother moved out two years ago. Makes no sense to cook for two, she says. Even Cristian's chilaquiles aren't as good as my mother's, but Dad comes in to town faithfully once a week to get his fill and the salsa-bathed tortilla chips are still my favorite breakfast food.

The door bangs open rudely as Travis makes his grand entrance. He thinks the heads that snap around at the sound are glad to see him, as if people like to hear the loud crack of a flimsy wood storm door against a cheap metal dining chair.

"Whoo." he says, shaking the outside air while kicking the door shut with the back of his heel. "Cold as a jackalope's asssstounding tail...whoops. Mixed company." Travis nods to each woman in the restaurant, as if it's a gallant thing to do and but for the feeble sex he would have let loose. He has given the same witty little joke about the outside temperature many times before. Celia and I ignore the gesture and Travis' entrance and sip our coffees.

No use. Travis makes a beeline for a chair at our table for four and unceremoniously and without permission, flings Celia's purse onto mine on the other open chair, meanwhile swinging the seat around so he can straddle it backwards. It's an odd habit somehow related to his false sense of machismo, and I choke a little on my coffee as I read my thoughts in Celia's eyes.

"Good morning, Travis," she says, smiling politely. He nods to her but his eyes are on me.

"Just couldn't stay away from your little mocha-pot this morning, huh?" he asks, as though I've come to his restaurant to interfere with his cook's work.

Rumors are that Travis left an ex-wife and ex-kids behind in Texas and the fifty-something-year-old's self-conscious attempts to suck in his gut and over-impress suggest that he is in the market for a new little woman. He brags about having quit smoking last month but his yellowed teeth and constant gum-chewing indicate that it may have been too late. How great it will be when Cristian is his own boss. Out from under the thumbs of jerks like Travis.

Celia looks up from her coffee. "Well, of course, Travis. Lainey's sweet husband is quite irresistible— why thank you, Cristian. We were just talking about how we women come here just to ogle you." Cristian slides my plate under my chin and I try again to make eye contact.

He ignores me and addresses Celia, "Really? Thought it was my cooking."

"Thought it was MY restaurant, and MY menu."

Celia ignores Travis. "Well, Cristian, I must admit that if you came out of that kitchen empty-handed we'd get tired of you pretty quick."

Travis or no, I've got to do something. I can't stand Cristian's smoldering silence to me. I grab his hand and pull it to my lips.

"I'll take him with or without food," I say. Celia nods in approval, and Travis grunts and pushes up from his chair, bumping our table and making coffee splash out of our cups. He doesn't notice or maybe care. Our plates of chilaquiles have totopos (stale tortilla slices), green sauce made from tomatillos, and shredded white cheese and are topped with a fried egg. Cristian told me that the cost analysis of Mom's recipe, which he adapted for the restaurant, easily allows for two eggs per person or a half cup of shredded chicken. But to Travis the extra protein represents income, and he cut it to one egg only.

Cristian used to slip in two when the boss was out, but once Travis came in and yanked a customer's plate away while he was eating to shove it in his cook's face. The man, lying, swore that he'd taken his friend's egg and that he'd never eat in Travis' greasy spoon again. A week later he was back, because, where else are you going to eat if you want hot food?

As Travis is spinning toward the kitchen Cristian leans over and deftly plants a kiss on my lips. I'm forgiven. He heads back to the world of stoves and chop tables.

"Isn't forgiveness wonderful?" asks Celia.

I open my mouth and shut it. How?

"How did I guess what was going on between you two? Once, I was married, too. But it's more than just a guess. Sometimes I hear a kind of warning or pre-whisper of words that would be good to say." Celia speaks quietly. So quietly, I have leaned in close. It feels like we are spinning, out of context of time and place with only our faces, sound, and attention, in the midst of the vortex.

"There's no explanation that I have found. It's not a physical condition; nor is it a paranormal thing. Well, maybe it's outside of normal, but I don't mean like bending a fork with your mind or something. It's a gift for knowing something real but not for altering reality." She's serious. "Maybe I'm crazy. Or maybe, Lainey, you have had a little taste of something like this recently, yes? Lainey, after that lightning strike you said something about praying for a sign. When you open yourself honestly you are likely to find a new reality."

Reach out and touch the fork. It's there, where it should be, on a solid Formica table. Lift a bite of spicy crunch to your mouth. It's mushy. Take another bite from the edge of the plate, that way the tortilla is still sticking out, dry. There's the crunch. Look around the room; ugly paneled walls, cheesy paintings for sale by local high school kids featuring melting eyeballs and weird looking girls' faces penciled by boys too shy to study the real thing. Celia's hands are shaking.

"I'm sorry, Lainey. I don't mean to scare you."

"I'm not scared."

"You're lying."

"Yes, I'm lying. I've been sort of seeing and hearing things. …Since the lightning. …And I was having a hard time with my son, and suddenly I had a really clear memory of something that used to happen to me and I knew why what he had done bothered me so much."

"God is getting a hold of you, Lainey."

We stare at each other for a while. A teenage waitress refills our coffee cups. Cream or sugar? Neither, because it would be the disgusting dusty powder this time. I drink it black, and it grounds me in reality. "So, what? I have super powers now? Or am I just psychotic?"

Celia leans in again and smiles. "I don't know if I'd say super powers. Really, Lainey, I don't know if it's even anything out of the ordinary at all. I mean, if we knew how to harness the amazing gifts we're given, perhaps everyone would have 'eyes to see' and 'ears to hear.' Life is hard and being a parent might be the hardest thing of all. Doing it well takes superhuman strength."

"So," I ask, "Did you have a psychic vision, or what? Is that how you knew to come over and help me in the parking lot?"

"No, Lainey. I was coming out of the store and I put my bags in the back of my car while you parked catty-corner to me, and that's when the lightning struck. I saw the big light bulb explode and the electricity shooting down the pole and sort of bouncing toward you while you leaned over in your car door."

"I dropped my keys and was picking them up."

Celia nods, taking a sip of tepid coffee. "I thought so. And I felt a kind of pop myself just as I shut my hatchback. Like flipping a light on after shuffling across the floor. Anyway that's when I ran over to see if you were okay. Do you want half of my egg? I am getting quite full."

"No thank you, Celia. I'm not even eating my own."

"What do you want, Lainey, most in the world?"

"Peace." I don't know where that came from but now it seems to float in the air between us. A balloon of a platitude. I exhale. "I just want peace, I guess. I mean, for everything to work out. With Timber, especially, in school, and with our res—for my husband's career, and for my brothers and my best friend; all the people I love…"

"So peace to you means things working out?"

"Yes, I guess so."

Celia smiles distantly and sits back for a moment. "That's interesting, Lainey, because I grew up in a community where the word 'peace' only meant 'not war.'"

I nod. "That works too."

"No, no it doesn't. Not really, because peace is more than the lack of something, and I think it's also more than just 'things working out.' For one thing, peace isn't possible without conflict. It's bigger and fuller than that. That's why you're searching so hard, Lainey. And me too, I searched a long time myself." Celia's hands are still shaking a little. She looks at them too and chuckles. "You have no idea what it is like to get old. A little excitement and my nerves are all over the place."

My heart has begun to race a little, too. I hear it resounding in my ears: palpitations, Vanji once told me, with a long Louisiana accent. As I realize it so does Celia.

"Oh dear. It's from the jolt, I'm sure. Let's talk of something different for a bit so that you can calm that down a little. Maybe my spastic hands will slow as well. Tell me a little about your family—if you don't mind?"

A new group has come in and settles at the large table between the corner where we perch and the rest of the dining room. They appear to be government administrators of some kind, and some are wearing stick-on name badges. Words like "grant proposals," "homecare," "HMO," and the presence of our local county Medicaid nurse give the impression that they're meeting about the health care center we voted to build last elections. They speak in shouting voices, pent-up laughter and humor exploding after an early morning of meetings.

I turn back to Celia. Now we can hardly hear each other. "My heart's okay. I'd really rather hear about you, Celia. Why were you in Panama? Why did you come back?"

"When were you in Kingdom Kids, Lainey?"

"Kingdom…? Oh, was that the kids' club? Well, it must have been like twenty years ago, because I went during second and third grades, maybe, and I'm almost 29. I remember they sang the Hippie Birthday Song, and I got to wear the Hippie Hat when I was eight and again when I was nine."

"Oh, the Hippie Hat. I love that hat."

"Don't tell me you still have it?"

"We used it last week for little Tommy Troyer's eleventh."

"Well, I sure felt the honor on those two birthdays." I pause. One year the friend who'd ridden the bus with me moved away and without her parents asking mine for permission I had never gathered the courage to go back, even though my brothers still went once in a while. Eventually I convinced myself it was the stuff of little kids and forgot to even want to go. "You once gave me a little book with no words and colored pages."

Celia nods absently. "And how is your heart today?" she asks. "Are you walking with the Lord?"

"Maybe you don't remember me there? At the club?"

I have to lean in uncomfortably close to hear Celia over the din. "Oh yes. I remember very well."

"It's a good thing I went to your club," I confess, "Because Cristian wouldn't have married me otherwise. He'd promised his mother, see, to marry only a born-againer."

Celia locks me in the gaze of her good eye. "But Lainey, how is your heart today?"

We're not even friends, are we? She is overstepping some social boundaries. How is my heart? It is still beating a little too fast, actually, and maybe that accounts for my confusion. I take a long swig of too- cold coffee. Celia drops the interrogation by squeezing my hand and clearing her throat.

"Okay. You asked me about Panama. It must have been a few years after you quit coming to Kingdom Kids that my husband of thirty years was killed on the highway returning from work in Denver. He was hit by a semi that jackknifed near Rosalie Road."

I remember. Everyone was talking about the truckload of cell phones all over the hillside. "I'm so sorry. It must have been terrible."

"Yes, well, anyway, following a bit of a break down, I decided to go to the mission field. My husband was mostly a good man, and I did and do still miss him. I wanted to be far away from constant reminders of his absence. I ended up at a lovely little camp on the ocean, where I lived in a cottage and hosted groups, along with a couple who were natives to the area. My Spanish never really caught up to what I wanted to say, but many people spoke English and all in all we got along wonderfully."

"Why did you come back?"

"A new host family moved in so I wasn't needed, and I realized that, in the first place, I had been kind of running away—again, and it was finally time to come home. You see, Roy was a military man, and our marriage itself was a kind of rebellious act on my part. As a young girl I was tired of life being defined by the don'ts and lacks, so I went out looking for the war, in a way. Fell in love with a man in uniform and married on his first furlough." Celia smiles thinly and places her napkin, folded in thirds, on her plate.

"Peace is not the absence of war, nor is it the presence of war. It's bigger than a smooth-running ship-shape household. I believe that it does have a lot to do with family, however. Grandchildren, of course, were another reason to move back to the States. I'll tell you more someday," she adds, condescendingly, I think. She seems to have forgotten the super-power stuff which is what I really want to know. But we both know our time is up for the day. I see Cristian glance at the clock on the wall as he slides a dish across the counter to a waiter.

"I suppose it's time to go get Timber?"

"Yes, Celia, I'm afraid so. The school only offers half-day kindergarten unless you pay extra."

"We must do this again. This was wonderful, dear."

"Thank you," I say, crumpling my napkin and attempting to mask my disappointment. I really wanted to know why I can suddenly almost see and hear through walls.

Cristian comes over nervously. "Lainey, you've got to get going or you'll be late for Timber. I'll take care of the bill on my break. Travis is okay with it. Go."

We stand and put on our jackets and pick up our purses. Celia touches my bad hand and a spark passes between us.

"Don't worry," she whispers. "It's good. It's all very, very good."

She's right. I know she's right, but I rush for the safety of my jeep while the tears pour down. I am watching my nine-year-old self recite the sinner's prayer, and I'm feeling the weight of twenty years build up since that day. What happened to that innocent little girl? Life and reality. The jeep smells funky, and I vow to clean it out when Timber and I get home. Maybe that's what I'm like. Stinking old food accumulating in the cracks of my life as a happy wife and mother, and pretty soon the entire world will know through their noses how fake I am. They won't need bionic vision; ordinary noses will serve just fine.

For the second time in a week I speak a prayer. "So what? So what do you want from me? I stink; I'm a mess, and I don't get it. Give me a break, would you?" I cry the whole way up Crow Hill, but once I've turned left toward the elementary school I'm down to sniffles. Just say you're sorry, Lainey. Even to God. Let the tears wash those sins away. A grand ponderosa catches my attention as I pass. I note its individual needles shining against a sapphire Colorado sky. There is an obvious design to all this. Someone planting seeds. Spinning molecules on the tips of his fingers. And if nature, why not my life too?

"I'm sorry," I say. And I'm smiling.

Chapter Seven

THE BOY

Colors. The boy could never remember the right names of colors. He could never remember anything, which just proved that he was stupid. He tuned his classmates out by leaning on his hand so only the quiet ear was open and he let his eyes lose the edges of things. Maybe he could refuse to be a superhero, but he could still use power kind of backwards to help him control the world by just erasing it.

Some colors were good and some were bad. The space around the boy was mostly good, the warm color of construction machines and big trucks. Broncos: yeah, team. The boy tried to fill his mind with that color and maybe remember its name, but little-girl colors kept on slink-sliding past the walls of the reading corner. They were colors like gumdrops or wildflowers, and when he was looking close at the tiny petals of a picked plant they were okay, but today these cotton-candy hues were just making him nauseous. Another flash whirled by and he reached out to stop it.

And then the boy was standing at the big desk beside the teacher because the fizzy-dizzy color was just a skirt on a little girl, and she was sniffling next to him with a bump on her knee from where she hit it when she fell down. Because he knocked her down, she snuffled. The teacher was talking about gooses and ducks and explaining AGAIN the rules so that the boy would understand. The boy was not in trouble, the teacher said in the voice that meant that he actually was. The boy didn't try to

explain about her color getting in the way of his color. He remembered the game and he wanted to play, but he wanted to be
the whirling swirl, running-spinning on the outside while everyone else sat, hard-bottomed legs crossed, waiting and waiting and
thinking of colors.

Wanting them to touch him. But knowing anyway, no one
would pick him to run. Finally the teacher's lips stopped moving,
and she sat and waited for the boy to say what he was supposed
to say now. But he wasn't sure. He had been pressing the loud
ear shut while she talked so most all he'd heard were squishy
sounds. He had, however, been noticing the sky, and he knew for
certain that it was blue.

"Timber...?" said the teacher.

And it came to him: "Purple. Purple dress?" But the little girl
just rolled her eyes and said, as she moved back into the circle,
"No, dummy. My dress is lavender."

After school the boy was happy. First off the teacher did not
give him a Major Write-Up about tripping the purple-dress girl
and then on the bus he found a seat that had no one in it until
after he sat down, and Taylor asked really nicely to sit beside him,
and when he said okay Taylor showed him a special sticker collection on the inside of an Eagle Pride assignment notebook.
Taylor said if he was nice and if Taylor still rode this same
yellow school bus next year the boy could choose two stickers of
his own to start out with, if he wanted.

The boy wasn't always sure who his enemies were and who
were his friends. Sometimes at recess he would be worried about
what to play and suddenly realize that he was running together
with other kids and laughing. More often he would watch others
play while he sat alone. He decided to make a magic Like Me
force field, and everyone would have to be his best friend. Share
his lunch. Sit together. That was why Taylor was being so nice,
because of that force field.

Even so, the boy was not quite sure. Taylor said something he didn't understand, and laughed. And then it was Taylor's stop and the boy sat wondering.

At home the father said, tired-voiced and watching TV, Please Just Go Play Outside, and the boy wondered again.

LAINEY

"So, Vanji called while you were out," calls Cristian from his station at our kitchen sink. The pile of dirty dishes is higher to his right than the clean dishes in the drainer perched atop a stove burner. He hates the backwards set-up, but the stove is pressed in close on the left and there is nowhere for dirty dishes to hang out except on the counter space on the right of the sink. If Cristian were here all day long instead of me, the dishes wouldn't have to worry about it, because they'd be bathed right away and would spend more of their time stacked in cupboards. Cristian speaks over his shoulder to remind me that he has been washing dishes and fixing lunch while I was out back picking some of the newly bloomed wild lilies for the lunch table.

But I'm being paranoid and mean-spirited for no reason, except the monthly reminder of my womanhood. Can't even make a baby, so why should I have to suffer this? Cristian dries his hands and comes to swing a leg over the stool beside me. His face is completely open, without ulterior motives. Can I blame him for washing dishes? I want him to wash dishes. Why do I always think the worst of everyone?

"These are great." he says, fingering a waxy blossom.

"Vanji called? Darn. I hate to miss it." I rub his shoulders and thrill at the muscles he flexes for me.

"She's still there. I said you'd call right back. But wait—" Cristian puts his hand on my thigh as I begin to rise from the barstool.

"Lainey, I think something is up. I know, something is always up, but...she didn't sound too good. I think she might be drunk."

"Who the drunk-skunk stinking-punk?" The door bangs behind Timber.

"Nobody, Timber. And don't talk like that. And please take your boots off." Timber has already taken one step too far, but he freezes and tries to pull off one boot while balancing on the other foot and hanging on to the open door.

"Timber," shouts his dad, "Shut that door. You're letting all the heat out." But our son can't balance without the door and the shoe thing is complicated, and he falls in a heap and cries. Once again, mud is everywhere.

If Cristian hadn't just lost his temper I would have. But when he does it I can see so much more clearly. Now I feel like yelling at Cristian instead. Just shut your mouth, Lainey. I quickly brush some of the biggest chunks out the door after removing Timber's other boot. He hugs me and runs stocking-footed to perch himself on my stool while I set the boots in the old cookie sheet that I placed on the floor for muddy melt-off. Cristian has gone back to washing dishes.

"So, should I call Vanji right away?" I ask carefully, crossing the room to the counter.

"Yeah, of course. Just, try to make sure she's okay. If I say I'm worried about her she gets all defensive, right? And talk her into coming for Easter."

When we began the process of getting licensed to foster/adopt we had to list what we hoped for, couldn't handle, could manage, etc., in a child. We both had said we hoped not to have to deal with the agony of a terminal illness; each of us hoped for a child of color, and, each worrying what the other might think, we admitted we wanted a boy. For me it was easy; just thinking about my older sister makes me nauseous, but I adore my stinky, loud, boisterous little brothers. Cristian loves Vanji immensely, but he has already been her surrogate father and says he doesn't need another "daughter." I occasionally have to remind him of this, when we get those lines blurred in our own relationship.

As I look for the phone handset I think how some of Cristian's fears for Vanji are valid. After all, she lied constantly about how great things were at home, as she nursed her mother and mothered herself through middle and high school. Cristian heard between the words in their short phone conversations but ignored his fear and pretended to believe them. He still berates himself for not acting on his impulses and throwing away his life to go home to Honey and Vanji. In truth, his little sister had threatened that if he ever came back to live she would run away. When Honey died, just as Vanji was about to begin her senior year, Cristian quit his job, executed the (humiliatingly televised) body removal and funeral, sold everything in their rented rat trap, and took his sister to Boulder for her last year of high school, while he did a stint as pastry chef for the university food service. He says he doesn't think he could handle another teenage female. Ever.

His employment got her a reduction in tuition once she began college, and scholarships paid the rest. That's where I first saw him. He was standing at a huge stainless-steel sink reverse-dumping silverware from basket to basket for a second sterilization in the steaming clanking washers. When he reached up to pull the three-sided door down, I gasped out loud at the sweat and steam pouring in rivulets around his muscular gray-black shoulders. I felt like such a little child compared to his maturity. How dare I think he was hot?

I already was a little child next to Vanji. I'm a few months older, but she was forging her mother's signature on welfare checks while I was still practicing mine by dotting the "i" with flowers, hearts, and stars.

Timber scoots the stool to the sink and then scoops a handful of bubbles and blows them at his dad. I find the phone, under a discarded pair of Superman undies. I don't even want to know why they lay discarded on the kitchen counter. I motion to Timber to pick up the sudsy banana peel he just dropped on the floor near the trash can. He ignores me and moves out of my reach. He also takes my "shush" to mean "rev your engine louder."

"Hey chickie-babe." I can hear from her response as she greets me that something is wrong. But she's not drunk. I don't think she has ever even tasted alcohol, and yet her brother is always afraid she is a closet lush. Stepfather hangover, I suppose.

She's not talking to her big brother now, so she has no need for pretenses. It's funny; she doesn't care if I tell him everything; she just can't tell him the bad stuff herself. "They dumped me." Vanji starts to sniffle, and as always when she cries, her nose plugs up. The congested whimpers do make her sound drunk, somehow. How can Cristian not know this?

Because Vanji has sworn off men on the off- chance they might lead to procreation, which she has also sworn off for the same reason she doesn't drink, I understand immediately that the "they" who have dumped her must be employers. She's a loan manager, and even though she doesn't like her current bank, she's amazing at her job. I have a hard time believing that any boss would let Vanji go. But it could be agents. She moonlights singing. I don't quite get the whole music industry thing, but last month she was practically bubbling about a night job singing at a blues bar. Something about a new singer who is doing duets with her. Besides her beauty and intelligence Vanji is also gifted with unbelievable vocal chords. She can adopt just about any style she feels like.

"Did you lose your gig?" I ask, shutting the bathroom door be- hind me and perching on the edge of the tub. Only way to get a little peace around here.

"Dumped. Lainey, they might as well have thrown tomatoes at us. Our first big shot…"

"I'm so sorry, sweetie. Who is 'us'?"

"Oh. Just my band, uh, my new group, you know. You'll hear us soon, promise. Our sound is too pure. Too pure, Lainey. This…this guy, he goes: 'so we were hoping for hoarse, you know, gospel-type.'"

"So is it a race thing?" I don't know the ethnicity of her band, and I don't dare ask right now. Timber crashes in, slamming the bathroom door against the wall.

Vanji bursts into a string of expletives, and I cover the earpiece. I make signs for Timber to go away, but he is jumping up and down, trying to take the phone from me.

"I wanna talk. I wanna say hi Aunt Vanji."

"Stop it. No, not you Vanji. Well, yes, you should stop too but I mean Timber, who's looking for a beating. Go away or leave me alone, please." I turn my back to Timber as I make my way back to the counter.

Vanji blows her nose. "It's okay. Let him talk to me for a second. It will cheer me up. And I won't cuss, promise." Reluctantly I give in.

Cristian wipes his hands off on the towel and surveys the clean dishes with pride. I realize for the first time that he really is telling the truth. He kind of likes washing dishes. He whispers an apology for letting Timber bother me and pulls him off the phone, interrupting a crazy diatribe about someone who can probably even fly. I take it with my left, since my right is still a tiny bit tender beneath a big Band-Aid. "What's that, Timmy-poo?" she is saying.

"Just me again. I cut him off."

I'm listening to Vanji moan about her review at the club as the boys head outside. The breeze that cuts in behind them is still chilly, but the sun shines brightly on that muddy entrance area. Beneath a stack of junk mail on the counter I spy a single M&M, left over from our poker game the other night. Doesn't gross me out. I love that little burst of chocolate, when you make yourself suck without biting and the coating gets almost sharp.

"Did they actually fire you?" I finally ask, swallowing. I mean, the girl can do gospel, if that's what they want. She can make you run the aisle and scream hallelujah or woe is me if she feels like it.

"No, but, well, it was just a one-time gig and I don't think we'll be invited back. I mean that guy just sits over in the corner smirking like he knows something…"

I can still taste a hint of chocolate along the sides of my tongue. Yum. "So, what, this guy is the owner or your agent or what?"

"Nah. He's just some regular at this bar I guess."

Vanji can make me crazy sometimes. She's so dramatic she probably really will make it as a singer. When a real crisis hits she is the coolest person in the room, but everyday ups and downs flip her around like a yo-yo. Her voice is back to normal now, and she kind of laughs it off. She tells me I've helped her get grounded and put the thing in perspective. Another friend told her the same thing, but she didn't listen to him. Him? Vanji doesn't easily invest herself to the point of calling someone "friend," and I've never heard her use the term in a masculine context. This is big, but I am afraid of spooking my girl so I decide not to pry. Yet.

"So did Cristian tell you about my little incident with electricity?" I'll save the restaurant news till I know she's calm enough to take it in.

He didn't. I tell her, leaving out the part about having asked for a sign just before it hit. "You are crazy, girl. Who gets hit by lightning?"

"I know, right? That's what your brother said."

"And are you okay? Have you gotten checked out, like, your heart and everything?"

I tell her about the ambulance and exaggerate the kid's qualifications a little. No, I don't need to go to a real doctor, but thanks for the concern. By the time our conversation is over, though, I've pretended that I will go and Vanji has pretended that she doesn't care about one heckler's rude remarks. She doesn't say any more about her mysterious new friend. But it makes me mad, this secret friend. It's like some dishonest thing has seeped into our relationship. I hang up slightly frustrated but at least with a promise that she'll come up for Easter dinner and stay the night, according to tradition. I was hoping for a sister to solve all my problems but I feel more like Vanji has just used me in that role.

Cristian peeks his head in the door to see if I've hung up, before allowing Timber to burst back in. Their faces are flushed and they're happy. This time they hang onto each other while getting their boots off, and most of the mud is corralled on the tiles and in the tray. Then they run to me and, one on each side, press their icy cheeks against mine, giggling like girls.

"You boys." I say. "I don't understand you, but I love you. And yes, Vanji is coming for Easter."

Chapter Eight

THE BOY

It was the middle of the night. The boy's eyes shot open and he sat up in the rumpled Murphy bed. The cabin was very dark with only the sliver of a moon showing in the highest part of the big window where no curtain reached. Besides that silver thread, there was a small reddish heat which forced its way through the air vent on the top of the old woodstove. That red light hit the boy and made a gleam in his wide-open eyes. His hands pushed a heavy quilt off his legs and they swung in tandem over the edge of the bed. In a fluid motion the small body slid out of bed and stood pajama-ed on the rug. He took a mechanical step toward the red light.

Lights were falling all around. Magic lights with super powers. The boy walked through a meadow of light, reaching towards light as if catching butterflies. Just like butterflies, he couldn't seem to catch any. His heart was breaking, and his eyes leaked, because the light was precious and powerful and he had to have some. Then just as he grasped an armful of glitter he saw that it was actually a reflection of firelight on small pieces of colored foil, glued haphazardly to an evil smiling face. The mask from school. And the horror and failure of the object and the project and his dream came together and he was awake almost. And the boy felt a power fill him after all, and he turned the iron handle on the front of the woodstove and he poked the coals with the poker stick just like his father and he flung the hideous mask into the open maw.

With no words, the boy made a magic chant that could destroy evil and bring back showers of light. The boy danced without knowing he was dancing, a slow step-slide while he hummed his magic hum-thumping hummer. A piece of tissue paper caught fire because he wanted it to, and he flew and slid around the room and the universe night sky fast and slow, light and dark until suddenly he was jolted like the lightning bolt back into his old home cabin. Awake now, with ears and eyes open widely.

On the floor was Rabbit. And they were running towards him.

Yelling. Always, they were yelling.

LAINEY

I'm standing in the restaurant. It's our restaurant, and it is completely filled. People are chatting happily with each other all up and down the long plank tables, passing baskets of McDonalds burgers family-style. I'm actually, I realize in a panic, standing on a table, and the swinging antler chandelier is about to hit me. Then I smell the smoke. It's curling out from the kitchen. In fact, I can't even see in the open kitchen door because it is filled with plumes of gray. Cristian? No one seems to notice or hear me, even when I try to run down the table and step in bowl after bowl of thick, sticky ketchup. I think my hair is tangled in the antlers because I am pulling and going nowhere. Timber. Where is Timber?

"Lainey. Wake up. You're having a bad dream. What the heck—smoke!" And Cristian has leapt from bed beside me. Sweat drips between my breasts and my heartbeats are all over the place, syncopated black notes. Hazy consciousness. Crashes and bumps as

Cristian descends the ladder, and then yelling and crying and I'm still trying to pull myself into some kind of awareness. I smell it now, the stench of burning trash or an overheated engine. Cristian stands beside me again, and we're moving together, slowly, down the ladder. Then I'm wrapped in a quilt on the couch and Timber is sniffling into my belly, soaking my pajama shirt with mucus. The cabin door is open and frigid air bites my cheeks. Outside is only black. It's the deepest black the eastern sky ever gets, which means even far-away Denver is still mostly, finally, asleep.

Cristian curses and mutters and Timber, beside me, begins a grating wail. As my cheeks freeze, my mind clears, and I see the smoke-filled loft and the ceiling fan slowly rotating, moving the cloud through our tiny upstairs window vent. In the fireplace in front of us is a hideous face; half-burned but colorful strips of tissue paper curling down from an evil snarl. The smoldering mass smells of burned white paste and papier-mâché. Something wicked this way comes.

"Fire! He plays with fire, in the middle of the bloody night?" Cristian fumes.

Timber jumps up. "I no play with fire. Is in fireplace where fire goes. You hate me. I stupid. I just a stupid dummy like Taylor say. I no can do nothing. Why you no throw me away?" He holds Rabbit in his left hand and throws him at the woodstove. There's a clink when the bunny's glass eye hits the cast iron, and Rabbit crumples to the floor.

"Stupid Rabbit. I gonna pull you ears off and stuff 'em in you mouth an'…"

Timber now stands in the middle of the floor, with the quilt I had been wrapped in falling off his skinny frame. Cristian continues a weird dance with an upside down broom, I guess trying to help move the ruined air out of the cabin. He ignores Timber. Neither of us will say it. We both know that Cristian slipped the smoke detector's nine-volt sideways when I burned a tray of cookies in the oven a couple of months ago. We both bear the guilt, but each of us wants the other to feel it.

"Timber," I yell. He turns, slightly. "Get your sorry self over here now. Not only did you try to burn the house down in the middle of the night and now almost ruin your favorite toy, but now I am freezing and you took the blanket. I am so sick of this crap. How are we supposed to run a restaurant when we have to constantly worry about what stupid stunt you're going to play next?"

"Aaah, you hate me." And he drops the quilt and runs for the open door, shirtless and barefoot with thin flannel pajama pants. Cristian intercepts him and takes him down in a football move. I realize I have jumped up, but there is the quilt so I grab it and wrap myself back up, shivering in the depth of my bones. I am sorry. I am so very sorry. The boys lie there for a few minutes, chests heaving, before coming to join me. Cristian grabs the blankets off Timber's bed on the way and we huddle, broken and breathing shallowly, while the slightest red line moves across the black of the gaping doorway and slowly, slowly, breaks into dawn.

Chapter Nine

I still can't believe those words fell out of my mouth this morning: let's go to church. We awoke cotton-mouthed with eyes bleared from smoke and cold and angry pain, three Claysons tangled together on the couch, blinking to remember what happened last night. I looked from Timber to Cristian and said it, like you might suggest pancakes or grits. And stranger than my suggestion, stranger even than Timber's middle of the night attempt to destroy his ugly art project and almost gas us all, was Cristian's prompt decision.

"All right, everyone. Get dressed, nice, now."

And somehow we were sitting on long wooden pews with people all around and in front of us, and most of them we already knew. We even knew the preacher, by sight at least. The disconcerting thing was all the smiling. Noticing us, newbies in this place, those smiley faces got even brighter, and it was almost comical. I wanted to make an announcement after the preacher's lesson; that it was nice but we're not joining up or anything, but then I looked at Cristian and he was in. Like, transformed.

So here I sit in the Crow Barre with Celia, in the middle of another bizarre transcendental conversation, and I can see Cristian's glowing face outside the window where he stands near Timber, who is doing short sprints to make up for spilling a glass of water. Well, not for spilling it. That would be cruel, of course. He's training because of his reaction of screaming like a maniac that it was not his fault but mine because I always make him do everything bad. I bumped his arm, he insists, even though I am sitting opposite his chair, which was next to Celia, before he knocked it on the ground in the middle of his tantrum. He was angry because I told Celia about the smoke last night. "You always tell," he screamed. "Why can't you just shut up?"

"Dad has always said it is dangerous, this church and religion stuff." I speak quietly, almost whispering, in the Crow Barre dining room, filled with people who have also just come from Sunday services. Celia looks at me, not near but right into my eyes. Her left eye has the smidgen of a cloud in it and drifts just slightly away. Her right eye pierces my soul.

"He's right, of course. Religious tradition causes a lot of division. Seeking God, now, that is different. That saves the world." Celia sits back a little. I cross my legs and the table joggles, causing our empty dishes and glasses to clink. Suddenly she leans forward and that right eye grabs me again.

"No, I'm sorry. That's just a matter of semantics. Let me try to explain what I mean. Organized religion can be dangerous on a political level, but that's not what really scares people even though it probably should. History is full of failed attempts at state religion, after all, and just look at the Middle East today. But I think that what people actually fear is profound personal change. People who can be counted on to act one way suddenly act another. When you go beyond religion to seek God—or rather, when God gets out of religion and seeks you—now that is when we get nervous, don't you think?"

Nervous? Yes. Don't I think? No. When have I ever thought about this stuff? Never. But I am thinking now. My soul burns. Glancing beyond Celia I see the couple at table seven staring at us open- mouthed and snap my own jaw shut. Celia is oblivious and continues, following a reinforcing sip of tepid coffee.

"When moral law takes precedence over politics, priorities rearrange themselves. We become new. What could be more dangerous? So yes, many people, from communist to conservative, are petrified of religion. They are so scared of spiritual things that they would use any means of force, coercion, or ridicule, to cut the spiritual craving from every human heart."

She's insane. But so am I, apparently. I feel that actual ache she is talking about, spiritual craving. "But you can't."

"No, you can't cut out your need for the real thing. The person of Truth. The person of Peace. Lainey," adds Celia, leaning in so close that her white curls cover us both with a halo of holiness, "do you believe those simple words you spoke so long ago…are you still willing to take that narrow road?"

Vaguely, I am conscious of choice, of a host of different religious traditions and cultures. Why this one? Why now? A ribbon of cloud is visible beyond the window, a celestial pathway. I choose.

"Yes, I believe."

"Then you are already being remade." A gazillion skin cells fall off, and I am naked and red. Blood courses strangely into and out of a tender but mighty heart. This instant, this breath, the words hanging in the air in front of Celia's lips, my lips—this, then, is Truth.

"Celia," I whisper, cautiously, "Is this thing big enough for Timber?"

She turns to look out the window. Bright sunshine glints off a parked semi, and Cristian gives a high- five to Timber, who has apparently completed his final sprint. I can see Timber's lips moving, and he lets his dad put an arm across his back as they return to the restaurant. Birdsong is so strong in the pines that even in here it covers the soft-playing country station from the kitchen. Each note is separate, vibrating through the cosmos and tickling my inner ear. My ratty old cardigan hovers like silk over bare skin. That blanket of peace. Celia smiles. And I do too.

"I am." Echoes in my mind.

Peace never lasts. We have paid and are making our goodbyes when gravel spits beneath the tires of a two-tone (if primer counts as a color) Bronco, and Timber squeals "Gwam-Pa" in an annoying baby voice. Cristian shuts the car door he has been holding open for me and strides toward my flannel-clad father, who has flung his door wide the moment he decided to park, but as usual, before the car is done moving and turned off. My mother, on the other hand, adores making everyone stand around waiting while she retouches lipstick, straightens her hair, and fluffs her scarves, before ejecting a dainty paw for the closest chivalrous male to gingerly touch whilst the queen alights. It's a good thing my parents are self-sufficient because if they had to live with us I think I would have to be admitted to a loony bin before a week was out. I can't remember if they've gotten worse or if they have always been just like this.

"Stay back." I warn, as usual. I glance around but don't see Celia. She's probably already driving down the highway.

Dad stands by the Bronco, and as Timber runs to him he raises his hand in a stupid salute: "How."

My skin crawls as Timber freezes stiffly and repeats the gesture, and then does the stupid movie battle cry of slapping his mouth with his open palm while screeching. I'm glad our adoption was finalized years ago, because I'm sure this insensitive behavior would have been grounds enough for denying my family the privilege of raising a Native kid. After their ceremonial greeting Timber busies himself smashing Rabbit's face into the gravel landscaping along the edge of the parking space.

Cristian knows the drill by now so he has already shaken Dad's hand, like some random stranger, and is waiting at Mom's side of the car. He has a theory that she likes to hold three minutes of time captive, so the sooner you get started...

"Didn't answer the phone," accuses Dad, and stops to cough and spit phlegm. "So we went by the place. But I guess you were here. He pulling Sunday again?" Every word tugs at that blanket on my shoulders, and the more I fight to hold onto that peaceful feeling, the faster it dissolves away. "He" is my husband, Cristian. We've been together for ten years now; you'd think Dad could say his name. And the very idea that our whereabouts are any of this man's business…

Just as my imaginary blanket drops away and the burned flesh on my palm threatens to set fire to the rest of my body, I feel a soft hand and there is Celia. Breathe deep, she whispers. Or maybe doesn't, but I do. And in one breath I am okay again. Better, anyway. I am being remade, right?

"Dad," I say, "This is Celia…"

"Vonderbrandt," she furnishes.

I decide to go for broke. They want to know where we've been? "We went to church this morning and then stopped here for dinner. Cristian's not working today." Dad coughs again. He sounds really horrible, but that's usual for him. A lifetime of shivering in hunting blinds, warming his house with a fireplace, and of course smoking is starting to catch up. When he finally stops choking, I see that my mother now stands slightly behind him, on Cristian's arm, awaiting her introduction to the group. She doesn't get it.

"Vonderbrandt-- Are you Roy's wid—ahem—Was Roy Vonderbrandt your husband?"

"Yes, I am Roy's widow. You were friends?" Celia smiles and looks Dad directly in the eye as she had looked at me a few minutes before. She reaches to push a curly white wisp of hair off her forehead, but the breeze sends it back again. My dad zips his jacket higher.

"Sure. Roy was a good guy. One of the best pancake flippers we had at the Hall." He means the musty A-frame where ancient vets sit around complaining about politics and sharing hunting and fishing lies. They still have a monthly breakfast, although what they're raising funds for is beyond me. Maybe they are equipping a militia to teach those whippersnappers in Washington a thing or two.

Mom makes a desperate plea to be included by faking a dainty sneeze. Celia notices and steps back, widening the circle (which was plenty wide enough to begin with) and extending a smile. Her hand would never reach now, and it's unclear if my mother would shake it or kiss it or simply look at it anyway.

"There is no doubt you are Elena's mother," Celia offers. "I can see where her beauty comes from." It's the wrong thing to say, of course, and my mother looks stricken. She touches her cheekbone.

"I didn't sleep so well last night," she explains. I know what she's thinking: How bad must I look to be compared to Elena?

"Me either. Timber tried to smoke us out."

Timber yells, "It over. You no supposed to talk no anymore." He begins to wail, but a touch from his daddy miraculously calms him. My parents ignore our outbursts, as we have nothing to do with their agenda.

"Next week the kids will be home. All of 'em, and..." Another dramatic pause while Dad coughs and my mother finishes for him.

"Angela, she is coming. She will need our guest room. Probably you can find someplace for your brothers at your house."

"We have two blow-ups you can use," adds Dad.

Cristian physically steps into the conversation but he touches my arm, lightly, on the way and meets my eyes. The thermometer drops a few degrees and I try to remember to breathe.

"Mr. Morse, we will be kind of tight already, since we are expecting my sister Vanji for the weekend. Perhaps it would be easier for Angela to stay with us since she is also a single girl, and for your sons to stay at your place?" I would die of shock if we didn't all know that Angela says she is coming every single time she talks to my parents and yet hasn't been "home" since before we were married. Has never met her brother-in-law or her only nephew.

My mother's cheeks deepen in outrage. I have always thought my mother prejudiced against Cristian. But why would she be? Isn't it more likely that she's simply angry that she keeps hoping for what she knows will never happen? It's not about me and Cristian, it's Angela. Suddenly my burning indignation is replaced with pity.

"Look, Dad, whatever you need, we will do. If Brad and Joe want to stay with us, they can." The younger boys will come, but just for dinner, and then they'll leave at the earliest opportunity. We all know that. We also all know that Mike will not be here. Until he can come home with success and a trophy he can hang on the Morse family fringes. We have danced this dance many times. Dinner will be at our house, changed from the folks' at the last minute, because…well, any number of things could be given as excuses. Vanji, too, is sometimes a toss-up, but this time I am going to play all my cards. Too much has happened for her not to come and stay long enough to catch up. This time I made her promise. She is, after all, my best friend and more of a sister than my sister ever was.

There's a break in the conversation as a Safeway truck passes, air brakes squealing, leaving the odor of rubber and burning electronics thick in the air. The sun is in my eyes.

Celia, who had subtlety positioned herself out of the conversation, is re-introduced to my mother, who actually responds in a polite and charming fashion. Celia steers clear of complimenting me again, but talks of Timber's luck in having his grandparents close. Her own grandchildren are growing up in Kansas and California now, and it just kills her to have to choose whom to visit. All those years in Panama, it was one or the other and always hurt feelings. She's just going to stay here alone this time. These gas prices have made travel so much more costly, you know. My mother listens with interest.

Timber has reached the limit of his ability to stand around. He begins to gather small stones from the lot and place them, one atop another, on the hood of the Liberty next to Filthy Rabbit. Not only might he scrape the paint, but I know what Travis will say if he sees him. The greater danger is probably what Timber could do with the stones, with cars speeding down the highway right behind us making wonderful targets. Cristian notices too, and we take our leave. It's no surprise to hear Celia inviting all of us to church next Sunday.

"It is, after all, Easter," she asserts. "Everyone goes to church on Easter." Close to my ear she whispers, "I almost forgot. I have a little something for you." And there is a tissue-wrapped book in my hand, and we're in our Liberty and heading away from my parents and toward our home. I open it and it's exactly what I expected. A guide book, she said. Holy Bible, it says.

THE BOY

The boy listened to every word Celia said. A group of children sat in a circle on a bunch of old beanbags in the corner of a small classroom. She read a story, but she wasn't really reading, she was telling a story she already knew word for word. The boy stood hands on the doorjamb leaning out into the hallway, but he listened especially hard, since he knew she was just Celia for him and not Missus Celia, like the girl with dirt-colored hair kept saying. He listened because he had met Celia when the lightning struck his mother and danced in the air. The boy knew that this was a very special thing between himself and the old lady, and he did not want to share it. He hoped she wouldn't mention anything in front of the other children. He was ready to run if she did.

Instead, she talked to him alone but made it look like she was speaking to everyone, as though she were an ordinary teacher. Celia spoke of a boy who was good and obedient and the listening boy wanted, more than anything, to be the boy she talked about. That boy, Celia said, grew up to tell people, I am the Light of the World. What does that mean, asked Celia. The way to go? Truth and goodness? Yes, thought the boy. Yes, that is it—light-of-the-world falling through the air full of miracles. Both of us have super powers, thought the boy. And he wished the other boy could be his secret friend.

Chapter Ten

"Who left the milk out!" It's not a question but an accusation. Timber and Cristian both glance up, disinterested in my same old mundane complaint. So what if today is Easter and Mom's stress level is blinking red. What do they care?

Neither of them left the milk out; it's just that neither of them put it away. Why would they? Mommy will do it. I stick the carton in the fridge, wiping the splotches of already thickening spilled milk off the counter. I'm even angrier because they use this stupid expensive lactose-free milk. I use yogurt. Cheap, bulk, vanilla yogurt with my daily grape nuts. There's a sticky O on the edge of Timber's bowl and rather than eat it, he flicks it off, laughing as it sails across the kitchen to bounce off my hip.

"Ooh. I got her butt, Dad."

"Nice. Ten points."

"No, twenty-gazookan points. Hit the butt. Smack a butt." And he's lining up more little bits of cereal to launch.

"Stop it," I scream. "Are you going to clean this crap up?" To Cristian: "Don't you think I have enough to do without you encouraging him to trash everything? Boys are so stupid."

"Dad, she call me stupid."

"She called me stupid too. Maybe we are going too far, huh? Let's get out of Dodge, pardner." Cristian is trying a puppy dog face and he's patting my hind quarters, "Where did that Cheerio get to?" and hoping his charms will work but my face is still hot and I will not be appeased by silliness. Cristian takes the not-too-subtle hint and swings Timber up sideways, and they go outside to sweep the porch. It's not about them, I know. It's about my mother, calling, as expected, to beg off for hosting today's get together. All because of Angela.

Mom had a week. An entire week to cancel, and she waits until the "morning of." We were swamped enough because Cristian's already cooking practically the entire Easter meal. And my mother has the nerve to drag me out with this charade that she was actually going to host. Little updates, all week long, about how Dad had finally gotten around to fixing the front door, cleaning the flue, even moving the junk 4-wheeler around back. Cristian had to help with shovel duty on Thursday, filling the odd holes in the driveway. This just in case Angela were to show up in a flashy little sports car or something. You know how those rental places can do things. No, Mom, I don't, and neither do you. When have we ever rented a car? And when has Angela ever come home? And now, now this.

I was a senior in high school the last time I saw her. She stole my car. Technically it was not my car, but I was the one who used it. Piece of crap Ford Taurus with a broken taillight. I used it almost exclusively because it was a stick shift and Angela was too lazy to learn, Mom was too old, and Mikey was too aggressive. But suddenly, sometime after that girl died at the high school and everything seemed to change, Angela developed this interest in learning. I showed her a couple times but the jerking hurt my neck and I was embarrassed that someone might see us. Also, I suspected she was up to something. She was.

Angela was supposedly taking classes at the closest community college down in the city, but she never worked on anything at home and her class hours seemed awfully flexible. Also I heard her demanding cash from our father, because the admissions office couldn't do checks. Could he be any more dense?

The guy was named Troy. Or Scott or Todd. When they left, late at night, I saw Angela's silhouette against the headlight of my car as she slunk off. I am sure—99.8 percent sure—there was a little bulge below her prized upper bulges. The kind of bulge the doctors say I will never achieve. The kind of bulge one expects to hear news of, say four or five months down the road. Three months down that road we still hadn't heard from Angela. Dad was talking to detectives. Mom was sure I had made up the story about her voluntary middle of the night escape. And then, the day of my graduation when, rather than dressing up to attend, my mother was tearfully constructing one of her disturbing little Mexican shrines to Saint Angela, with that daughter's mortarboard cap as the centerpiece, flanked by her prom and graduation photos—two different guys, even then—at that very moment the first postcard arrived. No return address.

> *Hey, You-All, Greetings from sunny South Carolina. You wouldn't believe how hot it is here. Suckers! I bet you still have snow. Sean sends his love. (He might be The One, Daddy!) I'll bring him up to meet you-all (like my accent!) for the 4th of July if we can both get off work. It's a great job! I will be loaded soon! Tootles, Angela*

No "Sorry to miss your graduation, Sis," no "By the way, I'm having a baby." And she didn't. At least, she has never mentioned a kid in the half-dozen equally brief notes she's bothered to send since, or the more recent smattering of phone calls. In fact, she's never mentioned me or our brothers. Once she sent a whiny note that included a post office box number in North Dakota where money should be sent, because how could she expect to find work without a decent outfit? One wondered, how can you expect to find work in North Dakota even with a decent outfit? That time, she made a blanket statement about men being jerks. This was enough for my mother to relieve Angela of all guilt or responsibility. This is about love. Angela just loves too much, or the wrong men. The poor thing.

So many times I have wanted to throttle my mother and make her see the truth. Angela loves too much, all right. She loves herself. She obviously didn't love her baby enough to give it life. She obviously didn't love her parents enough to tell them she was leaving.

And she obviously didn't love our brothers and me enough to care about our lives. Instead, she behaved in a way that caused our father to clamp down on any dating and almost all social activities for the rest of us. Of course, by then I was almost gone from home anyway. But I was saved from Angela's rabid promiscuity—ha, like that was a threat. Cristian was my first and last love, even if he is a slob who is making double the work for me on this solemn day of family torture.

While I'm mentally regurgitating this litany of hurts by Angela, dirty dishes move through my hands and into the drainer. When I squeeze the rag and hang it on the faucet, it is Angela's arm I am thinking of, and I wring it a little tighter than usual. I wish Dad had brought the tables he has promised so that I could get them set. But Timber would probably just go careening through and knock something over anyway. I shuffle through the cabin again, picking up all the knocked-down magazines and pillows that I have already picked up twice today.

Thinking, still. Rubbing the emotional wounds. Big surprise. Dad called Angela last night, for the first time since she left, what, twelve years ago? Dad wanted to see if he could get Angela to change her mind and let him pick her up from the airport after all. When she called last week she had said, "No, Daddy, don't be silly. I always rent a car. I will be there; if I'm running late just save me a little plate, please."

But for Christmas this year we gave the folks a new phone, with caller ID and stuff, thinking it would help them weed out those lecherous telemarketers and old-people scammers. Suddenly, for the first time since she ran away, Dad had a way of recording her number. Silly girl, she always seemed to mix up a number or two when they'd ask, or the system was so new she didn't know the number yet, or she was calling from work... Anyway last night Dad remembered the new phone's features, and actually found the number she called from. He dialed. A teenage-sounding voice answered and said

Angela Who? And then shouted, "Frank, it's for Jelly I think. Some old guy." And a man told Dad that she was gone to another job. Where? NASA. Where do you think? And who are you anyway? Jelly doesn't have any family, she told him that when they first met. Bailey, Colorado? No, no one is going to Bailey. Wrong number, you schmuck.

And you are a schmuck, I think, as he tells me all this early in the morning, his voice muffled. You have been a schmuck for a long time now. Mom can't host. She's trying to digest this news. Would we mind?

And I do, I mind so much I could scream, but the sound of my daddy's voice transferred over the fiber optics of the phone line is so hurt, so bruised that I say sure. They are still going to visit the church this morning. It is, after all, Easter Sunday, and everyone in town will go. Except that none of us has before, I want to add, and how will we have time to be ready? Brad is going to be up by one, even though his apartment in Boulder is almost as far away as Joe's condo in Colorado Springs. Mike, who already admitted he won't show, lives only an hour away in Denver.

The truth is I expected this, because something always happens. Even though signs were stronger than ever before that my parents might actually go through with hosting; the driveway cleaning and all, I still knew deep down that it would all fall apart. Anyway there's that tiniest little relief in knowing that Timber can't break or dirty anything that he hasn't already broken or dirtied, and none of it will belong to his grandmother.

Dad left it to me to tell the boys, and they wondered why I bothered to call. Family dinner is always at our place, despite whatever they are told initially. Joe wondered what would make anyone think Angela was coming, despite whatever she said. And as I expected, Mikey bowed out. We don't need Dad asking a lot of questions, he told me. This isn't the time to play 'fess up to all your broken expectations. So I learned another family secret: Michael the star quarterback is not currently playing any sport at all and has a girlfriend that he's afraid to introduce. Maybe he doesn't think we will approve of her. I begged him to bring this mystery woman, and finally got a half-promise of a future meeting with just Cristian and me.

"I really like her, Lainey. I can't lose her to the family weirdness until I'm sure we can both take it. By the way, you haven't been hit by any more lightning this week, have you?" Ha ha ha.

So here I stand, with a Cheerio mark on my butt and a rag in my hand and a thousand worries in my head. The boys come back inside, cheeks aflame from the morning cool. Cristian coerces Timber into "coloring" all over an old magazine on the floor under his folded-up bed. The house is clean, or at least as clean as we ever get it. Cristian's food stands before me, ready in a variety of dishes that will fit together in a warm oven while we do the church thing again.

"Well?" he breathes in my ear and I scrunch my shoulder to itch it. "What do you think?"

I know what he means because I was about to say the same thing. The one unknown of the day. The Wild Card.

"She'll come," I say. "I told her…I need her." I start to cry and Cristian holds me softly. My beloved Vanji. Little motherless thing that mothered me better than my own. I don't think that "friend" is supposed to be a bond stronger than blood, stronger than sister, but to me it is. I love Cristian in a different, maybe bigger way, but Vanji will always be my bestie.

"HONK HONK." echoes Timber, leaping across the cabin. She always does that for him. Honks twice, fast, and lightly. He's ripped the front door open and is yanking on her car door, even as the dust is still settling. We run behind him, just as excited as our six-year-old.

"Whoa. Tiger-Tim." she laughs, trying not to trip on the monkey now attached to her kneecaps. "You, boy, are bigger every time I blink."

She freezes dramatically and stares at me. "Lightning. Lightning? Who gets struck by lightning?" Vanji is going Caucasian today, with her relaxed hair pinned up from her face and pulled into a low ponytail. She wears a tight purple t-shirt and indigo jeans to show off her perfect figure. She's cruel, this pseudo-sister of mine. Knows exactly the effect she has on my hormone-riddled little brothers.

Cristian pecks her cheek and folds her fashionable new handbag (someone's been self-pity shopping) over an arm as he hooks his little sister with the other. Get these tears out of my eyes. But they are flowing now, and I'm getting to that snotty choky state.

"Just a sec," I call, running back inside to the bathroom. Cold water on my face and Vanji's bony little hands on my back. My heart is slightly irregular, still. The blood in my veins reminds me of newness. I am aware of dirty blood pumping in and clean blood pumping out. Getting zapped and remade, being washed clean. I decide to let go of the anger towards Angela, the anger towards my parents. I'll wash it down the sink.

"We were afraid you wouldn't come," I sniffle.

"But I said I would. I ain't Angelina-Jo-look-at-me, you know. Or is she really here? Is that why you are crying?" Vanji's eyes go wide at the thought. She's been through all the family milestones: our wedding, my brothers' various graduations and big games, Timber's arrival and adoption, birthdays, and has never once met Angela. How could she? Angela's been gone forever. Since before Vanji and I met. Angela's faded into a Morse family myth. Wherever she is.

We kill a few minutes side by side on the couch, sipping coffee with real cream and waiting for Timber to first wind up and then deactivate. It's impossible to have a real conversation while he is the center of attention, but if he doesn't get that time right off he'll keep trying and that's even worse. I wonder sometimes if he doesn't share my mother's genes after all. Vanji is so perfect with her nephew. She says it's because she gets to come and go, and no doubt that is partly true. So many days I wish I could just go. Timber has shown her every page in the magazine he just destroyed with crayons and is looking around for something else with which to impress his beloved auntie.

"I maked a mask at school, was green and blue but I burnt it in fireplace stove and Mom was SO mad because of smoking up everything cause you can die more from smoke than flames but not lightning because Mommy no is dead and Daddy hit me really hard. And it was no cool it was stupid how come is why I burn it up POOF 'cause sometimes I can't do nothing but I want butterfly lights so I go burn the mean guy. And look." And he's rolling around doing somersaults which is his latest physical skill. Vanji glares at Cristian.

"Cristian didn't hit him. Timber, you had better stop saying that."

"Yeah, huh. Him hit me and me fall down in snow and mine finger turn blue." This, slightly muffled as my son continues rolling around, bumping our legs and the sofa table.

I'm starting to tense up again. "Okay. That's enough. You are hurting me and Aunt Vanji. And your finger was blue from the paint on the mask and you didn't even go outside, you just tried, and Daddy stopped you by tackling you and I am serious about not saying that we hit you." Even Vanji's presence can't keep me from seeing red again, already. I wish I could keep my calm. Earlier I was ready to punch Cristian over the cereal and milk. Now I want to hit my kid if he says one more time that I hit him.

"Aunt Vanji is a Panda-ji. A panjie. Is a pansy?" Timber tilts his head and smiles, but Vanji frowns and nods no-no.

"Let's not get into name-calling, Timber, honey. When you start rhyming sometimes you say real words, and sometimes they aren't good ones."

"Panda? Pansy? What's a panda-zee?"

"Time for church," says Cristian, and we look up, surprised.

"Really?" says Vanji. "You all are just gonna go off and leave me here?"

"No, you are coming with us. Timber, smooth your hair and your shirt. Lainey, want that?" he nods to the "guidebook" Celia gave me a week ago. I haven't cracked it yet. Well, I fanned the pages and found a ribbon sewn in marking the middle of the book of Isaiah. It did pique my interest, simply because Isaiah is Brad's middle name. But I didn't have time. I don't want Celia to ask me about it, nor do I want to look like I belong there, so I leave it. Vanji stares at us with her lips apart.

"Are you seriously doing this? I am in blue jeans, big brother."

"Yup, little sister," says Cristian, guiding her toward the door, "we are. And don't worry about jeans. This is Bailey."

THE BOY

Auntie Vanji was the best aunt in this whole world. I got you, babe, she said all the time but the boy's name was not Babe. It wasn't Timbertoes or Timbuktu, either, but Aunt Vanji was funny and the boy liked it when she came up with a new name for him. He wasn't supposed to call her names, though, because he was just a little kid and might say bad words on accident. But most of all he liked to know that she got him. You and me, we understand each other and we've got each other's back, right? Right.

Of course Vanji didn't ask the boy, or his parents or anyone, if he would like to ride in her car. She just leaned in for a cheeky-cheeky rub and nodded toward her…space shuttle. The boy gasped. Better than the ride in his mother's rocket ship. He lifted the portal, jumped up, and felt a little rip in the too tight and too scratchy but don't make a fuss and wear them anyway pants he had to put on that morning. He smiled a little because that would be the end of that after all. Aunt Vanji heard it, he thought, but it looked like she thought he farted so he said Wow. Who farted? And then spread apart his legs so they could see the rip in the middle of his bottom.

The boy's mother would have made him go back in and change but Aunt Vanji just said Keep your legs together and don't be flashing anyone in church, 'kay? Being with Aunt Vanji made the boy so happy he started to make some baby animal squeak sounds, but even Aunt Vanji didn't like those 'cause honey I'm driving. Be a flower instead, she told him, and make your face just blossom out like it's morning and the sun is coming up. It was the most beautiful thing the boy had ever heard and so he began to cry, softly. But she thought he was sad about the animal sounds and started to apologize and explain about loud things outside only and everything just felt ruined.

Aunt Vanji pushed a button then, a kind of hyperdrive and she and the boy flew out of their seats into the starry darkness of space and holding hands they used their rocket booster packs and then suddenly they landed in the parking lot of Celia's church and the boy had forgotten to use his super-mind-powers to tell something special to Aunt Vanji (I love you most in the universe) and the parents were walking up and the mother might see the rip and yell at the boy and then Aunt Vanji leaned in super close and whispered You are my sun and moon, little man. I got you babe. And he realized that he must not have forgotten to send the message after all. His smile felt like a flower blooming, all the way into the building.

Chapter Eleven

LAINEY

We are kind of late, and apparently everyone really does go to church on this particular Sunday, because the auditorium is packed. A piano plays softly. The heady scent of lilies fills the air. The stage is white with bouquets, and a backlit cross hanging in front is draped in a cloth colored the yellow gold of fall aspen leaves. Last week the cloth was purple. Luckily there are lots of other people filing in and looking for spots because I hate standing out. Still, I feel an embarrassed warmth crawling up my neck onto my cheeks.

A pony-tailed man in a biker jacket scoots over so that my parents and Vanji with Timber can all squeeze into one row, and Cristian and I slide into a small space diagonally behind them. Vanji shoots me a look over her shoulder. This is a great location to observe reactions. Vanji has wrapped herself in a gorgeous scarf that makes her jeans and t-shirt look more formal than my out-of-style sweater dress.

Timber is tugging her arm and talking too loudly about a puppet he saw when we were here last week and how someone put his name on a poster and he already got a gold star just for being there and it's so good we came back because he will get another one today. If she wants he will see if they will let him keep it to give to her instead of sticking it after his name.

Celia is here, of course. She greeted us first thing, while we were still walking through the door. She has both her daughters and a pack of teenage grandchildren at her side, and is glowing with happiness. Using busyness as an excuse, I never returned Celia's

Tuesday call. Now I feel guilty. What if she was asking for help with something since her family is unexpectedly here? I was simply trying to avoid talking about myself and faith and things that make me uncomfortable.

I watch Vanji squirm. She pops a TicTac or something in her mouth and I appreciate the minty odor more than my neighbor's lavender perfume. Cristian is stuck on the lilies. "Smells like a funeral home," he whispers.

The Thorndove clan fills half a row. I blink: Julie and Billy are holding a tiny parcel between them, smiling and cooing down into it. Cristian sees, too, and nudges me. I have been so self-consumed this week, worrying about my heart rate and the dust in the rocks around my chimney, and making hard-as- rock rolls to counterbalance all of Cristian's perfect culinary delights, that I completely forgot about their baby. No one called us. It can't be more than a week old, but still.

The service begins now with louder piano music and then a greeting, and the pastor beams at our friends. "Well, Billy," he says, "Let's see her." And the new little family traipses to the front and they uncover the baby's delicate face and she yawns, and he makes a joke about long sermons. Her name is Sally Jane Thorndove, they say, and everyone says "Aw." She was born just Friday night. Rippled whispers prove that I was not the only one not in the loop. Maybe there was no loop.

Bill Senior sits proud; puff-chested like a bird in the winter with his little old wife folded in beside him, tucked under a wing. I look at my parents' grave faces and wish they would feel that way about me. Or even each other. I wonder if they are disappointed that their grandson is not of our flesh. But now Timber is making too much noise, and I watch as my mother leans across my father to touch him or hand him something. He looks up, surprised, and smiles at her.

"Thanks, Grandma," he says in an outdoor voice. She touches her finger to her lips but seems to be smiling. Or maybe she is grimacing. I don't know what he has, but it keeps him occupied until they send the little kids downstairs to get them out of the sermon.

I listen to every coo and gurgle from tiny Sally. Pages shuffling somewhere behind me grab my attention. There is a wasp's nest in the corner of a tall opaque window across from us, and I can see tiny shadows buzzing around it. My heart races and I hear the intonations of dozens of whispered comments, the hum of a microphone left on by the choir, and something like clinking glasses in a back room. I'm not sure, but I think I hear the buzz of the wasps' wings as well. The milky light falling through the window is pure, somehow. I hear myself think: this is being alive, aware.

Just as my butt goes completely numb on the wooden bench, the service finally ends with a boisterous song and a procession of children waving coloring pages as they march up the aisle. Cristian says, "What do you think? Should we do it?"

I'm just tuning back in, and the first thing I notice are Vanji's tears. "Do what?" I mumble, even as I move toward her.

"Weren't you listening? The Shackles Free rescue mission. Should we go along on Tuesday to help at the mission? He was calling for volunteers."

"Sure," I shoot over my shoulder. Now it is my turn to rub Vanji's back, like she rubbed mine this morning. I'm not going to ask what's wrong. Who am I to judge anyone's reaction to this stuff? After all, I tried talking to God and got struck by lightning. I've been spinning ever since, on the edge of tears myself. Vanji turns and we embrace for a moment, the hopes of a dozen years melting together in our arms.

"Right," she says, adjusting her classy ensemble. "Don't we have a feast somewhere to devour?" She smiles at my parents, shaking Dad's hand and leaning in a little with my mother. Probably whispering that she's sorry Angela couldn't make it. And now Vanji fully embraces my mom, which is something I have never seen before. Cristian strolls back, with Billy at his side.

"All signed up," he says. "We'll meet here at three o'clock after my shift on Tuesday. Timber can come, too." Billy is gussied up in something that is not plaid and his hair has been plastered down. He looks like someone from the Andy Griffith show, not his usual loose and comfortable self. Still, there is nothing stiff in his ecstatic expression. He's happy about seeing us in church, he's happy about Cristian wanting to volunteer at a charity, and mostly he's happy about his tiny new daughter.

"You have a new baby." I squawk. "You should have called."

"Don't worry, Lainey. Julie felt so good she just decided we'd keep her a secret for a couple of days and then bring her out today." Billy is smiling and probably genuine, but the tenor of his voice is somewhat insane from sleep deprivation.

"Where is she? Can I see?" and here is this tiny, perfect little girl-child with rosy cheeks and wisps of colorless down. "Oh, she is so beautiful. Congratulations." Billy beams and Julie, though tired, looks terrific. Timber waves his coloring page in our faces, almost scratching the baby.

"Hey."

"Sorry. Oooh. Look. A little little baby. But what for it got snot in that hair?"

"It's called cradle cap," laughs Julie, swinging Sally up to burp, one hand curling around the tiny skull. "Crappy crap? CRAPPY CRAP," and Timber looks at Vanji's wet cheeks.

"Why she cry, Grandma? She gots crappy crap? Ha ha ha." Somehow Vanji ushers everyone out of her pew, and Cristian pushes us up toward the exit.

Chapter Twelve

Brad lounges on my sofa, size-13 feet and a bottle of Coors propped on the cold woodstove, and some really obnoxious song on the radio. Help yourself, I think.

"Hey, little guy," he says to Timber, who inexplicably begins pounding on his back.

"You know babies got crappy crap—on top?" he asks, pointing to his scalp.

"Why do you think I don't want a girlfriend? Hey everyone. Wazzup?"

Mom beelines for the radio and shuts it off. The woman is in high-drama mode, smudged mascara and tightly pressed lips.

"Angela," she says tersely, "is not coming."

Brad snorts. "Really? And here I thought this might be the day… Come on, Ma, she never comes. I barely even remember what she looked like before her alien abduction or whatever. Who cares? We can still eat, even with your first-born stuck up there in Washington in her little coffee chain." At this our mother bursts into tears and heads for the bathroom.

Brad is stricken. "I'm sorry, Dad. What did I say that Mom doesn't already know? I mean, she never comes. She's too busy and self-important."

Dad clears his throat into a napkin that he quickly stuffs in his pocket before perching on the edge of the couch beside Brad. He gestures for everyone's attention. "I checked the number, after I called her back. It was not Washington. It was Colorado. Pueblo. There probably is no coffee shop chain. She's not even in another state." And another fit of coughing overtakes him.

Pueblo? She is just a few hours away and can't come home, after like a dozen years? To see her nephew? Her mother? Her father? Me? I was struck by lightning. I could be dead and she wouldn't even care. I taste the anger again and then, maybe for the first time ever I feel a new emotion rising up for my sister: pity.

"Has she been here all along, Dad?" He shakes his head. He doesn't know. Didn't even talk to her. And he recounts the conversation he had shared with me this morning. Jelly. The girl is calling herself Jelly? What is she, laughs Brad, a prostitute or pole dancer or something? And his short laugh freezes in space as we all think, together, yes, probably.

I picture a sleazy, wasted woman, too proud to just come home, and I am sorry for her. Poor Angela. Indeed.

Brad shrugs. "Well, didn't we all kind of guess something like that? I think Mike knows what she's actually been doing."

I see my dad's skin tone darken. Wonder where I get my anger issues. "What do you mean, Michael knows?" Brad slides slightly farther away from our father.

"Just, I don't know, I think she asks him for money sometimes. Something he said once, maybe. Who cares?"

I'm curious, too. I had believed the most recent coffee shop manager story, and I certainly never thought she was hiding out in PU-town, of all places.

Dad sort of slumps back on the couch. Vanji very tactfully diverts Timber out the doorway.

Dad speaks like a wounded animal. "We had this trip kind of planned. We were going to go up, surprise her. Maybe, you know, show pictures, of Lainey and Cristian and Timber, and you boys' big games, stuff like that." I go to the kitchen to get myself a Coors but think of Timber and grab a Mountain Dew instead. Six years without booze. It's all about modeling. Dad doesn't need to model. I hand him a bottle and think about Angela and the boys' banner games. Maybe it's the smell of Dad's Coors that reminds me; someone's secret spilled out on the high school stands when their thermos was knocked over, perhaps. Suddenly I am back there, years ago, and I can almost taste the pride.

We were sitting in the stands for Michael's first big game, and we were stoked. Dad had even painted half his face blue, which was terribly embarrassing but, at the same time, filled me with happiness. And Mikey came through for his pops by choosing and executing play after amazing play. He was only a sophomore and everyone was talking about his future. Angela was there, and she was smiling too. But she was looking past Mikey to the senior half-back who was waiting to take her out after the game. In all the excitement no one realized she didn't come home until the next morning. When I let the dogs out I let my sister in. I wonder, is this the past my dad hopes to recreate? Sounds to me like she's still living it.

Brad's cell phone rings, and it's Joe. He just got off the RTD and wants a ride up from the bus stop. "Don't be a pansy," Brad teases. "It's only like a mile—can't you walk it? Oh, I forgot, swim geeks need water to move." Even as he talks Brad is moving to the door, signaling Timber to come along.

"Pansy...Pansy," chants Timber. I follow out into the thin sunshine. But Brad has come on his motorcycle and short distance or not, I will not allow Timber to go without a helmet. I still say no, even when Brad offers up his. Who would drive if Brad's head got snapped off or something? And hasn't Brad just had a Coors in his hand? He says I'm ridiculous, points out that the bottle is whole, minus about half a swallow, and shrugs at his nephew, who is now mad at me. Thanks for that.

I plop in the deck chair awaiting their return and giving time for Timber's tantrum to subside. Cristian and Dad's voices drift out to us, as they discuss the relative merits of gas versus old school charcoal grilling. Meanwhile the smell of lighter fluid smoke drifts through the evergreens, from someone's distant barbecue. Timber breaks rocks against each other. Forgetting that he's mad at me, he rushes over to show me the "gold" he's discovered, mica flakes around a pure quartz center.

Soon Brad is back with Joe, both looking handsome with wind-bitten cheeks and tousled hair. The two youngest Morse boys have always shared puppy dog dispositions along with their GQ features. They are lady killers. We all blink as we step into the darkness of the cabin and then my mother is pressed in an embrace with her young-est, tearing up despite herself. Brad tells about a couple of deer they passed on the side of the road. He gives a hilarious pantomime of a buck thinking about whether or not to cross the road in front of Brad's motorcycle. If the story is meant to relieve my anxiety over his death machine it fails.

"Just missing Mike now," says Joe, who has travelled all the way up from the Springs. He doesn't mention Angela, and no one else cares to bring her up. It registers how very close Joe must be living to our sister. I think of that ugly Taurus. If Angela hadn't stolen it maybe Joe wouldn't have to take public transportation to come to a family gathering. Not that it would still be running. Actually, Joe doesn't have a car on principle. If Dad knew his son was waiting for affordable alternative fuel he'd accuse Joe of being a tree-hugger. Which he is. It's Dad's fault anyway, for teaching us all to love the natural world.

Mom seems to have composed herself as she offers drinks. Joe and Vanji have greeted each other. Vanji saw Brad at Christmas but it's been longer since we were together with Joe. She stage whispers an accusation about men being exempted from church when she was forced to go.

Brad quickly changes the subject. "So, dude, lightning. Who gets struck by lightning?"

"Yeah," chimes Joe. "What in the heck? Why were you grabbing a lightning rod anyway, Lainey? What were you thinking?"

Cristian's eyes are full of concern while he replays his version of the event, even though he wasn't there and seemed to forget almost immediately that anything happened. I've tried to downplay it myself and only mentioned it twice this week because my hand hurt. Anyway, it's nice to have a little sympathy, and I gladly show the scar to my brothers.

Timber jumps up and down with his hand up. I haven't told his story, just to Cristian, when he asked about the tear streaks down his face. The lump on his head only lasted a couple of hours and wasn't even visible with that messy mop. Why not let him explain what happened? I tell him to go ahead.

"Flash go bang. And Mommy have light stars, and I get some super power (shh, is secret) and then I be stupid and go Timber-is-a-tree-falling BOOM. Cry cry and break my crappy crap. Ha." While he jabbers he swings his uncles' arms and pulls and twists his body so that even the gist of what he wants to say is lost.

Mom turns her head away to avoid the entire unpleasant subject. To my mother, the worst part of the whole thing was seeing her name in the little write-up in our county rag. "Victim Elena (Morse) Clayson, daughter of Jim and Ida Morse of Harris Park..." Shouldn't surprise me that my life and death experience was earth shattering only to me, and yet I feel somehow slighted by the lightness with which everyone treats it. Lightning? Who gets struck by lightning?

Joe looks fit. He tells about training with Olympians and talks about kinds of dives I've never been able to keep straight. We really need to get down and watch him in the water. Timber would like that. Joe would like that. He is also doing something I don't understand, involving sales and shares and making a killing "just sitting around," he says. Brad, on the other hand, is barely paying his bills but buying whatever he wants anyway, working as a cashier at a sporting goods store. Both of them, and the rest of us, for that matter, are famished. It's time to feast. Dad has brought two doors and four sawhorses, and we press the couch and chairs up against the woodstove. With Mom's old lace table cloths and the crushed handful of fuzzy pasque lilies I picked out back, the place actually looks pretty.

"At least it doesn't smell like a funeral home," pronounces Cristian. Vanji punches him in the arm. She liked those church lilies.

Cristian directs the symphony of flavors he calls Easter Dinner and we feast. Only Mom holds back, probably upset that anyone has an appetite when poor Angela is slumming it in Pueblo, of all places. But that is not fair, I know it isn't. I can almost feel this switch click on, checking my thoughts, keeping me from diving in too deep. These waters are dangerous, change course. Judgment and self-pity are getting flagged. Note to self: ask Celia about this. I never thought about thinking before. Now, it's like I'm being held responsible for even the smallest whine or gripe. Part of the renewal, probably. Burn off the old blood, oxygenate the good blood. Try thinking a good thought for Angela. May my sister be well this day. Amen?

Finally, as the chairs are pushed back and the bellies are patted, so very manly of them all, Cristian asks, "So, Jim, how about you come along on this rescue mission thing? I signed up after the service and I have the number of the guy in charge."

"Damn, brother, did I just hear you right?" My thoughts echo Vanji's. This coming from the boy who hates charity. Won't give it; won't take it. And come on, aren't these places full of losers and dangerous men? The kind of men who choose to take no responsibility but feel entitled to be fed by others? Drunks and other losers?

"Uh, sure," says Dad, coughing again. This time I see pink before he hides the napkin. What does that mean? Blood, maybe? Something bad, I'm sure. Vanji helps me swap out platters of savory potatoes and green beans with bacon for pumpkin and apple pies.

Cristian rises and coughs. He nervously fiddles with his Stetson which had been balanced on the back of the sofa and it falls but he catches it and smashes it back in place. He bursts out, "We have big news."

Everyone freezes, and my mother and Vanji unashamedly check my belly. Then try to cover their disappointment, as soon as they hear him continue: "I'd just like to announce that we may soon be offering this same quality of gourmet food to the good people and poor slobs of the greater metropolitan Bailey area. We are hoping to open our own restaurant."

Joe and Brad are thrilled. We'll do great, it will be awesome. They are already reserving the place for their future children's birthday parties. My mom surprises me with a few kind words about Cristian's talent, although there is a slight warning about getting in too deep financially with this kind of thing. Vanji is quiet.

Cristian doesn't notice, because he and Dad and the boys are talking construction and remodeling. They are discussing where and how to find old-growth tree planks to replace a couple of rotted ones in the long tables. I catch Vanji's eye, and we carry dishes to the sink.

Before I ask she answers. "It's you, Lainey. I'm a little worried about you in this. I love that brother of mine, but I don't want to watch you melt into his shadow as some kind of kitchen slave. You are the best mama. How could you keep Timber the higher priority? I know how restaurants are. It's like the most time-consuming, least pay-off for your buck, kind of business there is. Except maybe hotels."

"Or farming," I offer, smiling.

"Or farming. Girl. You ever milked a cow? I'm telling you, that is not something you get over. Still, baby, you sure about this? This is a big thing. A big, hairy, all-over-your-life kind of thing. You wouldn't let it just swallow you up, would you? You wouldn't lose your creative genius?"

I blow some suds off my hand onto Vanji. Wipe my fingers on the front of my own t-shirt. "Wait a sec. You should see this." I pull out my "creative genius" and hand it to her. As Vanji rifles my notebook of ideas she starts to smile.

"Okay, okay. You are fine. This is what I'm talking about. You are so smart, Lainey. You've had like a week and you have a plan and projections and diagrams. And these colors are great. I love your sketches of the kitchen area. Not sure about those long tables, though. Won't it be strange sitting with a bunch of, well, strangers, to eat?" She laughs, melodically, and reaches up to redo my barrettes. The palm of her hand rests briefly on my cheek as she lowers her arm.

"Lainey, I just wanted to be sure you are not just getting swept along here. You'll be fine, you all will, and I absolutely cannot wait to have my first, complimentary meal."

"Complimentary nothing," scolds Cristian, coming around the table to look over my head at my notebook. "Family pays double. Right, guys?"

Joe answers. "Sure, bro, but only those of us who don't buy stock in the company."

He's serious, and Cristian has to copy down Bill Senior's numbers as well as the lawyers, so that Joe can check into investing some of his savings with us. Brad would, too, he says, if he had any savings. The thing is, skiing is so expensive. My parents even hum around a little, though we keep saying we are not asking anyone to do this.

Finally the sun begins to set, and the temperature drops ten degrees. Everyone but Vanji starts talking about heading home. Vanji will crash on our couch and head back to her place in Aurora in the late morning—she has Monday off this week. Brad will take Joe all the way into town to catch a direct bus to Colorado Springs, even though I would rather see him take the RTD since he has no helmet or leather jacket and they've waited until dusk. Cristian offers his junker. We could pick it up later in the week on a Denver run. Or Cristian could drive them tonight. They've been doing this since they were way too young to ride, however, and they laugh us off. We move onto the porch where we begin our goodbyes.

Suddenly my mother reengages with life. She and Dad will take Joe to the bus station. There is an argument but she wins. This is her youngest child, after all, and she will not be responsible for his blood spilt out. Brad shrugs and zooms away. Mom shudders slightly, thanks me for hosting at short notice, awkwardly pecks Vanji on the cheek while pinching Timber's, and climbs stiffly into their old Bronco behind Joe. Dad pulls his door shut as he accelerates out of the driveway. And this is safer?

It's the first time, I think, since Angela left, that I've seen my mother so concerned for any of the rest of us. It's Easter, and there's been an uprising.

Chapter Thirteen

THE BOY

The boy opened his eyes in bed and thought up a list of enemies: Taylor who sometimes made fun of him and Brian who always did and all the other children whose names he could not remember but who had hair the color of cats and pink skin. The boy and his father were maybe the only people with dark skin on all the whole mountains, and the father's was even darker than the boy's. Sometimes classmates were friends but usually enemies. Since they hated him. Also teachers and the principal and the dentist just because the boy punched him once.

Friends. All his best friends had come to the house for dinner this day. Auntie Vanji, best in the world. Uncle Brad and Uncle Joe who he didn't see very often but when he did they always punched a little too hard and then felt sorry but made the boy feel tough and strong and cool like a rap star. Grandma was a special friend but kind of secret, since her praise was always whispered, just for the boy alone, like the tiny caramels she fed him when his parents didn't notice. Grandpa, too. And Celia, even though she wasn't there today. Old people didn't scare the boy. He supposed they all could see his new invisible super cape and they played along with his disguise as an ordinary boy so that other people wouldn't guess.

Everyone the boy knew either loved him or hated him. No one just only liked him. The sheet covered his face and he blew it up and away sweaty-wet because of the hot woodstove fire since it got so cold when all the relatives left. All the friends. Everyone but Vanji who was sleeping on the couch cushions laid out on the floor. The boy wished his uncles and aunt went to his same school and class and then he wouldn't have to count friends and enemies because everyone would be a friend and no one would hate him.

Today was a very good day said his mother when she tucked him in and kissed him softly, like the first taste of an ice cream cone. He thought about all the day and then remembered going to church and Celia in the sunshine room talking about the one good boy who became a good man and got killed for it. Is it good to be good, he wondered. Celia heard his mind words and said in his imagination: Yes, yes it is worth it to be good. The boy would have beat up the bad guys when they came to kill the good man. He could have been the friend, standing against the enemies. He would not have run away like those others. He would have stood and stayed.

The boy became invisible and slid out of bed and into a cape and flew all the way there, to where people were hurting the good man and the man looked at him and loved him and with secret mind-words told the boy that he could go ahead and go to sleep, the work was already done. And then the boy slept.

LAINEY

Cristian is buzzed with the events of the day, but I am burned out. His eyes glow like fireplace coals in the dark of our bedroom loft. We're both in bed, but he sits half uncovered while I stay flat, tan flannel sheet and cotton blanket pulled tight under my chin. Every time he gestures he pulls the covers away, and I am cold and annoyed. He drones on about his trip to Shackles Free. He loved it.

My dad loved it. Dad is already looking at making some kind of commitment to go down every other week to teach basic carpentry. Just what the world needs: more dowel racks for drying out Ziploc baggies. I've already got two on my washer, and they don't really even work for drying the socks and bras I have permanently draped there. And I may be poor, but I didn't grow up during the Depression and I'm not about to wash out a slimy plastic bag.

The rescue mission has this system, Cristian explains, with levels for time served cleaning and staying sober and stuff like that, which get more advanced and can include actual college credit, and the success rate is phenomenal for this kind of thing, and I just want to tell him to shut up. Who cares? All I picture, as he talks about this place, is our son Timber, himself an addict, grubby and long-haired, trying to make his way in the world. After our rough afternoon it seems like he's headed on a path to failure. Alcoholism or prison or something. His odds are so bad. I can't stand it anymore. I interrupt.

"Whoopee for you, Cristian. I know you don't care, but guess how my evening went? Timber was all riled up and out of control since he got off the school bus. Because he was so hyper I didn't come along with you because we couldn't trust how he'd behave and I knew we wouldn't be able to stand to be with him in the car." Cristian nods; he was there. "Well guess why he was so upset? Because he's about to be suspended. The vice principal called tonight."

Cristian does care, and he's upset at my delivery and my lack of faith in his concern. He makes me say I know he cares before he lets me continue. My ears are still hot, but he's right, it's not his helping this Shackle charity thing that I'm upset about. I take a deep breath, pull myself onto my elbows and then pull the covers as high as I can.

"So this kid he mentions every now and then, the new one that came in at Christmastime, turns out this is a girl Taylor, not a boy Taylor."

"No way, I've seen him—her?" Cristian wraps his body around mine, softening my resistance by force.

"Me too. I thought she was a boy, but actually she's a tomboy. Anyway Timber says she is just trying to get him in trouble, but she says he is pushing and hitting on the playground." My shoulders, then my arms loosen beneath my husband's warmth.

"Lainey, are you sure? Timber knows to never hit a girl."

I roll my eyes. "Better for you to teach him never to hit anyone, you sexist pig."

"Maybe I should teach him to hit his mama when she mouths off to his papa." Cristian's hands cup my breasts and he nuzzles the space between my shoulder and my ear. But now we're getting silly and this really is serious. I have to pull Cristian back to the topic at hand, keep him from getting back onto his Rescue Mission twelve-step whatever, or overly turned on. If he keeps going I'll never get the assurance I so desperately need. We have got to have this conversation.

"So maybe I am exaggerating about him getting suspended, but things are serious enough that we have to go in to a special meeting with all his teachers. It's set for Friday. The appointment is at 9:30 in the morning." I'm leaning fully into his chest, now. No more acting tough.

"Right in the middle of breakfast rush."

"Yup. Sorry. I tried to change it and felt like I was the one getting bullied—this is when they do these things, this works perfectly for all other parties, there is really no other option, blah, blah. There is one good thing. Timber's teacher, you know, Miss Say Everything in a Positive Way, told me not to be too worried. She said she believes Timber is a sweet kid and there is always more than one side to these situations."

I snuggle deeper while turning my voice to my husband. "Oh, Cristian. What are we going to do? How do you discipline someone for being mean? Spank them for hitting? Yell at them for name calling? How can we be raising a bully? I always thought Timber was the one being teased. That's what he keeps saying."

Cristian slides farther under the covers and pulls me tighter. "Who's to say he's lying? We always assume the worst, but he does tell the truth, almost always, right? Anyway, what can we solve now? Nothing. Let it go, Lainey." I give in to the snuggle and silence. After a few minutes Cristian speaks again.

"I want to tell you something else."

I make a sound that he interprets as a go-ahead.

"These Shackles Free guys, the last-year group, they have completed the entire program, which includes teaching the first parts to new guys and putting up with a lot of crap. Some of them even earn an associate's degree in business from Metro. After their detox phase, nine months to a year, I think they said, they study and work, hard physical labor, for eleven hours a day, six days a week for two solid years. They get a tiny subsidy and their room and board."

"Child labor laws?" I wonder. "Sounds cruel."

"These are grown men. And the work keeps them busy. No time to miss their addictions, no opportunity to get back with the bad influences that got them in trouble in the first place. And when they re-enter the real world they have this work ethic that employers can't believe." Cristian lifts my chin to see if my eyes are open so I squeeze them tight.

"Faker. Lainey, listen. I want one of these guys for the restaurant."

Is he insane? I am bolt upright with no memory of sitting up. Bring a bunch of drug addicts and drunks into our brand new venture? Our own son, at six years old, is already practically on the road to destruction and my husband wants to bring in this kind of influence? Tattoos and piercings, shaven heads, history of rape. My stomach begins to turn.

"Number One. We don't even have a restaurant yet. Number Two. How do you find low-cost housing up here for employees like that? Number Three. How can you think of bringing in that kind of influence for Timber? When he is in trouble already? Number Four. Do you want to find me raped and murdered some day? This may be the worst idea you've ever had. Ever."

Cristian just smiles his seldom-used but most aggravating Father Knows Best smile and pats me like a kid. He's already decided, and he will just wait until I come around. Rather than throttle his skinny black neck I give him my back and a couple of inches of bare mattress, blankets clenched firmly in my fists.

Chapter Fourteen

Timber hums, which is good, because it's the first nice sound he's made today. I glance in the rearview mirror at my boy, who seems to be counting posts or something out the window and making long smudgy marks with his finger for each one. Stop. Don't say it. I will wash the window later and bite my tongue now. We don't need any more drama. As I pull into the carpool lane, however, I have to speak. Our bully review is tomorrow, and I have this need to do something.

"Remember, Timber, be really nice to Taylor today." He kicks the seat.

"You always saying that. You always saying that. All the time and I be nice nice nice to him. I no done nothing and you is always yelling."

"Say 'I am nice to her,' Timber. Taylor is a girl, remember. Maybe she gets upset because she doesn't want to be called a boy."

"Argh. You always yelling at me. Stop yelling. You is so mean." All this time he is kicking and kicking the seat in front. If he rips the fabric… And it is our turn for the aide to open his door and he jumps out without a goodbye and stomps, two-footed, in the only mud puddle in the wide walking area in front of his temp building class, splashing the aide who glowers at me. I pretend not to have seen.

You deal with him, I think, savagely, gunning the engine a little more than I should on my way out of the parking lot. Through the windshield the road opens briefly with a meadow to the left and just then the sun makes its first break over Old Baldy. In that instant I am conscious of my role in the little tussle with Timber and feel my lips moving: I'm sorry. I lost my temper. And the calm and the shafts of sunlight glint off my side mirror and through my blinking eyes and into my heart. Forgiveness maybe, or peace. Or something close.

THE BOY

The Test sounded easy. The boy liked the nurse because her hair was as black as his but shinier, and also she always gave a sucker to kids who got a Nurse Pass when they felt sick. The boy had gotten suckers twice this year. She said look here at this poster and point with your finger which way the E is facing. When she brought the poster close in, he could see what she meant by facing, but when the chart was on the wall it turned white by magic, and the boy had to use super powers to guess what the invisible Es were doing. Then she said hmm. And the boy said huh? And she took him to another chair in front of a machine with earphones and let him pretend to be a rap star. All he had to do was lift his hands whenever he heard a bleep which was so easy he didn't need to use any extra power.

Pretty much it was fun, until he went back to the posters and tried some others and she put some funny clown glasses on his nose and then Ta-Da there were pictures on the poster. The reason this was not fun was because Taylor came in next, since their names were T names even though their last names were not next to each other.

Taylor pointed at the boy in the funny glasses and laughed so hard snot came out. Nurse said sure, these are funny but they help us see some things clearly, and come on now, Taylor, it's your turn. But didn't let the boy stay to laugh at Taylor in the funny glasses. He had to go back to class down the long hallway full of student work by bigger kids who could write their own words, all the way out the front door and down a hill to his temp classroom. But he knew where to go, he had promised the teacher, and he could do it himself. Was carrying a paper with numbers and letters that the nurse made for his mother which was Very Important. He knew it said he couldn't see the right things on the magic poster so he ripped it in half and smashed it up and stuffed it in the trash can beside the bathrooms.

He took so long by the bathrooms that when he looked up there was Mrs. C. coming in from outside and Taylor coming down from the nurse's room. Perfect timing, said the teacher, which was better than Where Have You Been, so he took her hand. Taylor glared at the boy and grabbed the teacher's other hand, just to show him.

At recess Taylor was still being mean, so the boy ran to his favorite climbing tower and scrambled to the top to sit alone. But Taylor followed him anyway and said do you know why we had to go to the Nurse? Since we have bad eyes and probably need glasses and yours will be uglier than mine. Timber! said Taylor. I am talking to you stop ignoring me. Timber! The boy kept his eyes almost but not quite shut and watched Taylor climb up to the top of the wall where he perched on the little platform. Pressed in close beside him at the top, Taylor screamed again, so loud it hurt even the boy's squishy ear: TIMBER! TIMBER IS A TREE FALLING And Taylor's arms stuck out to the side like a T. Like the painting on the Sunday school wall. Like the good man on the bad tree.

Chapter Fifteen

LAINEY

Billy meets me around back to unlock the old Whippoorwill, and I see Julie in their car, so I go first to greet her. The morning sun kills the first layer of chill, and I slide my arms out of this ratty sweater as I walk toward Julie, tying it around my waist. I'll need it again in a minute when I step into the cold restaurant. Julie smiles when she sees me coming over.

She had been almost apologetic a couple of months ago when I saw her in King Soopers, fat-bellied again–but with a look that seemed to say she knew that this time, this one would make it. Apologetic because of Timber, I figured. People who work so hard to have their own biological babies seem at a loss to explain themselves when they see me with my adopted son. Personally, I don't get the clone thing. It wasn't a big deal to me, not to carry on my family's genetic code. Maybe having four siblings has something to do with it. If our gene pool dies, it's not my fault. Cristian loved his mama but hates the man who knocked her up. His decision is almost out of spite, I think, to stop that bloodline. Anyway, who's to believe the recent bunk about Nature beating Nurture? Love conquers all, right? This week, however, I have had some doubts.

What if ? Would our biological child have so many physical problems? I had to sign permission for hearing and vision screening, and I am just as sure as the teacher that the tests will show Timber with problems in both. Plus the baby talk and nonsense words and the fact he still doesn't even know his colors.

My moon face looks back at me, reflected in Julie's car window. Even as Julie rolls the glass down, jerkily with her left hand because Sally is nursing and she's reaching across, I can see my countenance changing, rearranging from a serious glare to a friendly smile. I don't look at myself much, but when I do I usually see a disturbing reflection like this. Gross. This is me. Furrowed brows, tight lips.

Just like my mother. That disapproving stare I grew up with glares into Timber's face every day. No wonder he thinks I'm always mad. I am. Or almost. At least, it looks like I am. So Timber has genetic faults. What makes his any worse than mine? Quite possibly they are almost the same, anyway. Anger, lack of focus—sure would think he is my natural son in all the wrong ways.

"Good morning, Lainey. So wow. Were you as tired as me when you first got Timber? I mean, I would kill for a few hours of sleep in a row, you know?" Julie smooths scraggly hair from her daughter's face and then her own. Peas in a pod. Now that's the beauty of biology.

"You don't want to know." She doesn't.

"Yes, I do. What was it like when Timber was little?" Sally stops nursing to stare up with round eyes and milky lips. Julie readjusts and begins to gently pat the baby on the back, burping her.

"Well, if you remember, Timber was about a year old when we got him. He would nap about an hour every morning, two to four hours each afternoon, and ten hours at night. He was a cat, I swear. Sleeping off his hangover, Cristian said. But me and Cristian, we are not night owls. We both need our rest, you know. I don't think we could have handled a newborn."

Julie laughs. I must be kidding, she asserts. I am not. She has flipped the baby to the other side and covered up with a hand-knit blanket. "Oh, I hate you, Lainey. You were right; I didn't want to know. The most Sally has slept in a row so far was four hours one afternoon, and then my dear Billy woke her up because he wanted to put on a different dress to take pictures."

113

"I did not," Billy joins us, leaning beside me against their car and shading his eyes from the sun. Julie laughs. "Did so. You must have had Barbie envy in your childhood, Billy."

"Actually," I can't help but add, "there was that time in second grade…"

"Watch it, Lainey." Darn. It is such a good story.

Billy steps in front of me and pulls back the blanket to gaze at his little girl, exposing Julie's breast and embarrassing me. Another part of natural progeny that I'm maybe not so sad to have missed. Except that her once smallish breasts are huge. I could have used that growth spurt. Do they last?

Julie is slightly embarrassed too, having only been flashing the world for a couple weeks now, and she covers herself and smacks Billy's hand, with which he has been smoothing down a fru-fy collar on his over-dressed child.

"Don't you have something to unlock?" she accuses.

"Done. Here, Lainey, you might as well keep these. Dad's meeting with the lawyers today and since Cristian said to set things rolling you might as well get started."

This is news to me but I try not to react. "What about county permits and stuff?"

That's part of what they're talking about, he says, and since Cristian went to the meeting this morning (more news to me), he should have a good idea of what to expect, and all first-hand so there isn't confusion. Billy hands me a rusty lock along with the key ring. In case I can't get the door to shut all the way; there's a latch across the outside that I can secure with this padlock.

"Congratulations again," I say, as Billy gets in and puts his key in the ignition. "I am so happy for you guys. You deserve her. She is adorable."

Julie touches my hand. "So is Timber. You have a great kid there, you know. I hope you'll share your parenting answers as Sally grows."

Answers? That's a laugh.

Billy and Julie and baby Sally drive off in a scatter of gravel as I tramp over clumps of dead grass to the door. The air tastes fresh and healthy. Bits of green are shooting up here and there in the frost-killed yellow patches. Better clean out the parking lot too. Wouldn't want someone to pop a tire on an old broken piece of metal hidden under these clumps. Beside the back office door I notice something new. Not new, but that I didn't see on our other visit. There's a lean-to along the right hand side, butting up against the log wall. That explains why there is no window along on this side of the dining hall. The three walls are simply hand-hewn planks of oiled pine nailed to posts, and tarpaper shows through the chinks and spaces. A tin roof slides out from under the eave of the real roof and stops a half-foot over the edge of the long wall. The warped hollow-core door has no lock so I pull it open.

Something scurries. Ach. Lots of cobwebs in the space; it's dark and full of rustic chairs. At the far end is an exposed porcelain toilet and along the sides, beneath the tottering legs of stacked chairs, are two bunks. It's a little bunk house. A jail cell. A home for Cristian's convicts. Another creature scratches to my right and I shudder and shut the door.

Once inside the restaurant I copy, as close to scale as I can get without a tape measure, the layout of the whole place in my little notebook of ideas. I label walk-in, dining hall, separate M and W one-seat bathrooms, kitchen, office, rapists' quarters. Even as I pout I know Cristian will win. Worse, I know he will be right to win. Don't we all need second-chances now and then? Catching that same moon-face glare in the reflection of an ancient speckled mirror above the sink outside the toilet closets I force my face into a ridiculous smile. Maybe if I practice in private it will get easier.

The picture windows, only partly un-boarded, call my attention. The big windows look to the southwest, so a sunset or at least twilight view should unfold as the valley before me lights up each evening. The craggy rock formation on the far-east horizon should outline like a wood print. It will be gorgeous. I know it will. It's like finding a forgotten twenty at the bottom of my purse. I almost call Cristian: come and enjoy the view. Let's make love on the table and watch the sun go down tonight. But if there is any watching the sun go down from now until early summer when the days finally length-en, Timber will usually be included. I sigh. Some days it's hard to remember just what is so great about parenthood.

Beep. My cell phone. It's the school. I need to come in right away and get my son. He's in the principal's office. There has been an incident. I need to come get him. Now.

THE BOY

The office with the hum lights is always way too bright and smells like bandages stuck in your socks and washed accidentally in a clothes dryer, but at least the nurse has popsicle sticks. There's no popsicles on them, though, probably because she forgot to put them back in the 'frigerator ice place and they melted. The boy glares at the girl who isn't a boy too but yells and belches anyway just because she is glaring harder and has a broke-up arm that's all his fault. Except that glaring makes his eyebrows hurt so he turns away to play with those sticks, even though it's supposed to be only one to say AHH and make you taste summer nights after the picnic is over. The nurse is here too even though she's clicking on the glowing laptop and so he is kind of careful about pulling the sticks up out of the glass jar. Some of them stick together like they do sometimes and he holds his breath as they bonk onto the table under. The girl named Taylor sees and motions with lips squeezed shut and hands saying gimmee gimmee, all excited about the joke to the nurse who

116

doesn't notice so the boy takes two then three from the pile on the table and leans back, casual and easy, to hand the sticks behind Nurse's back while she's tap tapping. That Taylor girl, she smiles at the boy.

Chapter Sixteen

LAINEY

Palpitations. Heat. It's not even May yet. We stoked a fire last weekend. Shouldn't be so hot today. The elementary school entrance hallway stretches up before me but the sides are caving in. I reach to steady myself but the walls are too far away. My fingers tremble. Timber pushed Taylor off some playground equipment. Taylor's arm may be broken. She's on her way down to the hospital and Timber is in the office waiting in shame, for me to take him home and fix it all. Each thought is a jagged breath.

It is so hot. The shaking in my hands spreads upward, and everything is shaking, and all at once, everything is bright.

My brain reboots to a burst of antiseptic-tainted air and giggles. The school nurse has placed a cool rag on my forehead as she reads my pulse. Has got a gentle touch. She smiles. "Getting sent to the principal always freaks me out, too," she confides, winking. I think she is the younger sister of someone in my class but with her hair now dyed an unnatural black. It's unlikely, because there aren't that many of us natives around. But not everyone runs as fast and as far as they can. Some of us come slinking back home. She hands me a glass of water to sip. I am surprised to see Timber here, twisting back and forth on one of those tall doctor stool things and sucking on a tongue depressor.

"Wow Mom. Lightning go POW again?" he asks with a grin. A kid laughs behind him and surprise again; it's Taylor. She has short cropped dust-colored hair, which looks like she cut it herself, and a dirty face streaked by tears. Her left arm is propped on an examining table at her side and she too swivels on a stool.

"Hi," I croak to the girl.

"Did you really get zapped or did Timber just make that up?" she asks.

"Yeah, I did, but not today. I have no idea what happened to-day."

"'Cuz a me," she smirks proudly. "Bet you fainted 'cuz Timber broke my arm 'snap' right in half." The way she's swinging the unsnapped members of her body around casts doubt on the "right in half" claim. Already, though, where her long-sleeve t-shirt is pushed up above the elbow, you can see ugly black and blue marks. It takes my body a couple of days for bruises to color that bad. Maybe this kid is just super-sensitive, and every little bump hurts or at least bruises. Or maybe my son really has broken his classmate's arm. She grins sweetly to me, the nurse and Timber. If she's a faker I don't see it.

There's a sudden gust of stale cigarette smoke and the glass door to the nurse's office bangs against the outer wall as someone swings it out, way too wide and hard. The someone is cloaked by several layers of flannel and gabardine. This gruff figure fixes bloodshot eyes on Taylor. Its voice is grating.

"Think I don't have a damn thing to do but run down to your school for some damn emergency every second? Get your shit." The voice is male, but like Taylor herself it's hard to tell. She cowers, slightly, and glances at the nurse for confirmation.

"Mr. Lowden," says the nurse, "Our policy is to have all sus-pected broken bones X-rayed. We need to take her down to the clinic in Conifer where they can do that for us. I only called you because we don't have your signature on file authorizing us to take her in." She holds out a clipboard and a pen.

The ballpoint and papers clatter to the floor as Mr. Lowden vio-lently knocks them from her hand.

"What you can do with your damn permission." He glowers at Timber and me and grabs Taylor by the allegedly broken arm, dragging her from the office. She winces but doesn't make a sound. "She'll be back tomorrow, and there'll be no damn X-rays. I can't be babysitting when I got work to be doing." He focuses for a half-second on me, then sees Timber.

"That the little punk what pushed her?" Instinct takes over; I slide my body in front of my boy. Mr. Lowden notices. "Your kid, huh? You just tell him to watch his back." He shakes his daughter, again, by the bad arm. "What you waiting for? Get on out of here."

The nurse cries after him, "I gave her acetaminophen, but if you have some ibuprofen it might help her pain and swelling."

The door has clanged shut, and the nurse puts her head in her hands for a moment. Timber spits chewed up slivers of wood into his palm.

"Would you excuse me?" asks the nurse. "I see the counselor is ready out there now, and we have some calls to make. Oh, and Lain—Ms. Clayson, you should get your heart checked out just to be sure."

Timber and I leave the nurse's office and the principal steps over to greet me.

He is really tall, which always intimidates me. And he has that good-ole-boy look that freaks me out. Makes me imagine burning crosses in front of our cabin. Maybe his grandfather. Maybe his father.

"Hi, Mrs. Clayson. Thanks for coming in today. Sorry you had to witness that…" Despite appearances he has a clear, friendly voice and I imagine he is very good at his job. Kids respect tall men, too. Timber plops onto a sofa out in the main waiting room. Relieved of his stick he just swings his legs hitting a coffee table stacked with books with each swing. The principal motions me into his office, which has a glass door open to the rest of the larger office. It makes me feel safer, somehow, and less panicked while I get a run-down of the "incident." No adults actually saw the push, but the two kids were shouting just before and kept yelling until only a few minutes before I was carried into the nurse's office. Who carried me? I am afraid to ask.

Other kids report that Timber constantly asks Taylor if she is a boy and that Taylor called Timber the "n" word after Cristian came in one afternoon to help chaperone their annual nature hike. At least, she called him something bad that had to do with skin color. None of the other kids would actually repeat the word, which speaks really well of our school, the principal thinks. Timber has never mentioned this to us, but then, I hope he doesn't even know the word. Tone of voice would have been enough to tell him he didn't like it, I suppose.

The principal is distracted; keeps looking through the window at the nurse, who is on the phone and talking with her hands. He explains school policy and why they have to send Timber home today. He is welcome back tomorrow but it's provisional. Any other aggression against any other student, and it is an automatic week-long suspension. Like the guns and knives policy they have a zero-tolerance for bullies. There's even a shiny poster behind the principal's head announcing this fact. It rubs me wrong. It's like the slick way news stations describe international conflicts. A war doesn't count until it has a catchy name and workable logo. I am totally against bullying, but this bully happens to be my son. He's not an idea, he's a kid with issues who is trying really hard to be good.

"Timber fixates," I say. "He doesn't mean to keep calling Taylor a boy but he is having a really hard time accepting the fact that she is a girl. We're working on it..."

The principal knows. They are working, too.

"Sounds like Taylor will be in school tomorrow too," I say. "Is that a good idea?" I mean, what if Timber pushes her again and the sensitive arm is hurt worse?

"She is safer here," he says, quietly, then corrects himself. "I mean, our nurse can keep an eye on things; check for further swelling, and try to convince her father to let us get X-rays."

"That was her dad?" I was sure it must be an uncle or stepdad or heaven forbid, a foster father. There is a can full of sharpened pencils in front of a picture of the principal's family. It looks as though he has an Asian baby. Interesting.

"Yes, he and Taylor's stepmom got custody a few months ago. Taylor was in foster care down in the city before. It's a rough family. But we're keeping an eye on her now." He corrects himself again. "I'm sorry. Despite how badly he may have been provoked, the fact is Timber must not push and shove. What we need to work on here are coping skills for Timber. How to act rather than react; anger control strategies, how to respond in situations such as this. I would like to keep that conference we have scheduled for Friday, but also invite the school psychologist to come in and offer some suggestions specific to Timber. What do you think?"

Guilt from a shrink. But what do I know? It's taken me almost thirty years to start to learn this confession-and-forgiveness thing. Maybe there are more tricks to parenthood I've been neglecting. I try to smile. "Sure, that would be very helpful. We obviously aren't sure how to handle all this."

Timber and I are not even out the door before the principal steps into the nurse's office. And it clicks in my mind. No one bruises that quickly. Poor little thing. The anger at what she may have called Timber melts in a new compassion for a wounded child. Lesson number two: stop pre-judging people.

The air is fresher as we leave the school. Approaching the car Timber says, "I do push, Mom. Taylor say 'Timber is a tree falling.' and he goed like this and I push." I can't stop the tears. Timber cries too, but I don't know if it's from sorrow over what he did or if he's crying just because I am. Timber in an orange jumpsuit, walking down a hallway. Timber slapping his wife. Is the God thing big enough for Timber?

"Sorry, Mom. Now you is mad." Timber looks through long eyelashes while I stand with my hand still on his car door.

"Not as mad as Taylor's dad," I mutter.

"Not that damn mad." he says.

It's wrong, I know, to take a suspended kid anywhere but straight home to lock him in the closet, but I have got to see Cristian. I need to process all this with him. I need his hand on my hand or cheek and his approval of me as mother. I am drowning in the events of the morning. As we head down the road Timber gets a lecture about staying in the car while I go talk to Daddy for a minute, but he's humming loudly to prove that he doesn't have to listen to me. Why does he take every word of warning from my lips as a personal assault? Stop yelling, he yells, at every admonition, no matter how gentle.

I am just gearing down for the final curves of Crow Hill, when I blink in surprise. There goes the equally surprised face of my husband beneath the glint of a rock-dinged windshield, headed uphill, in the opposite direction.

What the— I know he had to be at work by 11:30. The clock says 12:03. I do an illegal U at the bottom of the mountain and accelerate, despite the unlikelihood of catching up to him and the distinct chance of an encounter with highway patrol. The Liberty could usually outrun the ancient Tercel, but it's a long steep pass. I do almost catch up just as he turns off the highway into our own driveway. The normality of our cars in the driveway quiets my beating heart. Inhale, exhale, relax. All is fine. I pull up close behind and automatically put the car in park, pull the emergency brake, and twist the key to off. But then I sit, stunned as Cristian stumbles out of his car and away from me.

Chapter Seventeen

THE BOY

The boy's mother had those grumble tears falling and wasn't answering the boy who said where are we going. Usually he would say it again and again louder, loud as he could to make her lips move words because even angry words said to himself were his. But instead he held Suspected Rabbit (that's the word Taylor taught him—suspected was what they did to kids who hurt someone at school like Timber hurt Taylor) by the arm tight twisted behind his back to march him home home home. No more school today, Bad Rabbit, for because of pushing. But Rabbit felt bad and said sorry sorry sorry so Timber let go, his arm spinning around straight so it wouldn't hurt like Taylor's almost-broke-off arm. And felt sad and held Sorry Rabbit in a hug and loved him. Like his mother loved him when she leaned over to buckle the seat and kiss his cheek even though tears poured down across and over. One of the big truck Sammy trailers used those screechy breaks and stinked the air all around and then there was the boy's other car and the father and the mother turning crazy driver and following home even in the middle of the day, when Timber should be at school but instead, because of his bad choice, was on this ride.

LAINEY

All is not fine. I can count the times I've seen Cristian cry, and now I have to add a finger. Can the school have called him, too? It seems as unlikely as the thought that he would be this distraught over school discipline. He's the cool collected parent. It's a bad place to be, one foot out of the car, with a crying husband outside and a disturbed son in the backseat. Who do you attend to first? How do you keep the boy from making inappropriate comments? Comfort the anguished husband?

Neither one wants my help. The car door supports my weight in the frozen half-in, half-out position of indecision. Sun beats the part on the top of my head. Wish I were wearing my sunglasses and a hat. At least there's no lightning this time.

"What are you doing here?" barks Cristian. He sees Timber. "Is he sick? Why were you taking him to Bailey?" I don't want to talk about Timber right now. I just want to know what happened with Cristian. He doesn't share; doesn't even provide an opening for me to ask. Doesn't speak to Timber, who refuses to get out of the car. Instead, he grabs a down vest from just inside the door, reaching his hand around as if afraid to commit his body to the sanctuary of our home, and marches off through the aspens. Where are you going? I'm not sure if I say it out loud or not, but he shouts back "Going out."

I can't trust Timber not to put the car into neutral or something, so I have to lean wearily against the front door until he tires of his rebellion and comes inside. "Rabbit is sorry, Mommy." he chirps, with a peck on Rabbit's cheek. It makes me weep. The cabin is cool and dark and doesn't offer the usual comfort of home. Chocolate might help, but I have none. I need to talk. Timber sucks calmly on a carrot but the powder keg of his emotions could blow again at any time.

Vanji is at work at her bank, Julie and Billy are too happily married to understand. Who can I call?

"Hello, Celia?" How embarrassing. Now, how do I hang up gracefully? But Celia is a steady voice on the other end of the wire, and I let down my guard, let myself cry to her while Timber re-watches a series of politically incorrect cartoons from the 40s. Why do we even have this trash? It was Dad's present: a box of dollar DVDs from a garage sale in the Ranchos.

Celia doesn't tell me anything, rather asks questions that make me see things in a fresh way. Has Cristian ever left before? No. Did he take a car? No, just went up the mountain where he goes to think. Oh. He wants to think first, before sharing whatever burden he holds. So maybe it's not about me at all. Maybe he is overwhelmed at the moment. And it strikes me, could the deal have fallen through already? As bad as that would be, I realize, it would not be the end of the world. We haven't invested anything yet; won't gamble every-thing.

While I talk to Celia a calm begins to descend. A new light. I hear jays fighting over the tortilla scraps I threw out the back win-dow last night. A cool breeze through that open window prompts me to shut it.

Celia stops me. "Lainey, let me pray for you." Her words flow like warm water, over my fears and doubts. Things aren't really that crazy; thoughts and ideas actually start to form into some sort of pattern. Notes in a symphony, maybe, or dots of color on the com-puter screen. "All things," she is saying, "we know that ALL things work together for good, for those who love…" And the front door and my eyes pop open and I interrupt: "Cristian is home, Celia. I need to go. Thanks."

Chapter Eighteen

Cristian crosses the floor, quickly but limping a little from hiking in those silly boots, and takes me in his arms without even removing his cowboy hat, which tips off as we embrace. Timber sees and runs to press himself between us, unaware of the nature of the drama but wanting badly to be the center of things.

"Not yet, Timber. We'll talk in a minute, but I want to be with Mom first."

"But . . ."

"Now. We need a little time. You go back to the TV now."

"But I seen it sixty-six gazillion . . ."

"Timber."

And he sulks back to the couch and Cristian settles onto the stool beside me, and we face each other and some new giant which threatens our happiness.

His eyes moisten again and he mutters a quiet curse. Timber does not hear.

"Was it the meeting?" I ask, breathless with fear, leaning forward on my elbows with my chest against the cool countertop. "Billy told me today that you and Bill had a meeting scheduled."

"No. And yes. The meeting went great. I kept saying the plan was preliminary and they kept complimenting its professionalism and completeness. You did an amazing job, Lainey. But Travis saw my car parked beside Bill's at his office." To avoid small town prying eyes they had held the meeting at one of Bill's ventures, the local well-drilling company.

"I was just getting started on the breakfast rush when Travis actually climbed into the Tercel and took my portfolio out. I was bringing out more coffee because the teen waiter didn't show again

127

and there's Travis, our papers spread out all over the table in front of him."

I can't believe it. That's some kind of crime—opening someone else's car and removing their belongings. Stealing, that's the word. Travis is a jerk, but this? I wait. Cristian's tears have not so much dried up as steamed off. He wants blood. He chokes through tight lips so I have to lean in close to hear.

"Then. He sees me coming, says 'Boy, you're fired' and pours a glass of water over everything. It's ruined, Lainey, all the copies stuck together; the ink is blurred…"

Timber or no Timber I am pissed. "You are kidding! The—"

Cristian puts his hand up. "I know. But what can we do?"

"Call Bill Junior. Get another copy. Have them sue Travis for the extra legal time. Find out how fast we can realistically begin and make a plan of how to live off savings meanwhile. I can try for a temp job at the library; I saw an advertisement on the bulletin board…

Cristian laughs. I'm a genius. He can't live without me. He wants me, now, on the counter if I'm feeling flexible.

"You psychotic schizophrenic. A couple hours ago you stomped off into the forest in cowboy boots crying like a little girl. I finally had to call Celia to keep from calling the police." This man is every bit as dramatic as his sister.

"It's just," he's serious again, black eyes shining in earnest, slender gray fingers intertwining mine, "I just saw all our hopes and dreams running off those pages with the ink. I had this math teacher in school, bigoted prig, said when he had to give me A's, 'Ain't gonna do you a bit of good, boy, getting these marks now. You think you're front-of-the-class material, but all you got is a back-of-the-bus life to look forward to.' I saw that smirk of his today, on Travis' face."

Cristian leans closer to me, and I cradle his head on my little never-nursed breasts and rock him back and forth while we both sniffle. My fingers massage his scalp, twisting his shiny curlicues of hair. Timber turns once to say "Aw," like we're little babies, and then goes back to the asinine cartoon. This is not the way the world is. This is not the way my life has been in Bailey. I brought Cristian here because it was safe. Who let Travis in? Who let Mr. Lowden in?

It's time, and I explain about Timber's aggression and the encounter with Taylor's dad. Simply putting the day's incidents into words gives me some kind of power over them. Yes, he pushed. But he was pushed, too, by the "falling timber" taunt. And that girl was hurt long before today's fall. Maybe the whole thing will bring abuse to light, and she'll actually get some real help. Maybe this stupid meeting on Friday will give us some actual help ourselves.

Cristian shakes his head. "Things suck all over, don't they?"

I arch my back and stretch my legs. "That's funny. When I was talking to Celia, she said the opposite. 'All things are good in the end,' or something like that."

"I bet it was 'All things work together for good.' It's in the Bible." Cristian rises to his feet and stretches, fingers laced and palms up.

"So, do they?"

"Remains to be seen, Lainey. I'm going to call Bill Senior. Get that kid to bed, please." It's 5:30. I point at the clock.

"Well, feed him then. Whatever. I want to wait until later to talk to Timber about this bully stuff, okay? I've got to deal with my own bully first." He pecks me on the cheek and takes his phone up into the loft where you get reception, usually. I turn off the TV and cajole Timber into helping me make macaroni and cheese, from a box. It's the "from a box" part that excites my son and brings him running to the kitchen counter. He gets to cut the hotdog.

THE BOY

Hot dog, is not dog, is snot dog. SNOT DOG. Ha. The knife is not the fork and spoon knife but a real live hunter's knife that slices through the air ZZOOSH, like that and that and cuts that snot dog's little tail right off. Tail and head—hah. And the fat little snot belly into a gazillion chunks of guts. Yum. This is going to be the best macaroni ever in the whole world because the father has stopped crying and he and the mother laughing and smoochy-like, and the boy has a real live killer blade in his hand and the snot dog is fighting Oh No. Grrr, ouch. It's biting back, but by slicing all those belly bits into teensy pieces the dog is subdued, quiet, not-a-threat and probably, even, dead.

LAINEY

Dirty chunks of hotdog make me shudder. Should have made him wash his hands first. I give Timber a colander and let him wash both his hands and the "meat" at the same time. He takes so long with water so hot that they've 'plumped when you wash them.' Gross. Good thing I have enough lettuce for a big salad for myself. Cristian can most certainly come up with something. I don't bother setting out dishes. To each his own, tonight.

My mom would never have allowed each family member to eat something different. But then, it would have been quite a job with seven different menus. Especially since our family exemplified the worst double standard ever. Angela and I were assigned dusting and vacuuming chores when we started school. Dishes were added, then laundry and cooking. The boys? Their manly chore list included chopping and splitting firewood and driving the bush hog twice in those summers in which weeds actually grew tall enough to be cut. These chores didn't begin until they came of age at twelve, and their jobs came with money. They were actually paid. The only thing that was the same across the board was menu—if it is not on the table, don't ask for it, and if it is, don't complain.

As I wash a few leaves of lettuce and peel a cucumber, I think of Angela living as Jelly in Pueblo. Jelly-stone Park. Jelly and toast. But maybe it's Geli or something slightly less tacky. Either way it sounds like an exotic dancer. Angela never had much poise in dance, but talent is probably not an especially important asset in the underworld of pole dancing. Anyway I doubt she's really a prostitute or porn star. I bet her scandal is much more mundane: a sleazy second or third wife, working at some minimum-wage job and cleaning some other woman's kids' clothing. Well, at least she got that training in our childhood.

Cristian tickles the back of my neck with a spoon handle. He has descended the ladder as a new man and is actually grinning now.

"It's gonna be fine. Bill couldn't believe Travis would do that. Said it just shows how desperately he needs me at the Crow Barre and how quickly we need to get this plan up and running. Suing him is probably not a good idea, unless he fails to provide me proper severance. But I don't even have to ask for that: Bill's guy will do it for me. And Bill Senior actually apologized to me on behalf of Bailey for Travis' racism, can you believe it?"

I can believe it. It's exactly what I had been thinking.

"Lookee me wiener, Dad. Ha, ha, ha. I chop it up. Is a snot dog, gross, get it, SNOT? Chop the snot dog wiener. Dad, why them call it wiener?"

Ugh. I take my bowl of lettuce to the counter. A few bacon bits and a glop of dressing and I can pretend it's a meal. At least there's no hotdogs involved. Timber and Cristian climb onto stools, too, with matching bowls of macaroni. I raise my eyebrow and Cristian shrugs. He isn't a great restaurant tycoon just yet, and anyway, there's no law that says a great restaurant tycoon can't enjoy a bowl of macaroni from a box with chopped snot dog wieners every now and again.

"Wiener. Dad said wiener. Ha ha ha." Timber slaps the tines of his fork, flipping it up to land in Cristian's bowl. The bite that had been on the fork is now sliding down Cristian's shirt.

"Come on now, Timber. That's too far. Why do you always push things so far?"

"Because I is a idiot. I not understand nothing. Wah." And he's down from the stool, kicking the bathroom door before I can blink. I look at Cristian. If he doesn't eat, he won't sleep. If he doesn't sleep, neither do we, and he is awful all day tomorrow, the day of the big inquest. We are too weary for this right now.

"Timber, please," I begin, gently touching his arm and trying to direct him back to the counter. Please, just a little peace to salvage this rollercoaster day. Please.

THE BOY

The Day Daddy Cried the boy wanted to be tucked in especially tight. He wanted to know that even though he was a terrible child and had brought misery even to his father, they would speak softly and touch his cheeks with kisses and say that he was a good boy. He wanted to be loved. Rabbit was in his arms. Sorry Rabbit.

I sorry, whispered, quiet. But his mother didn't say anything so he said louder give me some water. She sighed then and he knew he had blown it again. He was so stupid. Couldn't even do the right thing right. His father looked at him then and seemed to see a little better. He sat on the edge of the boy's bed while the mother came back with a teensy tiny drop of water in the bottom of the green cup. The boy did not like the green cup. It had an icky stain that looked like a squished bug. But the boy didn't want his mother to sigh and walk away so he took the cup from her and pretended but didn't really drink before handing it back.

She knew he faked and was leaving when he tried again. I'm sorry for to push Taylor-who-is-a-girl. But…and it took a long time and the father and mother were watching but almost done and going to leave anyway…but how come my name be Timber-a-tree-falling? Always they are laughing. And the boy squeezed his eyes shut so that he wouldn't see his mother and father and know what they couldn't say. Oh, baby. Was not expected, the way the mother came in and scooped the boy into her arms while the father, smiling, the boy saw with eyes open, touched his knee.

Do you want to hear your story? And he did, and they told a bedtime story that the boy kind of knew, because he had heard parts and whispers in grown-up conversations sometimes. The main thing about the story, said the parents as they began, was that the boy was loved. He was loved by lots of people, but none more than them. His Story, his happily ever after family, was theirs, too. They all of them, all three, chose each other.

And then the boy's own story. And he was the hero, and he curled down like a kitten when the mother told him about a little baby in a box that meowed. A huge swirling cloud threatening to pull it all into the whirlwind. Opened his eyes wide to see a strong and good fireman leaning over him to save him from that cardboard crib. Twisted a strand of his mother's hair in front of a rainy window when they met the first time. The boy had a lot of questions. He wondered about where a baby would sleep in a fire station if they left the box outside and how a fireman could carry a baby up the sliding pole.

Could he ever meet the old gramma lady that took care of him when he was still a baby kitten? What about the fireman?

Yes, yes, of course we should do that. How about the woman who wrapped him up to leave him there? And the parents were still and quiet and the boy worried that he had asked a wrong thing again. Meow, meow? he said, to make them forget about his bad question.

But the boy's mother, very quiet, said sure, maybe someday they could even meet that woman, Timber's birth mother. And she got up and went to the wardrobe that the boy was not supposed to open and slam shut and she reached up high to the top shelf and pulled out a couple of things and finally a fat box and inside was a puffy green coat and she brought it to the bed and folded it open and pointed at two words sewn onto the pocket. You were named after this coat, kind of, it is a brand called Tall Timber. The fireman first called you Timber and then the foster mom and by the time we got you there was no other name you could possibly have. You are the most perfect Timber in all the world.

It wouldn't mean much to the boy now, said his father, but everyone had a piece of paper called a birth certificate and the boy's paper said his real complete total name was Tall Timber James Clayson.

The boy stopped kicking the quilt off his legs and stared at his father. He looked to his mother to see if it were true.

Tall Timber James Clayson? Tall Timber James Clayson. Not Timber A Tree Falling? Definitely not. What means Tall Timber? asked the boy, forgetting already about the coat. But his mother pointed it out again. It is a brand name, but what it really means is all the giant trees in the forest. The highest ones. Ready to cut, maybe, which is where the falling down comes from. The woodcutter man would yell, Timber! to warn of the cut tree crashing to the forest floor, to be pulled to a mill and cut for lumber. Lumber made houses, furniture, paper, and fires. But tall timber wasn't always cut for wood. Sometimes the trees kept growing, taller and taller and making homes for birds and animals and shade and beauty.

That is Myself, thought the boy. Tall Timber Not Cut.

James was the middle name of his father whose birth certificate name was Cristian James Clayson. Also it was his mother's daddy's name which was the boy's grandfather, Jim. The mother was saying Jim was James, too, but the boy was not listening, saying instead Tall Timber Clayson.

The boy smiled at his name. He was Timber. Tall Timber. Once he looked like a kitten but a nice fireman took him up and a foster gramma sewed his lips together and his very own mommy and daddy picked him up to take him here—home.

Good night, Timber, they said to Timber. Good night Daddy. Good night Mommy, said Timber.

Chapter Nineteen

LAINEY

Together we push open the unbelievably heavy doors to the school building. How do little kids manage? I will be okay this time, I promise myself. This morning I drank a glass of water before we left the house and ate an egg with salt, two things my Southern husband suggested to keep me from fainting. He has had more experience with the spells of delicate belles than I have. The only time I've seen someone pass out without alcohol was my fifth grade Spring musical in this very building, and the three kids that crashed off the bleachers that day had all locked their knees, which I couldn't possibly have done while walking down a hallway. Must have been my heart. Blame it on the lightning. After all, who gets struck by lightning, right? Might as well milk it.

The secretary sends us down another hall which smells of white paste and carbon paper, two things they don't even use anymore, as far as I know, to a lounge-type room with an oval table in the center. We're the first, which is almost worse, because I'm not sure how to greet people as they come in. Do we stand up? Ignore them while they plop important piles of papers on the table?

It's like being at a doctor's office. I'm sorry, Mr. and Mrs. Clayson, but your reproductive systems, for differing reasons... So this is the extent of your son's facial reconstruction. I feel very good about the outcome and think you will too, once the swelling has gone down and stitches are removed...

"Good morning, thanks for coming in. I'm so glad you both could make it," says the principal, leaning down noticeably to shake my hand. I realize both Cristian and I have stood up after all. The rest of the staff people file in behind the principal so we don't have an awkward up-and-down time, for which I am thankful. They are young and professional. One is African American. Not the kind of teachers I remember from my days as a student. I bet they're grant scholars, fulfilling their obligations to Uncle Sam by teaching in our rural district.

The principal starts by saying that this meeting is not so much about yesterday's incident with Taylor, but was planned previously as a forum for everyone to put their heads together to see how we can help Timber succeed as himself. The best he can be, as it were. First, the speech teacher. She's a tiny thing with a blond bob who bubbles about our son's progress. The change is slow but steady. R's are becoming stronger, TH different from D. Sentence structure needs help. The teacher is quite interested in the way he fixates on sounds and words. She wants to be sure it doesn't develop into Tourrett's Syndrome. Indeed. So do I. Visions of Timber shuffling along a city street, pushing a laundry cart and shouting "Dirty damn wiener" easily come to mind.

She has our permission to try anything she wants that might help.

"I'd like to go next, if I may," drawls the male teacher. Except that he isn't a teacher. He's a counselor, temporary because, as I expected, he is on the Teach America program, having college loans forgiven by "doing time" in our little district. Cristian perks up. He knows this accent, though he has worked hard to erase it. The rest of the table sits back for a few minutes while the two of them banter back and forth. Both from Houma, Louisiana, can you believe it? Grew up on opposite sides of the township. What a small world. Cristian slips into the language and cadence of his childhood and I am fascinated and jealous. How is it this young man can pull the real Cristian out of his fake Stetson? Or the bayou version of Cristian, anyway?

Finally they seem to notice the papers being reshuffled on the table. The other participants have places to be. The counselor addresses us all, saying, "So I'll be seeing Timber now on a biweekly basis, and we're gonna work on anger management strategies, mostly due to the situation between him and the young lady in his class." He looks down at his papers. "But what I would like to know, is does Timber have a diagnosis for fetal alcohol effects or ARND, that is, alcohol-related neurological disorders?"

Cristian and I look at each other and shrug. We've heard a lot of diagnoses throughout the last five years. Attention deficit, speech delays, weak hearing, and now less than perfect vision.

"I haven't heard exactly those words, but someone told us that prenatal alcohol exposure is probably what caused Timber's unfused lip. But he's had all the surgeries now, and you can't really tell unless you know what to look for."

The young man pulls out some papers and leans to hand them to Cristian.

"What I'm talking about, though, are not so much physical effects, but neurological and especially behavioral ones. Timber is not at the same level, developmentally or socially, as his classmates, is he, Miss Cohn?" Timber's perfect-words teacher shakes her head. "With prenatal alcohol use, and especially abuse like binge drinking, we're born with a bigger burden than most. I say we on purpose, Mr. and Mrs. Clayson. I myself was born under the influence, though I suffer mild effects compared to many. In essence, the alcohol puts us in a kind of permanent state of drunkenness, or that's what I like to use as an explanation for my personal problems with short-term memory, and especially with my thick skull when it comes to learning something new or doing what I know is right but just don't feel like doing.

"Does Timber ever do stupid or harmful things for no apparent reason? Does he ever seem to shoot himself in his own foot by losing privileges that you know are really important to him?"

Well, duh. This is Timber, to a T.

He goes on, and everything he says strikes a chord. Inability to correctly read people's reactions. Not connecting simple cause and effect. Using lots of words to get around simple vocabulary, like that round thing on the door that shuts it when you pull.

The counselor's slightly hooded eyes are very round and almost buggy as he leans across the table, punctuating his sentences by poking his index finger on the cherry-colored surface. "Those sheets I just gave you may be of some help (poke) I didn't know if this would all be new to you or not. (poke) Here's a number, though, for the diagnostic center at Children's Hospital. (poke) You haven't undergone evaluations yet, have you?" The young man sits back, his eyebrows forming the question mark. "It takes several months to get it. Call now and I bet you don't get in until next August. But their evaluation would help the staff here in adjusting his individualized educational plan next year." He leaves us the packet, so that we can digest this information in peace, and I promise to call and schedule an appointment.

The room is hot, though not as bad as the other day. Finally the conference is over and we all rise.

No one even mentioned the word bully. Relief, but no, here is the principal, ushering us now into his own office.

As we settle into padded chairs he says, "What we are proposing is that Timber spend his recess time with the school counselor, the man you just met, for two weeks. A kind of recess detention, as a disciplinary action, but also an opportunity to complete a series of psychological tests and skill-building activities."

"Sounds great." Cristian nods. What's to lose?

But I am skeptical. Timber is only six. Is missing recess a strong enough punishment for harming Taylor so seriously? My questions remain in my head and I force a smile, thank the principal, and stand up from the chair. The gleaming poster, "Zero tolerance for bullies," threatens even when I turn my back and walk through the door.

TIMBER

Timber was allowed to go back to school because he was only under suspicion for one day. He asked his teacher, did she know that Tall Timber was the tall trees that make lumber for chairs and houses for birds? She did and smiled and was happy about the story of Timber's whole real name. She agreed that it was cool that Timber was called Timber usually and not Tall because that might sound a little silly. She even let him sit beside her during story hour by the orange wall and he squeezed one eye shut and looked around the circle at his classmates and said to himself in his head the colors the kids wore. Yellow. Blue. Purple, maybe? Pink. White. And lots of the boys wore mixed-up colors of the woods like in the clothes you wore for hunting.

Timber wished he could go hunting but he didn't know exactly what it was except you got a big long gun. Kids should not play with guns. Or fire. Ever. Ever again.

The color Timber wore was green. It was a t-shirt of a color of sand on the edge of a lake you could swim in with a big green dinosaur and since the t-shirt color didn't have a name Timber chose green for the T-Rex. Timber wondered about being green. Would you smell like trees if your skin was green? Would it itch?

LAINEY

Evening light filters through the spruce and Timber and I wear jackets against the cool. We're hunting pinecones for some art project. I actually read the note on time, this once. Timber tells me he has been having talks with the counselor at school, the guy from Cristian's hometown. Timber squints up at me and then rubs his ear. His hearing must be bothering him again. As soon as the nurse gets the results in we'll have to check about seeing a specialist.

"How come I be dumb drunk skunk?" Drunk? Whatever this counselor has said hasn't gotten through very clearly. What should I say?

"Timber, remember that Daddy and I chose you, that you weren't born out of us like a lot of kids are born from their parents. You had different biological parents who made you get born and then later we got you."

"But Dad is colored darkly like them teacher." Timber holds a pinecone in one hand and a banana in the other. He flings the cone as hard as he can towards an innocent squirrel, dropping the banana in the process. He picks it up along with another, mostly eaten pinecone.

"Daddy's mom, your Grandma Clayson, had really dark skin. Someone way back, a great-great-great- grandpa or something, came to this country from Africa. In Africa everybody has dark skin."

"You is the same, Mommy. Not like Miss Cohn." He stuffs fully half the banana in his mouth and I answer quickly before he can try to keep talking and spew it back out on me.

"Well you know about that already, too. My mom, Grandma Morse, is from Mexico. People mostly have dark skin there, but not as dark as Africa. Grandma's skin is darker than mine, because mine is mixed all together with my dad, who is Grandpa Morse and who, you know, is totally white."

He swallows the last bit of banana, mostly. "Grandpa no is white. He like orange, only not so much. Like, Skin Color Crayon." Whose skin color, I want to demand. I hate Crayola.

I hold out a bag for a pine cone, but he drops in the banana peel instead. "Anyway, Timber, we are all different. Everybody has their own special color, like their own special personality. Some of it comes from the genes of our…from our biological genes, and hopefully some of it comes from our REAL families, those people who take care of us. I love you, Timber-toes, and I hope your personality will be colored a little bit like me and a little bit like Dad, even if our skin isn't all exactly the same."

Timber jumps on a dead stick, laughs at the crack it makes, and turns to face me. He is still thinking.

"I wish," he says, "I wish I only got colored by Daddy and you. I wish I had your skins only. Mommy, why you crying, Mommy?"

Chapter Twenty

Cristian has been to the Shackles Free rescue mission with my father three times already, enough apparently to be on nickname terms with the place. The Shack, he says now. Today I am out of excuses, and Timber and I have come along to help. Dad stayed home this time. Under the weather, he says. Coughing his fool head off, more likely. As we near the place Cristian keeps glancing over and grinning at me, like when he chooses a present for my birthday that he is much more excited about than I am. My smile is trying for pep but falling short at about endure.

We have entered an armpit district in the midst of Denver's urban center. This is a part of town that forgot how green Denver is supposed to be. Railroad tracks and old tractor-trailers are the principle landmarks, with even the mountains hidden behind something that could have once been an apartment building. A seven-lane highway screams by almost directly above our heads on a fly-over. The ground is covered by either asphalt or crushed rock or broken cement.

"Cool." cries Timber, "A balloon." But it is NOT a balloon and I scream and grab his hand just before he picks up the condom. Nearby is a grayed undershirt and I yank him to the door before we can focus on anything else.

Cristian's Shack is a warehouse-type pole barn with a couple sad juniper shrubs at the entrance. There are bars on the windows but no more than a normal warehouse in this part of the city. Still, it's creepy, thinking that these men probably really do need to be kept behind bars. Cristian rings the bell and the door is opened immediately by a couple of men in dark-blue polo shirts.

One man, an obvious participant in the program, smirks and shakes my hand. He tells me his name which I promptly forget. "Welcome to the Shack. Glad to have you all here to help today; especially Cristian's wife. Hubba, hubba, hey, Beautiful!" He winks and I grimace. Cristian doesn't even notice. His attention is on the other man who must be the director.

"And I am Chauncey Grant, but please call me Chance. That's Mister Chance to you, young man." Timber grins. Chance is big. I think bear-of-a-man is an apt description. Blond or white hair is shaved short and a tanned scalp shows through the stubble. He wears a long-sleeved t-shirt under the polo but even so, tattoos peek out from his neckline and vine down onto the backs of his hands. One of those guys who takes his work seriously. If you're going to work with tough characters, be a tough character. Only, he has gentle, smiling eyes and it is obvious he is anything but mean. I bet he's actually a teddy-bear of a man.

As we start down a dark hallway strangely wallpapered with dated country patterns, Chance turns to the other man who is still ogling me.

"Stay at the front, man. We need you to open the door for the next volunteers." He and Cristian exchange a look.

"Sorry, Lainey," says Cristian, as we walk. "You just can't let that stuff get to you." The snake eyes or the compliment? He leans backward to whisper, "But don't worry. I'd never hire him." Oh, so it is one of them. Chance speaks over his shoulder, explaining the procedure for the soup kitchen charity that we'll be serving for today. Homeless men and some families straggle through a part of the Shackles Free building daily for a hot meal. Preparing and running this soup line is a part of the training for the men in the rehabilitation program.

"Timber. Stop." He's dragging his feet on the tile floor, one after the other, to leave black rubber smears on the otherwise clean white tiles.

144

"Tire tracks, Mom. Is cool." He keeps going, making ugly streaks. Cristian ignores us. Maybe a little male discipline would help now? Come on.

"Cristian. He won't listen to me." But we seem to have arrived at the kitchen and Cristian won't listen either. He puts on an apron and quickly changes into chef mode, dipping a ladle into the nearest soup pot and breathing in the aroma.

Chance hands me an apron and introduces me to a frumpy little woman who doesn't speak but appraises me quickly and mercilessly. Then she kind of snorts and turns, indicating that she finds me wanting. Even so it falls to her to get me going, and she points me to a cabinet and begrudgingly tells me what to do in a deep smoker's voice. But what about Timber? Chance asks if it is all right if he shows Timber what the kids usually do. There's a toy room nearby, but first he'd like to have him help with something. Sure, whatever.

As I count faun-colored melamine bowls from a cupboard, bringing stacks of fifty to the serving line, I doubt the wisdom of my decision. Sure, whatever? I don't see Chance in the kitchen so I step back into the hallway. There they are with a mop bucket; Timber cleaning up those shoe tracks he made. Chance sees me and pats Timber on the back, tells him he'll be right back, and motions me back into the kitchen.

"He's a good worker," Chance tells me. I snort. He can be, I say, but… Then I tell this man a little about the stuff we've just started reading about prenatal alcohol exposure's effects on a fetus, and how it seems like we might be getting some answers to the mystery of Timber's behavior. Chance nods. He says it's one of the hardest things with this program, getting men to admit to the ways their disease has not only hurt themselves but has ravaged their families. He's done a lot of reading, too, and some think that even a father's alcoholism can affect a fetus.

"And you'd be a fool to deny that your drinking doesn't make it tempting or provide justification for your woman, carrying your child, to also drink," he says. "Misery loves company. Don't drink alone." In between pauses he leans back into the hall and shouts encouragement to my kid. This guy is really good at what he does. I bet he's the favorite staff of the "inmates."

"Thanks for having him do that, Chance. I didn't like the marks but I guess my yelling at him was not very effective."

"No problem, Mrs. Clayson. Anyway, if he doesn't do it now I will have to later."

The cafeteria lady ambles near and mumbles something savage like worth their salt and I'm pretty sure she means me so I rush back to my assigned duty of counting and carrying stacks of bowls. Looks like a night of mediocre effort isn't going to impress this woman. With her it would probably take a year of consistent hard work to break down her mistrust. And I watch her as we work and think of scenarios for her life. Does she have family? How did she get here? Would she leave if she could?

The faces going through the line look just exactly as I'd expect. Mostly dirty, cowering beneath too many layers of clothing, suspicious. The Lowden family would fit right in. No one meets my eyes, except the kids. Older kids, younger kids; what I don't anticipate is how many children come through. Doesn't someone take care of this? Don't we have all kinds of programs for moms and kids and people like this? Well yeah, this is one of those programs. An electric current charges through my blood when I glance up to see my own Timber batting those long eyelashes and holding up his hands for a bowl.

"Thanks, Mommy." He chirps.

What if we were here like the others, begging for a meal, worrying where to sleep tonight? Shake it off, Lainey. Fill his bowl and smile.

Eventually the kitchen lady nods her head for me to go out and join Timber and the other diners. We just eat out there? Yup.

Not even the children share eye contact at the table. Mostly people just slurp the soup, pausing now and then to dip in a biscuit or crumble more saltines. It's a simple soup; potato, but delicious. A rescue mission staple, they say, because of the low cost per serving. We have got to put this on our menu.

Cristian slides onto the bench beside me. His forehead still has the crease that appeared a couple days ago when he was fired and Timber pushed Taylor off the tower, but his shoulders are relaxing. This charity gig has been good for him. Really, it is hard to bemoan our family's state of affairs while we sit here surrounded by so many who are suffering much more.

"This dining room is set up almost identical to the Whip, isn't it?"

Yeah, I think he's right. Our log tables and benches have a more pleasing lodge ambience than this sterile and institutional pressed-board furniture, but the number and way they are arranged is just about the same.

He says that's for flow, and I see right away what he means.

"Man," he says. "If you could get away with a soup-only restaurant…it would be a great profit margin. Lower labor outflow…" He stuffs a spoonful of soup in his mouth while I think about the idea he just planted.

I brush a crumb off my cotton sleeve. "You need bread. Everyone is eating either a biscuit or crackers."

Cristian sets down his spoon. "To make a complete protein."

He wants to use soup kitchen staff, why not make a soup kitchen? Upscale and chic, it could be just the kind of gimmick people go for, like throwing peanuts on the floor of overpriced steak houses. My brain goes haywire with ideas. I wish I had a tablet to start writing this stuff down.

"That's it." he says. "We'll start collecting Depression-era prints to frame—Civilian Conservation Corps projects. Serve in enamelware. The Soup Line. Or Soupline? Soups and breads, and if we can contract with a local baker, pie."

"I wants pie, too," yells Timber. All those furtive eyes dart up, expectant. There is no pie. We were just...

Chance gets us out before the lynch mob catches us. Thank goodness we were signed up only for serving. It's hot and stuffy in the kitchen now with the large countertop dishwashers blowing steam. The Shack's usual crew is chugging along so fast it seems they will finish before the last person is done eating.

While I'm hanging my apron back on a peg I see a woman I hadn't noticed go through the line. She's tripping on something and can't seem to answer Chance, who keeps asking if she'd like him to pour a bowl even though policy is against serving late. I stare at the woman, thinking of her age, her coloring, her facial features, and am chilled to think this could be Timber's birth mother. It's not the first time I have appraised a stranger with that question. A stupid one, of course. There was quite an effort to find the woman at the time of Timber's abandonment, but nothing turned up. Anyway, that all happened three hours south of here. And I'm glad, sickly glad of the fact that we'll probably never know her. I think I don't want to know this woman who would abuse both herself and her unborn baby with alcohol, and then just dump him. There are lots of tough stories. Not everyone gives in. I have a hard time seeing what benefit Timber would reap from having a relationship with this woman.

It's not even so much that I'm afraid of being too angry at her; it's more a fear of feeling sorry for her. And always, always in a bitter spot at the back of my throat, is the fear that someday she will return and demand him back. Horton the Elephant's Lazy Mayzie flown in to town to collect. Or a teenage Timber, mad about some perceived injustice, will run to find the woman who slipped him into this world. That's the big fear. Not the mother's abandonment of my son, but my son's abandonment of me.

Timber slams into me. He looks startled for a second, hugs me, and careens on across the room toward Cristian. The mystery woman has stumbled back onto the street, muttering all the way. She didn't stay for her bowl of soup after all.

At the big metal door to the outside world, Chance tells me to greet my father for him and hands me a gallon sour-cream container full of leftover soup to take to him for that sore throat. Cristian indicates he'll maybe call Chance this week. I know why he leaves it ambiguous; he's giving me one last opportunity to talk him out of this plan to use one of Chance's converts in our restaurant. Timber is buckled in and we strap ourselves. The car is still in the parking lot when he begins.

"So, Lainey. About our employment opportunity,"

"Cristian, did you see how that slime dog guy looked at me? How can you ask me to consider hiring these people? I mean, it's great they are getting some help and all and maybe they can get off the street, but do you seriously want to compromise our future to help some loser? No way." I open the glove box. Don't we have some gum or lemon drops or something?

Cristian has his lips apart, waiting for a chance to break in on me. "That guy is a first-year, Lainey. He's new, and yeah, looks to be a jerk with or without alcohol. Even if he was all the way through the program I wouldn't hire him. What kind of judge of character do you think I am? Didn't you hear me talking to Chance?"

"Just now when you were trying to set up an appointment? You probably have to okay all of this through him, don't you?"

Cristian glances sideways at me. "What do you mean?"

"Doesn't the program have something to do with sending them on?"

Cristian is quiet for a moment and I lean back against the seat so that he can watch the side mirror as we merge onto the highway. Seems to me they have been repairing this same section of the I-70 bridge my whole life and it has never actually improved.

"Lainey, I think you are confused. You seem to think Chance is in charge of Shackles Free. He's staff, yes, because all participants are employees, since they are working at the shelter."

"Chance is an addict?" So the tattoos and haircut and everything are not costuming for the job; but who he is for real? But Chance seems more of a counselor than a criminal and I have this flash of insight: maybe not all alcoholics are total dirt bags. And another: maybe some addicts actually get better. Why am I always so quick to judge? But if I can't trust appearances, how do I catalogue my life? I touch the scabbing on my palm. What happened to my supersonic abilities? Now I can't even tell the good guys from the bad. Or those worth saving from the hopeless. A voice in my head: Maybe it's not your job anyway, Lainey.

Cristian tries to make eye contact while still watching the road. I turn farther away from him. "Got quiet, Lainey. What are you thinking about? What is your take on Chance?"

"Take a chance, take a chance, last chance, second chance." yells Timber in a sing-song tuneless loop. I try to shush him to no avail. Cristian clenches his jaw as the volume escalates in the space inside the jeep. Two minutes pass. Five. Finally Cristian explodes, and I am happy that it is Cristian yelling instead of me and I feel somewhat superior. Until Timber starts kicking my seat and it's my turn.

"What the heck? You will rip the seats if you don't stop. I said stop. Why are you being such a little brat?" I can't believe I called him a brat. Even though he is acting like one. Help, I pray, help me do and say the right thing.

"But Daddy say he take away all my toys because he say so. I no do nothing. Why you hate me? You no love me."

Then I remember a word of advice from somewhere. "This is no time to talk about love, Timber. This is a time for you to calm down and be quiet. We are driving on a highway and it is getting dark, and Daddy and I are trying to have a conversation. You must stop talking for a while."

He kicks one last time, hard, and stops. I clench my hands but say nothing. There is a pause, we all hold our breath, and Timber yawns. We wait a few more seconds, and Cristian speaks.

"So don't you think Chance would make a terrific employee? You even thought he was the head of the program; that's how responsible he comes across."

Timber is still quiet and my blood pressure is descending.

I answer, somewhat grudgingly. "You're right. This time. I think Chance would be worth a cha—trial, anyway. He's likable and hard-working. Bailey people will like his look."

"I know, right?"

Timber has his hand up.

"What?"

"Can I ask question, Mommy?"

"You just did. What?"

"How come do Chance got stuff all over hims arms? Them tutus I seed."

"Timber," says Cristian, "It's time to be quiet again."

TIMBER

Timber's mom used to yell all the time. He would have to use his squishy ear to tune out the noise or it would bubble up like a bathtub with shampoo which you should never, never dump under the running water. Once he got super power, and a lot of the yelling stopped. Maybe it was his power or maybe it was his mom's, because the super lights that fell through the sky fell mostly onto her but him, too. Just not Daddy.

Daddy always had a kind of super power anyway. Most men did, Timber thought. Someday Timber would be a grown-up daddy and Mommy would be his little girl. Or maybe his wife. He always forgot. Timber hoped he would look like his new friend Mister Chance, who was very scary but actually nice. When they were dumping a bucket of mop water down the drain Timber told Mister Chance that he was going to have to get glasses and have another check about his ear and he did not want to have straws stuck in there or anything like Brian in school who was all the time home sick because his ears were too dirty. Mister Chance showed Timber a secret. A little thing that clipped on the back of his ear like a spy so he could hear better sometimes when it was loud behind him like in the dining room. He even turned it on to show Timber who held it to his squishy ear and suddenly Timber saw everything get real loud. Maybe having a thing in your ear wasn't so bad, decided Timber. Maybe it was even cool.

Mister Chance was a new friend. So was Taylor, because since Timber pushed her she had been really nice. She said she hoped he didn't get into too much trouble. Taylor wore orange a lot, because the Denver Broncos were her most favorite team, which was the same thing for Timber.

Lots of stuff Timber still hated, like getting papers all marked in red because he was stupid and got every question wrong. He also hated being hungry. That was a Worst Thing. Being hungry.

Timber was not a-tree-falling but tall trees in a forest. His mommy and daddy loved him best of all but other people loved him too sometimes. His favorite toy, Rabbit, which he kept forgetting to think about, used to be Timber's best friend. Now there were other friends. Lonely Rabbit. Old Rabbit. Maybe one day Timber would take that old rabbit to give to that baby Sally, since she was a baby and didn't have a rabbit to protect her or a brother, except Timber who would act like one until she got her own. Or if he got his own baby sister who needed a brother, then he would have to take care of her, first. Timber of the forest was good at taking care of people. And he would never hit a girl again even if it was hard to tell she was a girl like Taylor.

Chapter Twenty-one

LAINEY

Caw! No alarms are set this morning but a loud jay jolts me awake. It's not even seven, but now I am conscious of a bathroom urge which is too strong to resist, and once I'm up, what's the point of going back to bed? If I start a pot of coffee Cristian might breathe in the aroma and decide to get up. Only I don't feel like sharing this stolen slice of morning, so I quietly heat a cup of water and pop in a Red Zinger. Nothing like hibiscus flowers to get you going.

The front door screeches against the tile. A piece of gravel must be stuck under the weather seal. Anyway I freeze for a moment but there is no sound of life from either of the sleeping males. Good.

It's cool and I pull an old throw off the nearest chair to wrap around myself. Cocooned with my tea on the half-broken resin Adirondack that graces our porch I let out a long sigh. It's a short drive to the highway; really only about five car lengths, but it curves and a huge blue spruce is the perfect buffer. At this hour on a Sunday morning, it is not surprising that the only sound of traffic is a distant wheeze of airbrakes on a delivery semi.

We have the perfect location between the north-south sides of the twisted valley. Already the sun is ready to do battle with a cloudy sky, and its first perfect ray coincides with a flutter of blue wings. My awareness has diminished drastically since the bolt. The bird's flutter is beautiful, but I can't tell the number of beats per second. The heaviness of Timber's problems and Cristian getting fired seem to have dimmed the glow of my electrical enlightenment.

Or have I just tuned it out? It's been an intense couple of weeks. That first time we went to church the speaker kept pointing up at this huge cross made of railroad ties that hangs up front. There was some verse…kind of like the Statue of Liberty's creed. All you who are weary, come in for rest. Something along those lines.

Why not? I am weary. I am worried about Timber, and how to keep him safe from himself. How to guide him through life. I am worried about starting a restaurant when Cristian has just been fired. I am scared of bringing in a former drunk to work for us. I am worried about a lot of things when I stop to think about it. Can I have a piece of that rest? That peace again?

A breeze ruffles the fringes of my old throw and kisses my cheek. The sunbeam broadens and I will it toward myself until it, too, caresses my face. It's red inside my eyelids and I open them, surprising myself by that magical clarity. The mountain blue bird is back, not four feet away, perched on the rail that flanks my roofless porch. He fluffs in the cool of the breeze. My eyes feel the softness of the down and the delicate curving talons on his tiny feet. He might as well be perched on my hand, because I know the weightlessness of his little frame, as though he were one of those flocked Styrofoam figurine birds on my late grandmother Morse's mantle.

"Hey, little guy," I whisper.

His head turns and I see through the lens of his curious eye, heartbeat and muscle structure and blood and breath and life. Telescope my consciousness to the spruce, and the sap moves steadily, water up, carbon dioxide in, oxygen out. The earth itself heaves and stretches beneath my chair, my porch. Even the air, the space in front and around is not space. Movement! There is movement everywhere. Matter, or substance: Spirit! I'm dizzy and afraid. Crawling deeper under this blanket isn't helping, because it's no more solid than the wind. Beautiful, beautiful!

I need a grip. I need something firm.

A rock. I need a rock to grasp. And I close my eyes and open them, and the rock I see is a fake-leather-bound book with letters, NKJV, on the spine. I was reading in the afternoon just before we left for the rescue mission. Trying to read, that is. Timber had been demanding my attention. "Look at this. Give me that. Why can't...?" I guiltily remember slamming the book down and yelling at him about giving me just five minutes of peace. Great example. Way to go, Lainey.

Reality adjusts itself back to that place I understand. The norms I can handle. For the moment, atoms freeze into place. I have set down my mug of tea, so I pick it up. It's cold but flavorful and I down it in a gulp. The liquid passes through the parts of matter and spirit which make up me. Guilty me. Impatient Lainey who is too selfish to jump at the idea of giving a down-and-out alcoholic an opportunity to move on with his life. Too easily angered to be a good wife; a weary mother. The leather on the Bible must actually be real after all, because it smells good. I hold it to my lips, breathe deep, and open it. Come to me, and I will give you rest. Was that it? Yeah, that sounds closer.

That ribbon is still in the fortieth chapter of Isaiah. I read the whole thing. Whoa. Comfort is tied up with humility. Who am I? A grasshopper, hopping in the wrong direction. My lips part slightly as I half-whisper, "I'm just starting to get it. It's not about me, is it?" And I think, there is someone who holds the substance within the molecules. Holds it together. Probably can be trusted to hold me together, too.

I am grounded again, but light. So light. Is this the rest? The homeland for the immigrant? Simply seeing beyond? Looking? Trusting?

The phone rings. I step inside to grab it quickly, and whisper hello before the second ring can bother the boys, and I hear the words, "Your father is dead, Elena." A burst of sunlight breaks through the swirling nimbus just before the wave of grief crashes. God?

TIMBER

One day Timber woke up and his mom was gone already and Daddy spoke quietly and said that Aunt Vanji was coming soon. Daddy was watching Timber to see if he woke up on the right side of the bed or not, but hearing about Aunt Vanji made every side of the bed good! Daddy was still quiet and serious so Timber stopped jumping up and down and waited for what his father needed to say. Grandpa was sick, he said, much sicker than anyone realized. Timber made a sad frowning face because he loved Grandpa and wanted to show that he was sad about the sick part.

But being sick was okay because you could get special things and you didn't have to go to school. But sometimes, said his father, being sick means someone's body gets so weak that it just kind of wears out. It stops, like a broken car, and dies. Timber said that he hoped his grandpa wouldn't get that sick and put his hands together to pray like Celia did in Sunday school for a little sick baby whose heart was bad. But his father put his hands over Timber's and looked into his eyes and said he already did. Already wore out. Was gone.

Dead? Dead like the stiff little bird with no eyes under the rock beside the house? Yes.

Timber wanted to think about it and asked if he could see Grandpa's worn-out body. No, it was gone. Maybe someone hid it, like Timber's bird. But Daddy didn't want to talk about it and Timber made an even sadder face and tried to keep the frown on right even though Aunt Vanji was coming soon so that Daddy could go to Grandpa's house. To see the body? No, it was gone already. To be with Grandma, so she wouldn't be alone. Would they have to live there now, so that Grandma wouldn't be alone? No, she would be okay after a while. Things would get better.

Timber didn't think so. He had been looking at that bird for a long time, and it just kept getting worse.

Chapter Twenty-two

LAINEY

Brad and Joe are shell-shocked. They sit closer than usual on the sagging couch at Mom's house, staring at the television set, holding beers that they barely sip. Death is here too: a real being, hovering cold and threatening down the hallway in the bathroom where Mom found Dad this morning. My brothers have actually been peeing on the woodpile rather than use that room. I wonder what they would have done in the days of dead bodies in the parlor and stinking week-long wakes. Maybe that was better. No sterile ambulance crew popping the offending item on a gurney to reappear waxed and painted in a coffin or magically converted to a handful of ash.

Mom isn't talking either. When she does speak it is with the thickest accent I have ever heard her use, and the worst grammar. Must be that the Spanish of her unfortunate childhood is the only thing adequate to this crushing grief. I watch her now, clad in slippers and an old orange sweat suit, scurrying over dated linoleum and ragged carpets, needlessly busy doing nothing. She seems unwilling to sit and meditate on death. And why would she want to?

Dad once told me that all Mom's family were killed in a gas explosion. People were trying to steal from the gas line, divert it or something, and everything blew. Dad said Mom's whole village was destroyed. Left a crater like an atomic bomb. Mom had been off to market in a neighboring town buying beans. Came home to blood and body parts. After that she immigrated, which was probably a grueling story in itself, but Mom has never spoken of it, either. Never taught us Spanish, even. Mom is Mom only. Jim's wife. No, now she's Jim's widow.

When she left me with her blunt message at 7:12 this morning she had already called 911 to report his death. Dad died sometime during the night. He got up, coughing, as he has been doing for the last year or so, and didn't come back to bed. Mom either heard, or didn't hear, something but thought she should have, and got up to find him collapsed between the sink and toilet. His lips were blue, he was not breathing, and his body was already stiff. The thing she hasn't explained is what she did until 7:00 a.m. on the dot, which she felt was a decent hour to call the authorities. She didn't want to awaken anyone at the fire station, she said.

But what if he was still alive? Were his lips completely blue? Was there still a chance? No one has said it out loud. He was such a strong man. But there was the coughing. Lots of coughing lately, and that time I saw pink when he coughed. It must have been blood. Why didn't I say anything? Maybe he could have taken an antibiotic or something. But the thought is ludicrous, because Jim Morse went to a doctor a total of once in all us children's lives. He fell off a roof on the job, and the site manager forced him go to a clinic. It was a broken leg.

"A simple broken leg," he'd say, "And the damn doctor can't even do that right." Dad believed it had been set wrong, so he cut the cast off himself with a handheld jigsaw and limped for the next twenty years. I never saw him swallow anything more than aspirin and Tums. Pharmaceuticals, he insisted, have ruined our country and created super germs. Maybe it was a super germ that caught him in the end.

There will be the usual coroner's report and autopsy. Until then, I suppose, people can just whisper. I think of Cristian—can't help it––his head in my lap and me calling him, please, don't go, please stay… I shudder. It's the worst thing I can imagine. If Death needed a payoff I am glad it took my father instead.

But oh, do I miss him already.

Beneath the busyness of following my mother's orders is this ache. Beneath the ache is something else. An awareness of that movement that is holding it all together, maybe. The fear of God? Because still, tears and all, I am somehow held together.

Brad and Joe get up at the same time, to revisit the woodpile, muttering something about stretching their legs.

"If you are going to see a man about a horse, please wash your hands in the garage afterwards. You have been sharing that bowl of Doritos." They freeze, glare at each other, then me. How did I know? These guys are as transparent as the long-neck bottle of Coors on the chipped coffee table. And, I have a male child. They shrug. Joe looks wistfully down the hall.

"Joe, Dad isn't there. There is no blood or anything. It is just a bathroom. The same one you have been dirtying your whole life and Mom has been scrubbing. If you have to go, go!"

He goes.

It is cool in the house this morning and none of us has removed our coats. I nudge the dial on the thermostat up before turning back to the box of files we've pulled out of the closet to see what kind of things must be done, dealt with, when someone doesn't wake up in the morning. The scuffed dining table is piled with an assortment of boxes and stacks of junk mail. Every time my mother leaves the room, I slide five more catalogues under the table into a quickly expanding black plastic trash bag. The sheriff gave Mom a helpful brochure with some suggestions of documents and information to gather. I wish he had given it to Dad yesterday, so that he could have had it all ready. He's the only one who understands his filing system. Mom has begun to tune out. She is focusing on her cupboards and pulling out all sorts of canned goods, aligning them along the counter.

"Something to eat, Elena. The boys are hungry I think, and when Michael is come she will want to eat." I look at Mom and see a woman who just found her husband dead in the bathroom and wants to feed her kids because that's what moms do. I resist the urge to correct her English. I say, "Mamá," and she lets me rub her shoulders a little before moving away.

There is a sound in the yard and we all step outside to see Brad walking up the driveway, with his arm around Michael's shoulder.

"Ma," croaks Mike, seeing her, and she lets him embrace her. Bury her inside his huge frame. He's grown bigger than Dad, this artist quarterback who holds his motorcycle helmet out awkwardly while enveloping our mother. With his bronze skin and longish black hair shining in the sun he is more like the returning conqueror than a prodigal son. But his timing sucks. Why couldn't he have come at Easter? Let us all be together one last time for Dad?

Mom steps back and slaps at him. "You come like Brad on the death machine? You boys just do not know what is safe."

"No, Mom. Dad taught us way too good to be safe," says Brad. He nods to the open garage, filled with hunting and sports paraphernalia, our old bikes and unicycle and stilts.

"Dad taught us to live, Mom, to have fun," Joe adds softly. He has come out at the sound of his oldest brother's voice. I agree. Mom said "Be careful," while Dad said "Go for it!"

My Liberty pulls up. Cristian gets out alone, so Vanji must be at the cabin with Timber. Cristian approaches Mom, and they embrace awkwardly. He says he's sorry, and she says she's fine. Joe's stomach growls so loud we all laugh, and panic crosses Mom's face. Cristian offers to pull some snacks together as another car arrives. I notice only that it's a small red car, and then I see Celia's face through the sun glare on the windshield. She steps out balancing an aluminum foil casserole dish. Sun glints off the Saran Wrap and even cold, through the plastic and across the yard, we can imagine how delicious it will smell. Mike introduces himself and I wonder if it's chivalry or a desire to get hold of that pan.

"I heard on the scanner at the gas station earlier," Celia tells Mom. "I'm so sorry. Please don't think I'm nosy. Oh, I am too nosy! Forgive me! I had this lasagna all ready in my freezer. I was actually thawing it overnight because I had hoped to invite you all over for dinner today." She blinks back tears, "With this bag of rolls, there might be almost enough for everyone. I am so sorry, Ida. I wish I hadn't waited until now to make this invitation." They walk together into the house so Celia can start the lasagna heating in the oven.

Joel's stomach growls again. "Magic stomach," says Cristian.

Joe grimaces. "It's not growling because I'm hungry. Stupid Brad didn't wash his hands, and now I got diarrhea."

Brad grins. "You are such a pansy, you can't get sick in like two hours. You probably just drank too much last night, Butthead." The men slap at each other like little boys. Mike whacks them both with open palms on the backs of their skulls and they turn together in protest.

Babies! If I knew how I would roll my eyes. "What are you, third graders? You're in your twenties now, for crying out loud."

Cristian stands beside me on the stoop, watching my brothers tussle at the bottom of the steps. The sun has risen higher and the sky glows in that blue you can only find here in our Rockies. "What needs to be done, Lainey?"

"Probably nothing. The casket and plot stuff is mostly done; they got some package thing from the internet a couple of years ago, believe it or not. The pastor will come by this afternoon to make up the memorial service. But what Mom wants is the garage and yard cleaned up. She says she wants to sell everything."

Brad and Joe stop wrestling and Mike steps back up onto the stoop beside Cristian and me.

"What? This crap has been here forever," says Mike.

"It's our stuff! And Dad's shop! You can't just sell his tools!" Brad is almost in tears.

I rub my temples. "I don't think so either, but I think she's worried about people coming by." Like Celia. "Cristian and Dad did a lot of work before Easter, so really, I think if you just get everything rusty or poky or old behind or inside the garage, and get the doors to shut, she will be happy. I don't think it's auction time yet. Anyway she has only had a few hours to think about this. In my opinion she just doesn't want to feel embarrassed and she needs everyone to be busy."

Cristian wraps his arm around me as my three brothers try to visualize rusty treasures through my mother's eyes and begin pulling things around. He holds me for a second, whispers again how sorry he is, and then asks, should he go get the flowers? We spent all morning Saturday putting together three large plastic planters. Flowing baby's breath, forget-me-nots, and pansies. Hardy stuff, in case we have another late freeze. We wanted blooms to last all summer long on our porch, which finally looks the way we'd always envisioned. Except that our chair is broken blue plastic rather than wood. Someday.

"Yeah," I sigh. "Go get them. I love you." And I do. He kisses close to my ear, and says again that he's sorry. Jim Morse was his dad, too, in a mountain man "Yes sir, I'm sleeping with your daughter" sort of way. They had a love they called respect.

As Cristian backs the jeep out of the drive, Mike sidles up close to my shoulder. He asks me to show him what to do around the side, but he means let's go where the others can't hear. He wants to talk about Angela. He heard about Dad's caller-ID fiasco. He knows, he says, where she lives. He's seen her a few times over the years. He hasn't called her yet. He wants to know what I think, and what our parents' reaction was after Easter. Did they get over the shock yet? How will Mom react?

"If what? If Angela shows up? If Angela reappears from oblivion? What if Mom finds out she's a prostitute or something? Why does she even want to come? Does she think she's gonna get some money? I mean, it all goes to Mom, who happens to still be alive," I say.

"No, Lainey, you're wrong. Angela's not—it's not like that. Look. She's just, sort of, a failure. She has had a lot of crappy stupid jobs and crappy stupid men, and she is ashamed." Mike doesn't look at me as he speaks. He kicks a hole into the soft loam with the heel of his Puma.

"Would she even come? I mean, she obviously didn't care enough to come when Daddy was alive. When he worked so hard to prepare the house for Easter and she didn't have the decency…"

"Lainey, come on." Michael's eyes well up, and he turns away. "I didn't come either. Don't you think I feel like shit?" He should. They both should.

He says, "So now you know. Angela does not have a great job up in Oregon. She doesn't even have a decent job in Pueblo. She cleans houses. The guy Dad called was just some client—"

I snort.

"—whose house she cleans. You think you know, but you don't. It is just like me."

"No it isn't! You don't lie to me, Mikey. I know you aren't playing football anymore. I know you are studying humanities or something for a Masters. I know you work at the art museum…" We pull dead branches deeper into the woods as we speak. The turned-up soil emits the cool smell of hiking early in the morning.

"You know what Dad 'knew' about me? I was the star quarterback at Platte Canyon High School. I was the best sophomore to ever play. I helped us take State as a junior and did well with a poor team my last year. I played at CSU. Second string, because the coach was an ignorant prick (according to Dad). Since then? I coach at different levels, different teams, according to what Dad expects and how much attention he is paying. He wants—wanted his star."

And my second man in two days is crying. "I just wanted him to be proud of me. For what I am, not what I used to do. Tutoring kids in art; not my fake stories about the little kids league coaching."

He's right. I don't know everything about him. "You aren't coaching at all?"

"No, Lainey. The kids I talk about, they're all real. But I know them through the YMCA as their art teacher, not coach. And I have another job. Something new, something important to me, and I just never thought he'd approve."

"Mikey," I pause. Is this the right time? "What about your girl-friend? Why don't you bring her into this? She should know about Dad. Hear what people will say about who he was."

Mike picks up a jagged rock and missiles it so far we don't hear it land. "I don't know. I'll think about it." He yanks at a branch that is embedded deep in the soil until it separates with a crack.

"Might be good for Mom, Mikey, give her something else to think about. Even a scandal would be better than dwelling on the fact that Dad is gone. Anyway, I'm dying to meet her. I don't even know her name!"

"No," says Michael with a smile, "you don't!"

"Elena!" Mom's voice calls through an open kitchen window.

"Yes," I answer, annoyed. "I'm out here, around back."

Her tone is more appropriate to a slacking kid than the wife and mother and dutiful daughter I am. I took off this morning the second she called. I haven't even chastised the woman for her blunt, insensitive way of telling us kids: Dad is dead. Period. Come now. Period. I was supposed to take Timber to his end-of-year class picnic this afternoon. Dad didn't choose today to die, but neither does Mom seem to understand that his death affects us as well as her. Resentment is building and I need something stronger than these shallow breaths to overcome it.

Celia! She is still here and she steps out behind my mother's el-bow, her face full of compassion and love. I think of our bizarre conversations in the Crow Barre. Does she have any hope to offer my grieving mother? What did a gruff old guy like my dad have to do with the kind of Christianity Celia talks about?

"Elena," Mom repeats, softer. "Let the boys do this yard. We need you in here."

And that is how easily Celia becomes my mother's best friend. She shows up when she is needed and offers hope. Even though she keeps reminding all of us that right now we can simply grieve, she honors Mom's desire to get everything done first. Mom keeps insist= ing that we first must complete the logistics of death and then we can give in to the luxury of grief. Speak for yourself! I want to shout, and yet here I am, obeying her command to stifle my emotions.

Celia's been through all this herself so she makes the job of sort= ing papers almost easy. Now we have sticky notes saying things like "Mail to this address along with copy of death certificate." We even have a check-off list to date when we mail each thing or make a call, so we can follow up on stuff like insurance payments. I can use some of this system to better organize the loans and projections for the restaurant.

Our restaurant! In all the sorrow of the day I haven't thought once about the most exciting thing in recent history, besides that lightning blast which now, a month out, seems to have been some= what overrated. Dad is dead. That's a lot bigger than some little boom. And Cristian was fired. No one even knows yet.

"Mom," I say, to the back of her head. She has been wiping down the ratty laminate countertop too long and hard, and the finish is liable to completely rub away. "We told you about the restaurant?" I look to Celia who nods. I guess I told her, too.

"Well, we're thinking of calling it 'The Alpine Soup Line' and serving from the counter, soups and breads only; kind of modeled like the rescue mission where Cristian and Dad went down to volun= teer. Timber and I went along yesterday, and it is a pretty good set-up." I remember the tub of soup Chance sent for my father's sore throat, still on the floor in the back of the jeep.

"Obviously we aren't doing a charity here, but it will provide a nice affordable dinner. Hopefully become the place to eat, you know?"

Mom doesn't turn. Keeps scrubbing. Celia smiles.

"Sounds like a terrific idea, Lainey. When will you open?"

"Sooner than we wanted, probably." Should I tell or would it be too much on top of everything else today?

"Because I was fired," finishes Cristian, brushing dirt from his hands before stepping into the kitchen. Mom spins around, reengaging with the conversation.

"What is this, Elena?"

Ask him yourself, I want to shout.

"I'm sorry, Ida. But Travis learned about our plans for the Whip and fired me before I could quit. I had been hoping to work another month, while we got permits worked out, got the refinishing contracted and settled all the details."

Cristian stands in the open kitchen doorframe, one hand on either side as though holding pillars in place. I note his muscles, beneath a clinging rayon shirt. I love it when he wears that color—peachy salmon, almost pink. On my man, even a girlie color becomes masculine. He's going to open a restaurant, I think. We're going to do it. I speak. "So now we're hoping to push ahead sooner, to keep from using up our savings before we even start." Celia's mouth is hanging open. My brothers appear in the doorway behind Cristian, and they begin to curse Cristian's old boss.

"The worst thing," I can't help but add, "is that Travis broke into our car to find the folder of legal papers about the restaurant. He was spying on Cristian and then went out to dig up something. And he called him 'Boy.'"

"Sue his sorry Texan a—" Beep beep! The timely interruption in Brad's expletive is Vanji pulling up with Timber. Her timing, like everything about her, is impeccable. This has been a long day already and could have been much worse if I had to constantly monitor Timber's potentially inappropriate commentary. On the other hand, it has been a long day without my baby, and I am glad to see his furry brown head and bright shining eyes. He flies through the house and into my arms.

"Mommy! I love you!"

"Timbuktu! I love you, too!" I sit him down after a big hug.

"Mine grandpa be dead." He states his new reality and glances around enthralled. All his favorite people together in one place! Whom to greet first? I spin him toward his grandmother with a little nod. And he runs to her, and his smile disappears, and he bawls on her neck. And she grabs him tight, and she bawls too and I've never seen such a thing. None of us has. Vanji, in the doorway still, catches Mike's eye and they cough and hem about work outside, and Joe and Brad turn away, but Cristian catches me and we both cry. Celia puts her head on her arm, maybe praying, maybe remembering.

One little boy has just ripped a path to sorrow. That big echoing presence of our gruff but loving father has been relegated to a photo on the center of the kitchen table. I notice that Angela's dusty memories are gone from Mom's little shrine shelf, and I know that she must come. Cristian's hands are massaging my shoulders and I could melt into his flesh. It's strangely sensual for such a moment. I pull back. I need to talk to Mikey.

Pushing the front screen door out and stepping onto the small porch, or large stoop, I am struck by the beauty of the pots of flowers Cristian has brought over. This will help Mom. I almost run back in to get her but it's Cristian's gift, his sacrifice even more than mine, and he deserves to be the one to see her reaction.

I find Mike easily by following a quiet murmur. I step on cedar chips Dad put around the house for mulch a few years back, which have been unearthed by our dragging of branches. Their pungent odor mixes with decaying pine needles to assault my sinuses, and I almost sneeze. How nice that Vanji is here now. She is so good with empathy and will certainly have words of consolation for my little brothers. I stop for a second, curious to know what she might say. Mike is speaking.

"I was stupid, Vanj. I should have come at Easter. It wasn't his fault. It was me. I am such an idiot."

Vanji whispers something low. And I come around the corner to hear "I would have liked for him to know," just as I see Vanji lift her chin and Mikey lower his and their lips meet. My gasp knocks them apart like the blast of a mountain dust devil. We stand, we three, in a confused daze.

"I just came to say you should call Angela. She needs to be here," I say, stumbling as I back up into a holly bush. So this is shock. It feels very much the same as getting smacked by lightning. Pulled out of bed in a smoky house, hearing that your son broke a little girl's arm, and being told your father is dead. Except this shock is good. I think.

Vanji is caught but not repentant. She shakes her head, ever so slightly, while squaring her shoulders and sort of shinnying her neck to its full height. It's her peacock-girl fight position, and I'm not about to get in the ring. Mike stares at the ground but then raises a sideways grin.

"Not what you thought, hey, sis?" With his thumbs hooked in his back pockets, Mike's straight brown hair hangs in his black eyes and I think how much his nephew resembles him. Mike and I are the Mexicans, that's what Dad used to say. I haven't thought of this in years, but we were his "burrito babies." Not Spanish princess like Angela, not Scandinavian blondes like Brad and Joe. Vanji is Black today, tighter curls loping down her cheeks and smoky eyeliner with a shimmering gray-black blouse to accentuate the shadows of her skin. They are a beautiful couple.

But Mike's my little brother!

"Cradle-robber!" I accuse.

Someday we'll wake up in Heaven with Jesus? Yeah, something like that.

LAINEY

Dad's casket is already at the cemetery. I wish it was over with already. My eyes well up at the slightest provocation, and I am a little girl lost. The memorial service is scheduled to begin about six in the afternoon, as people get off work and make it up the mountain and out to Dad's favorite place, the A-frame of the local Vets. I am wearing a short black dress bought for me years ago. The back has cutout stripes in a style much better suited to Vanji than me. I've only worn it once before, to the symphony for the big date he had planned as the rest of that year's gift. This time I omit the slinky lingerie he got for me to wear under it. Anyway it's a hot day today and I don't even want a slip, let alone ridiculous spider-webby hose that are held up by a complicated garter system.

Vanji actually rolls her eyes when she sees me. "Kinda sexy, Lainey, but black? Should I go get my movie-funeral umbrella now, or what?" I'm propping open the door to our cabin for her while she pushes past with a large flower arrangement. Daffodils and white lilies. My favorites. She is wearing a colorful and even sexier sundress that says anything but "Let's go mourn today!"

"You should just leave those flowers in the car for now," I say, but she didn't get these for my mom, or to dress up my dad's tombstone. These are for me, she says, and stop that blubbering. She says I'll ruin my makeup and crush my hair, but there is no other shoulder I'd rather cry on. Vanji just lets me go for a while, cooing and clucking over my head like a mourning dove. Then the door slams and the porch boards creak as we step together, back outside, inhaling deeply

173

the fresh mountain air. I wipe my eyes and blow my nose. Take a deep, cleansing breath.

"Where's Mikey?" I ask.

"Am I your brother's keeper? Lainey, Michael doesn't answer to me and I do not text him about what flavor coffee I'm drinking. I don't know where that boy is at." I stare, unbelieving, until she admits, "Okay, so I did try to call this morning but he was already gone." Vanji pushes me to arm's length and looks in my eyes.

"Is this freaky weird? I mean, you already are my sister thanks to Cristian, and brother/sister, sister/brother—getting kind of inbred, aren't we?"

"Since when did freaky bother you, Vanji? Anyway what could be better than my favorite brother and favorite sister…"

A car pulls around the spruce and into my drive and everything freezes like an old Polaroid print.

I know that car. I've seen it somewhere. It can't possibly be, but it looks just like our old Taurus! Suddenly I'm positive it is Dad's car, the one I drove and Angela stole. Michael's dark form is visible in the driver's seat. All I know of my family history spirals into this moment as the passenger door swings opens and my long-lost prodigal sister emerges, weighing at least a hundred pounds more than she did twelve years ago. Her hair hangs in limp strings over blotchy cheeks, and her eyes are puffed and red. Her glance is furtive and she makes a motion to get back into the car she just climbed out of.

I lose my balance. Vanji grabs me, steadies me, and then gives me a tiny push. Suddenly I'm beside my sister Angela, and I want to embrace and we start to, tentatively, and then it is a real hug and I smell her cheap Jean Naté that I used to steal and deny using and I can barely fit my arms around her huge jiggly frame and I think "Jelly," and start giggling and can't stop. We both begin to hiccup.

Through my tears and crushed view beyond my big fat sister I see that Cristian and Mike and Vanji are greeting Joe as he swings off the motorcycle behind Brad, and then Brad himself dismounts. They aren't sure who I am hugging, but I see Mike gesturing, and then they know, and Joe comes running over but Brad shrugs and goes on into the cabin. Angela will have to earn Brad's affection.

"Welcome home," I finally manage, stepping back to let Joe say hello. He is courteous and shy, as you might be with an elderly aunt you didn't know well.

"Little Joe?" Angela is incredulous. She really hadn't imagined how much has changed. An awkward conversation between my oldest and youngest siblings follows, with Angela asking Joe asinine questions about what he still likes. No, he hasn't been into Star Trek for many years now.

A door slams. Brad stands, feet apart, arms crossed forcefully. His eyebrows make one angry slash across his pale face. He spits his words: "It's time to go to the cemetery. Celia just called, and she is leaving now with Mom. By the way, 'Jelly,' Dad died. It's actually not about you today."

And I thought I was the one with the grudge.

Angela sways for a moment and then swallows and nods. Mike punches Brad in the shoulder and they scuffle before roughly straightening each other's dress shirt and tie. Angela squeezes back into the Taurus and the springs creak as the vehicle lists violently to her side. Joe coughs a laugh and someone gasps.

Timber asks loudly, "Why for that lady gotta be so fat, Mommy?"

Vanji whispers in my ear, "You should have seen my momma," and she and Cristian and Timber and I climb into the Liberty. My recently returned sister didn't even ask to meet her nephew. Or her brother-in-law. Or my sister-in-law. She didn't ask me anything. Maybe she'll never be able to care about anyone much beyond herself, but for the moment she cares about me. And that's enough for now. I can still taste peace, even if it is a little saltier than before.

Brad and Joe somehow squeeze into our back seat before Mike gets back in to drive the Taurus, and we caravan a couple of miles down the road to the graveyard to help our mother bury our father.

Chapter Twenty-four

Opening night at the Soup Line. Clammy hands; angry surf pounding in my ears. My heart hasn't raced like this in the two months since the big zap. Breathe, Lainey! It's my wedding all over again. Standing in a stuffy back room, glancing at Dad, who was even more nervous than me, just before he hooked my arm with his elbow and dragged me down the aisle toward Cristian. Thrust me at him. Here, take her! Just let me sit down!

Today there is no flowing or crinkling white mess. Just a comfortable turquoise-and-brown peasant blouse and my favorite jeans. Timber matches me in the totally cool Indian headdress t-shirt we bought last winter in Ouray. I chose the color theme, turquoise for the aprons worn by Cristian and his crew, which so far consists of Chance from the mission and two temporary girls from the high school. Blocky red-and-black buffalo plaid makes a nice contrast with the curtains and centerpiece ribbon, or at least that's what I thought a few weeks ago when I chose the finishings. Today I am not sure of anything.

Opening night. I've already forgotten my lines! Timber grabs my hand and says come on and he drags me through the office door and into the dining hall. The last of the remodeling was only just completed this morning and we worried that we'd have to serve around the construction crew. I spy another one of those yellow plastic things the electrician dropped and snag it up quickly along with some curlicues left from a drill. The new wall and serving counter looks amazing, and despite the last-minute panic I think we'll be fine.

We have filled clusters of red balloons for every kid who comes in, and these balloon trees are tucked into three corners. That is

Timber's job; to identify kids and give them each a balloon. My job is to be the consummate hostess and pass out Come Back Again dollar-off coupons.

The place isn't exactly packed yet, at a quarter to five, the official opening time. But our various family members, most of whom we haven't seen in the month since Dad's burial, along with the Thorndove clan easily fill one of the ten tables. I wish my father were among those gathered. I still can't get my mind around the fact that all four of my siblings, as well as Vanji, are here in one place. My entire family tree! Mike and Vanji look way too comfortable together while Brad flanks Mom protectively, steering her away from Angela who drove the two of them here in Dad's Bronco. Joe glances at his cell phone again. It was sweet of him to come, but it seems he has something he'd rather do. Bill Senior and his wife and Billy and Julie still glow with the newness of babydom, and they all smell like Johnson & Johnson shampoo. Baby Sally travels with an incredible amount of accessories.

"She is so beautiful, Julie! And look at that smile!" I never saw my baby's first smile. Or heard his first babble or laugh. It's a dark, deep feeling that settles down beside the anxiety of opening night. The doors are still shut and I'm already crushed! Julie hands me the baby and rubs my shoulders, quickly and efficiently. Sally flashes her brilliant, toothless smile. I am refreshed in seconds.

"Maybe someday," Julie whispers. She smiles toward Timber. A little sibling? Adopt again? Another child? Ha! Anyway, to dream of another would be asking too much. Despite Timber's issues he is so...so wonderful. Soft brown flesh and shining black eyes. To love a child, hear the gears shifting in his mind as a new idea forms—the amazing ways he puts words together sometimes—is such a gift. He's a gift I don't deserve, and I feel that I fail him so often. I smile at Julie, knowing that someday means in your dreams.

Cristian can't stand the pressure anymore. With ten minutes to go he swings the doors open to the general public. Smiles and laughter. People say things to me that I don't quite register, but I know I am smiling back because my jaw hurts.

The aroma of fresh sage is the strongest, I think, but thick black coffee in an old church percolator is a close second. Cristian's goal, of course, is to eventually get a huge shining coffee contraption. The coffee sits on the counter beside a glass water dispenser. Always full, always free. At least, that's what we'll try this first month. The carbonated-beverage contract didn't come in, and we decided not to apply for a liquor license, so making a big deal about fresh coffee and ice water being free will hopefully deflect people's complaints about the lack of choice.

I step to the side for a second, letting my aching back rest against the curves of the hand-hewn log wall. We worked so hard, yet the wood still looks pretty dingy up close. What it would take to look great is sanding, re-chinking, re-staining, and sealing. For the moment, we have chosen not to do all that. I am supposed to be keeping an eye out for any potential food critics, but I have no idea what to look for. Could be the mousy guy with a bushy mustache, or the bald guy who could be one of Chance's old bike buddies. Maybe the overdressed woman with a cell phone attached to her ear. The important things, I think, are the slurps and clinking spoons and quiet compliments. The laughter of the people going through the line at the counter, conversing with Cristian about which soup to choose tonight.

"Sure, take the Aztec tortilla and try the potato bisque on Monday, if I still have it!"

"You might not have it? Give me a bowl of both now, in that case! I can't take a chance!" And the hefty guy from the hardware store balances two big bowls as he makes his way to the first empty seat, which happens to be next to my own chubby sister. Good thing we didn't define place settings. Guess there actually is a plus for open benches.

"Jelly" as she honestly calls herself now, settled in quickly. Somehow her "night on the couch, Mama, if it would be okay," has stretched into a month. She did get Mike to take her back to Pueblo once, to "tie some things up." The things needing tying up seem to be a scattering of possessions she brought back up in black plastic trash bags and disgorged on the frilly bedspread of our childhood room. Lucky for her, Mom and Dad only gave one of the beds to the VA scholarship fundraiser sale a few years back. Luckier still, it was my sagging bed they got rid of, and her special Posturepedic they kept.

Angela is laughing with the hardware man now, enjoying Cristian's jambalaya. Our mother sips daintily at the tortilla soup, eyebrows raised as she secretly appraises her eldest. She hasn't voiced an objection—that I have heard—to Angela's re-entry into her life. I suspect that once the reality of her fallen angel set in, she decided to go ahead and accept her daughter as she is: overweight and not overly exciting, but one heck of a good cleaner. The archetypal single Latina daughter who sacrifices her future to care for her widowed mother. Maybe. She still has barely spoken to Cristian and shows little interest in getting to know her nephew either. Forget it. It very literally is her loss to be so wrapped up in herself. But she is helping Mom, so maybe she's not totally self-absorbed. Maybe she just has trouble absorbing too much at the same time.

Angela laughs again, a snort that sends a spray of soup back into her bowl. If there's anything more devious in her plan, I don't see it.

TIMBER

Timber, how handsome in those glasses. You look smart, kiddo. Bet the girls are going to love you. How does it feel to hear better, huh?!

All the questions, screamed at him, from the uncles and that fat new lady and even his gramma and favorite Aunt Vanji and people he never saw before, ever, not here in the restaurant or at school or anywhere in the world. Timber tried to keep the right face up with teeth showing, cheeks tight like a smile but it was hard and then Mommy passed by and looking not seeing said stop snarling like that Timber it looks ugly and don't keep taking that new hearing aid in and out of your ear like that because you are going to lose it. She said that because it cost a gazillion dollars which Timber knew because he had it in his ear on the way home from the doctor and his parents talking forgot now he could hear it all if he wasn't humming. Better be worth it! one of them said and Timber knew that meant probably Timber was NOT worth it. So broken. Thought about that story of a baby in a box with a cat face and knew now that the line under its nose was just a little tiny part of the huge brokenness of the boy Timber.

Are you Timber? Red-haired and snotty, the boy who spoke. The lady said you would give me and my sisters free balloons. Gimme those balloons, four-eyes. Timber knew that four-eyes was on account of the new glasses because the doctor told him about that. Told him sometimes other kids would think it was a funny nickname but they were just ignoring kids and Timber was supposed to say something then that would make it funny but instead tears hot angry filled up his insides and began to spill out. He pulled back the arm with balloons for the children but that boy reached up, bigger, and pulled his arm twisting sore and stole three whole balloons and dropped the arm like a burning stick and just walked on away. That hearing aid tucked against his ear and rubbing shouted back the red-headed words: ha look what that little retard gave us! And the boy who was called Timber pulled the strings of the balloons down close to himself and crawled under the desk in the corner and pulled the thing away from his ear and folded the glasses on top of it and picked up a

181

crayon and a dropped-on-the-floor menu and started drawing. It was a stupid picture, of course, but at least you could tell it was a really big sammy truck that weighed more than a house and under it was left just red marks from the hair of the boy who got runned over and over by that truck because anyway, the red haired boy was the stupid one what didn't know better than to stand in the middle of a highway.

LAINEY

But where is Timber? I run into the kitchen to ask. Cristian shrugs. He's around. But it takes fifteen minutes to find him, and my heart races and my palms sweat, making the faint burn scar glow pink. How many cars have come and gone tonight? He could have been taken by anyone. Or gone too far into the trees and gotten lost. Or stumbled onto the highway! But suddenly Cristian is beside me, telling me everything is okay. Timber is here. Turns out he's been inside the whole time, curled up beneath the desk and drawing pictures of something he calls a Sammy Truck. His giveaway balloons are pulled in under the desk beside him. I knew this would be hard, but now I wonder what we were thinking. Chance puts a hand on my shoulder.

"Relax, Lainey. Nothing happened. You got a smart kid there, and he'll be fine. Celebrate! You guys did great tonight!"

I want to believe him, but I also want to punch him!

Just then I notice the sky. It's lit by a spectacular July sunset, perfect to tie off a long summer day. It means that we have just about reached closing time. Everyone notices the sunset and there is a collective "Ah!" as an incredible orange ball of flames sinks slowly into the silhouetted mountains. Red, orange, and black like a cheesy painting on an old VW bus or a surfboard or…the mountain sky at sunset. There's a moment of calm before I flip the switches, bringing our antler chandeliers to life and bathing the place in a whole new warmth.

All the people are looking at me now, so I do a little curtsy, and wave my hand to Cristian. He also takes a bow and the room erupts in applause.

"Bravo! Great opening! Good job. Don't you all love these guys?" Bill Senior walks toward us, clapping heartily. "Timber? Where are you? Come here, kiddo."

He puts one hand on Timber's head and the other on Cristian's shoulder. Timber still has three balloons tied to his wrist and they brush against Bill's face. "I am proud to introduce the Clayson family and Bailey's new best eats; give it up for: The Alpine Soup Line!"

Chance grins like the Cheshire Cat and thumps his hands together. He and Cristian will stay late to count the night's successes, but the rest of our family members are taking their leave. As the remaining patrons file slowly out into the dark, I start to prepare Timber for the fact we have to go now, too, since keeping a bedtime schedule is of paramount importance. Five more minutes! He whines. I agree. Anyway I wanted five minutes with Celia.

She is smiling in that proud motherly way that gives me an odd urge to kiss her cheek. I don't act on it. She's still been hanging out––if old people can be said to hang out—with Mom. It makes me a little nervous, since maybe our relationship will change somehow. But she is as genuine and direct as ever.

"Lainey. Stupendous. Simply marvelous!"

"You must have had the jambalaya!"

"Yes, I actually did have the jambalaya, but they all looked great. And I mean everything; the ambience, the idea, the service. Even the industrial strength coffee that will keep me up for the next 17 hours!"

"Thank you, Celia. That is very kind of you to say." Celia's lazy eye swims out farther than usual and I blink, trying to refocus on the better eye without seeming to stare.

She puts her arm around my shoulder and we turn back to the window. The sky is indigo now; the cliffs cut out of black poster-board. A few thin clouds glow pale above the horizon. Suddenly a star or maybe a planet appears, gloriously bright, and then more and more.

"Can you feel Life?" she asks in a whisper. "He's singing you a love song."

It's a beautiful thought and I close my eyes.

Celia speaks again, with her favorite question. "Lainey Clayson, how is your heart?"

"My heart is good, Celia. It is real good." But there's a cloud across my son's face, and I wonder how his is.

Chapter Twenty-five

Despite Cristian's late night counting up and closing down with Chance, his eyes are open at seven when I open mine. Lying there with my cheek pressed on a lumpy pillow and our noses almost touching, I think I have never seen anything more amazing than my husband's face. His hair never changes, morning or night, wet or dry. His eyes shine bright and youthful and wise. He smiles.

"Hey, Lainey! Good morning. How does it feel to be Bailey's premier entrepreneur?"

"I dunno. How does it feel to be Colorado's Number One Soup Chef?!"

His fingers trace the corners of my eye, down my cheekbone, trail tenderly off my chin.

"Feels sexy." And his lips are over mine, hungry. I yield completely, but he suddenly stops. I open my eyes to see that he's rolled over onto his back and stares at the ceiling, a grin busting across his cheek.

"A Grand, Lainey."

Say what?! But he's in a different mood now, and I turn over onto my back next to him and let him have his way. Conversationally.

"One-thousand dollars is our gross pull for the night. Not counting the wait staff's tips, of course. You won't believe this, Lainey. Every bowl of soup sold for five bucks. We couldn't have had two-hundred visitors, because I know some people ate two bowls, but all said we sold exactly 200 bowls! No charge for the drinks, and the breads were free for opening night."

"Exactly 200? Weird." It's windy this morning because that tall aspen is scratching the window pane again. A woodpecker laughs somewhere beyond.

"Yeah. But it's too simple. I mean, I felt sort of rinky dink with no drinks; no desserts. Did we just put on a church fundraiser or open a restaurant?"

I don't know. I've never done either. People were happy.

"It was nice, Cristian."

He turns to me and his little-boy eyes sparkle. Finally he feels the pull of pheromones and me here, ready. He traces my face again and this time, keeps going.

Where to watch fireworks is a big discussion. Should we hit Como, which is a little almost-ghost town farther down Highway 285, or follow the crowds to the hillside above Evergreen Lake? I vote Como since I haven't been in years. Cristian and I went there on our first Fourth of July together and, well, we didn't watch the sky. Timber whines. He probably wouldn't even care, but since I said we're going he's sure it's some kind of punishment. I hate how he thinks I want the worst for him. As if going to see fireworks is a drag. But five minutes later he seems relatively calm.

His apology for the outburst goes like this: "Is not my fault. Is 'cause I wants to see fireworks."

"But we are going to see fireworks. It's what I said, in Como."

But I didn't just say fireworks, I said Como, and he remembers going to the railroad museum once and there were no fireworks. Make a mental note for this Friday's evaluation to ask if it's normal for him to be this literal.

Cristian is distracted, still thinking about the restaurant, I guess. I have to ask three times before he answers that, yes, he got a watermelon and left it in the Liberty.

We park backwards, hicks at a drive-in, with all our pillows and comforters piled up for a kind of bed. We have to squeeze sideways behind the back bench to see up and out. The darkening sky puts on a natural show as stars and planets and satellites pop out above us. If it weren't for the child rolling around and pinching our feet it would be easy to remember the romance of our last time here.

Cristian does anyway. He whispers in my ear: "That was the first time, remember?" Shush! Timber is right here!

Several parties start little campfires and the smells of marshmallows and hotdogs and many more suspiciously smoldering items assault us. Just as we're thinking to pack it in, the show begins. Pyrotechnics must get cheaper every year because this little town produces a show just as impressive as a big city display. The coolest thing is how it's all tied together with the beat of live music from a local bluegrass band to keep us rocking.

Snuggled together in our car, while color and light play above us and music fills the empty spaces, feels just about perfect. I am thrilled about the restaurant. Last night went better than we'd hoped, even, but still, better still, is this. Family. Cristian and me and Timber. Loving each other and forgiving a lot. As the universe swirls in sulfuric after-smoke, new lights continue to appear. Planned. The whole thing, perfectly orchestrated. My arm, still sleeveless beneath the blankets, encircles Cristian's chest. My fingers gently work his flesh and he flexes for me. I love you.

"I love you," I whisper.

THE BOY

Mad Rabbit leered at the boy from the other side of the jeep and so he grabbed him and twisted his neck around and around. Ouch, said the boy's mother when he rolled over her foot. Watch it, said the father. They didn't care that the boy was mad. They loved each other, not the boy, who was not even their own really truly son but a borrowed one who had no parents. Probably they wished the boy wasn't there at all. Then they could be kissy kissy however long they wanted. The boy hated the place called Como. It was a stinky place that tasted bad on his tongue. The sky was dark but there were still no fireworks and it was even worse than the Most Boring Museum in the world that was located somewhere nearby.

The parents were whispering to each other about the boy and how he was hurting their feet and taking their blankets. He knew this because the new thing in his ear made everything, even whispers, loud as he wanted. The boy once thought he had super powers but now that he could hear for real, he realized that he never knew anything. Was even stupider than he had once feared.

He could see now, too. Glasses plastic grey like old men, but not Grandpa, who anyway was dead, on the boy's face, scar under his nose and the "magic super-spy listening device" sticking out of his ear for all the world to see. Sure, the boy could see. He could see everything. He heard himself talking, knew his words came garbled like a baby. Knew what he wanted to say but only half of it came out. Saw people looking at him with expressions of loathing. Wishing he would be cuter. Or smarter. Or still and quiet. Not kicking seats, rolling on feet, impatient over fireworks.

CRASH! And the world exploded or maybe it was the boy's head. The black sky was suddenly brilliant. Too bright, way too bright, and a clashing breaking BOOM through the device in his ear, through his eardrum, and bursting his brain. He cried out, but the parents were gasping in delight at the show and thought he was too and didn't even notice the blood spurting out of ears, eyes, mouth and probably even bellybutton. It hurt so bad, and the boy ripped the thing from his ear and stuck it on Stupid Ugly Rabbit and pushed the glasses down into the hole he had just ripped in the neck by twisting too far. The grownups were kissing again and the boy quietly, without rolling on feet, slid Rabbit to the edge of the tailgate and with one final push sent him tumbling into the too bright darkness along with all the expensive things meant to fix the broken boy. He would rather stay broke. And even though now he would be able to see the blur of color of the lights without them piercing his eyeballs, he stayed buried beneath the oily quilt, kept his eyes squeezed shut, and pushed his fingers deep as he could stand into the tunnels of his ears, wanting darkness, wishing silence.

Chapter Twenty-six

LAINEY

Second night of Soup Line. Monday. Pans clatter in the kitchen as Cristian puts things in order in our own little home. Every now and then he yells "Five more ladles" or "A dozen oven mitts" for me to write down on his list for the restaurant, on a clipboard which I balance on my knee.

"Will anyone come? It would have to be new people, because who wants soup twice in the same week, right?" I feel a surge of panic and suddenly the wisdom of our whole platform is suspect. Why didn't anyone catch the flaw? We've already saturated the market!

"Relax, Lainey, we did the homework." Cristian comes behind me to rest his chin on the top of my head. Coffee begins to perk in the kitchen, filling our cabin with its strong scent. The charts and graphs are scattered on my kitchen counter in front of me, and I know the numbers even without my husband's finger pointing to them. The numbers are high, joyously high, for potential customers. Who are these people? I even have stats on that. White collar workers from the Denver Tech Center, defense contract peons, phone company techies, and more. People who work too long at difficult jobs to come home and cook. People who grab take-out in Denver and reheat it in a microwave for their spouse and children. They live in nooks and crannies in valleys that used to provide habitat for mountain lion and bear. They buy a half acre. Build their dream home. And turn around and try to make new laws to keep anyone else from doing the same.

"But," Cristian points out, "they are just like me. Fickle and easily assimilated. Acting overly loyal to local things like school to disguise their shallow roots." Cristian touches the brim of his cowboy hat in proof. I've never heard this honesty from him. I didn't realize he was even aware of what I consider his biggest character flaw, and here he is, making it work for us. They are us. Every resident in these hills did the same thing at some point or other. It's what makes us hang together and also what makes us suspicious. Protecting the pack, defending the den, hunting nourishment—these instincts seem often to come one at the expense of another.

I stretch back against my beloved. "Okay, so we already know that there are plenty of people who would eat at Soup Line, if they knew we existed and if they liked us. We are here, therefore we belong. But we are new, therefore we are suspect."

"We have to become old timers, and fast! Once people eat at a restaurant, they know that place. Once is all it takes, Lainey. Rope 'em in!" With that he kisses my cheek and heads for the door.

So. There is still a lot to do, and Timber isn't even fully awake yet. He had a terrible night, coming down off the high of enjoying the fireworks by behaving like a bear for the entire car ride home. I'm not in a big hurry to see what mood he's in today! I also need to finish cleaning house and organizing things here while Cristian gets started on tonight's meal. Calm down, he would say, everything will be fine.

Still. A July breeze saunters through the door he left open and ruffles my statistics. What if everyone just passes that huge "Opening Week" sign on the highway and thinks, someday we'll try that new place. See what we hear, first. See, hear…it's about taste, people! If they could just experience it.

"Timber," I call, cautiously, prodding the lump beneath his blankets. Nothing. Pull down the covers and there's that fuzzy little head, eyes scrunched tight in fake sleep.

If I try to rush him there will be a scene. Choose your battles, Celia said. Avoid meltdown triggers, said the school counselor. All day every day I must walk a tightrope. I long for the stress of school mornings where at least we had a few hours apart. Summer sucks.

I have been trying to give Timber a lot more leash and not over direct, to avoid oppositional confrontations. The glasses and hearing aid, both coming in last week just before the restaurant opened seem to be really helping. Timber has been walking around quietly, and I know he is absorbing information he never knew the world contained. And yet, I can't help but feel that something dark has been unleashed. Something was off last night. He said little but the glitter in his eye when I finally tucked him in was somehow disturbing.

I kiss his cheeks, whispering, "Wakey wakey, shakey bakey!" He squeezes his eyes tighter.

Five minutes later, he jumps from bed and runs straight for the bathroom.

"Brush good, go potty, and comb your hair!" I call after him. Making his bed takes a few minutes, and straightening the tiny house a few more. I finish getting myself ready in my bedroom mirror and head back down to wait for Timber.

Finally, the bathroom door opens.

"I am ready!" he shouts.

"That's correct!" I exclaim. "'I am ready' is completely correct!" The air reeks of Cristian's antiperspirant. Timber's hair is matted wildly. Must have used it as hair gel. Does it matter? It's a waste, it's an abuse of someone else's property, but it is only deodorant, for crying out loud. I ignore it.

"Don't forget your glasses and aid." A darkness passes over Timber's face, and I feel dread in my stomach. Come to think of it, where was the aid last night? And his glasses? What has he done with them?

"I no did lose nothing. You is a lying!"

Now I know he has done something. He's a terrible liar, fortunately.

Breathe, deep, and—

A double honk sends us both running for the door. That is Vanji's code, but why would Vanji be here on a Monday?

"Is her! Is Aunt Vanji!" And Timber is running right in front of her car, but she knows to watch and gravel flies as she brakes hard. She gets out and greets Timber sternly. His eyes well up. He's sorry. He will never do it again. He will stand on the porch and wait for her to stop. And then she gives him a huge hug and says that everything is fine.

"Hey, buddy. Happy fifth of July! Hmmm, smelling kind of strong here!"

"It's Cristian's deodorant, I think," I offer. Timber opens his mouth in denial but Vanji cuts him off.

"Why don't you run in and give your head another quick dip under the sink faucet. See if you can't get some of your daddy's goo out of there? I wonder if he would like you using it that way?" Timber bites his lip and nods.

"Sorry," he says, again, looking at me. "Sorry, Auntie Vanji. I no mean it. Not at all." Vanji kisses his cheek and he runs in to obey.

What's that taste? Oh yeah—jealousy. If I had lectured my son, he would be screaming back at me. But no, he'd never yell at Vanji. Maybe we just need a break from each other.

"Vanj," I whisper confidentially, while handing her my travel mug of coffee. "Try and find out what he's done with his glasses and aid. I have a feeling that he's hidden them somewhere."

She takes a sip and nods, but Vanji has not come up today just to solve my current Timber crisis. "Thought you would be over to Soup Line," she says, adjusting the neckline of her emerald scoop t-shirt. "I was just going to do a pull through to make sure the car was gone. So you're letting the man drive the Liberty, huh?" She points to the old Tercel. I nod my head toward the door where Timber disappeared to clean up.

"We were just on our way. Cristian left about an hour ago. We figure the Liberty looks better parked in the lot. What's up, Vanji? Don't you have to work? We already kept you from singing on Saturday. I don't want to be responsible for you losing your bank job!"

"Bank job? Lainey Girl, you make me sound like a criminal!"

I laugh and open the back door of the Tercel. I hope Timber will get his butt in gear and get back out here. "Well, 'loan officer' kind of sounds like fuzz then, doesn't it?"

Vanji turns to Timber who stands dripping in the doorway. "Which am I? Good guy or bad guy?"

He thinks she's the best guy. And she agrees. She's got today off, since she had some kind of audit work on last week's vacation day and they'd rather give make-up time than pay overtime. No one cheaper than a bank, she insists. Vanji is dressed like me in that she wears jeans with her t-shirt. I just wish I filled my clothes like she fills hers! I think of Julie's new baby boobs. If Vanji ever gets pregnant— it's a staggering thought!

"Besides," says Vanji, "You need help."

"Actually, Sister, we are doing pretty well," I answer.

"Actually, Sister, you don't have a clue! You are in serious shi— ny happy people place if we don't get started quick."

Timber jumps up and down, shaking the porch beneath him. "You was gonna say the bad word! Mommy! Aunt Vanji was gonna say ship! I know it!"

"You were going to..." I say, but Vanji glares at me. I'm over-correcting again.

"Yes, Timber, you caught me. Ships ahoy! Sorry. Lainey, we got some trouble. Cyber trouble. There was a good buzz going Saturday night after the opening, but starting early this morning someone is dumping a lot of crap online. My guess is Mr. C. Barre, if you get my drift."

"Travis?!"

"Travis is a ask-hole!" yells Timber. He could have heard that from anyone, but I think it was his loving uncles who were harping about Travis on Saturday at the opening. Timber knows better and he clamps his hand over his mouth in mock surprise.

We really need to get to the restaurant. The problem is that once there, all I can do with Timber is send him up on the hillside hunting rocks, which he is getting paid to line up around the building. It scares me, having him wandering around like that. After Saturday's episode of "losing" him for a few minutes, I made up a new set of rules about where he can be during operating hours. It's not like it's our property at home, where he knows every tree and hole and is very clear on staying far from the highway and on our side of the barbless wire fence. It's hard to remember to keep checking on him at the restaurant, and hard not to check too much.

Now, though, I need to see what Vanji is talking about. Timber will just have to do without his glasses and aid for an hour or two while she shows me what's up. Maybe he is embarrassed about Vanji seeing him with them, although up until maybe Saturday he had enjoyed passing his reflection, talking about how he looked like a superhero. Our laptop is at the restaurant anyway, because we are getting consistent signal there and so our internet card might finally pay off. I've been in the Stone Ages, according to Vanji and my brothers, practically off the grid since college. I may be the only person alive not linked in to social media networks. All I have is email, on the off-chance that I actually check it.

Time to change the subject. "Hey," I ask Vanji as I'm snapping Timber's seatbelt into place in the backseat of her car, "Did you and Mikey start, you know 'connecting' in person or on Facebook or something?"

She laughs. "You are off the grid, Lainey! You ever seen that brother of yours initiate a conversation? Especially with a girl? Especially with his big sister's sister-in-law whom he has crushed on since your wedding? Cyber space is amazing. He put up a song. I loved the song. I sang the song. I put me up, singing the song. Then he called. He could talk. In person, even! But his texts, Lainey. I am telling you. He is a poet. A song-writing genius." Vanji pulls out onto the highway.

"All along I thought the big secret was that he loves art more than sports," I add.

"Frankly, Lainey, his paintings aren't that good. At least, I don't think so. Critics don't think so; not even Mike thinks so. He is a terrific art teacher and the kids love him, but…it's the music, Lainey. Even his vocals are amazing. We go together; I think we really might be something good."

"Uncle Mike is the best!" shouts Timber. I see his eyes narrow in the rearview mirror. He doesn't understand exactly what we're talking about, but he suspects we're saying something less than flattering about his uncle.

"What's not to love?" asks Vanji. She pulls down the visor and checks her perfect face in the vanity mirror. I sigh and glance out the windshield, past the reflection of my own flawed features and out to the mountains beyond.

We whiz by a crooked Ponderosa pine. This is my game. If I am the only person in the world to actually see that pinecone, or that tree, or that cloud, it belongs to me. I feel stupid for not knowing any of this information about my brother. He is a pine tree, and I forgot to keep my eyes on him. It's just getting too hard to keep track of every one of these objects I own, let alone my people: Mike, Cristian, Vanji, Timber…

I stretch my leg along the edge of the car door. An old burger wrapper moves and I smell yellow mustard, proof that Mike has ridden here before me. Maybe my job is to merely appreciate the order in the universe, but not to decide that order. Bless them, not change them. We pull into the restaurant lot. I vow to be a better observer.

"Okay, baby girl. Let me show you what Travis is up to and how I've started fighting back." Timber waits until the car is stopped and off before unclipping his seatbelt. He takes Vanji by one hand and me by the other and tells us not to worry. Half his hair sticks up and half is still sort of matted down. The back of his striped rugby shirt is wet.

"I gonna punch that Travis nose and twist hims ears off! Him go be just like Dumb Ole Rabbit."

Yikes! But, where is Rabbit, anyway?

Chapter Twenty-seven

THE BOY

Run-Over Rabbit. The boy told the whole total truth to his aunt and so then his mother took him straight-away back to the scene of the crime. The price the boy paid for his tantrum? A ruined best friend. His mother prayed Oh No! Let us find these things in one piece, please!? And so they found a totally safe and sound hearing aid. Rabbit's ear was doubled over like he was keeping that thing safe on purpose, Since anyway he always did love the boy. But the boy's glassed got smashed.. One lens was cracked from top to bottom in a lightning bolt, just like the one that hit his mother in the Safeway parking lot. The other side was fine. The mother took the bent frames and squeezed and pushed against the inside of the car door and then even that brokenness was almost fixed. The boy kind of liked the lightning bolt, even though it made one glowy place down the middle of things if he looked right at the line.

The boy's mother didn't yell at all. She didn't even have an angry face. She told the boy everyone has bad days sometimes. She said how glad she was to know the truth. More than anything in the world she wanted to trust the boy, and this just proved she could. She hugged and kissed him and they sat side by side waiting before she turned on the jeep and he held the squeeze bottle Gatorade on his knee and thought. He thought a lot before trying to say it.

Are you really going a be loving me forever? he finally asked. As much as Daddy, mine love? Oh Timber! I love you as much as Daddy! As much as I love him and as much as he loves you! I love you both COMPLETELY. Not always perfectly, sweet Timber, but wholly.

What should they do with Battered Rabbit? The trash can. And it was time. Timber put the glasses on his own nose again and he could see as far as the end of things. Could Mommy see that well? Probably not. Even after the superpowers? And she looked at him in surprise because how did he know? But he smiled a little secret smile and held the hearing aid in his hand. He could hear just fine with his regular old passenger-side-of-the-car ear. This was the first time he ever rode in the front seat.

LAINEY

We have spent more hours walking around Como and eating lunch than I realized. The Soup Line is already open when we get there. Celia is just finishing an early supper. I explain how Timber and I had gone to Como to retrieve the lost things. Vanji has already left.

"I didn't even realize how loud those fireworks must have sounded to Timber, and I feel horrible that I was so unaware of what was going on with him."

"Why, Lainey? Are you a mind-reader?!" And she laughs and it gives me permission to have made a huge mistake without being the world's worst mother. "Frankly," she continues, "I think it shows real growth that you reacted so calmly. I think the Lainey I met in the Safeway parking lot would not have had such a gentle reaction." She touches my cheek, wet with a line of tears. Our eyes meet.

"Remade, Lainey. You are being remade."

Timber bangs through the door and runs straight to give Celia a hug. He sees my tears and hugs me, too.

"Guess what, Celia? Jesus keeped mine hearing aid safe and mostly too mine glasses!"

Celia holds his swinging arm. "I heard that, Timber. Isn't it wonderful? Say, would you like to show me your rock collection? I was just leaving but if you wouldn't mind?" Of course he wouldn't.

Since I am on register duty I have been sitting in front of the computer and marveling at the way Vanji has handled Travis' smear campaign. She's got this growing group of loyalists who help monitor the "airwaves." If Travis posts something against one of our advertisements, or even Google's Earth satellite photo Place setting, Vanji's group goes into hyper-drive adding however many positive messages it takes to boot his false complaints off the list. Damage control. Lucky for us he doesn't seem to have many friends.

Cristian whistles happily in the kitchen until the sounds of water filling a pot cover his tune. Vanji is still fixing the story for him, I think, just like the old days. Back then Vanji had to cover up the parts about their pounding landlord, leaking faucets, and overdue school fees to keep everything sounding perfect. Keep him from abandoning his own dreams to run back home and take care of them. But this time Vanji isn't covering up or lying, because our food really is great. Salty. That jealous idiot had the audacity to call Cristian's soups salty. "Put it outside for the deer," was one of his nasty comments. "This is the time of year they go looking for a salt lick." I'd like to put Travis outside, for the bear. But Vanji is putting him out, figuratively, and if I decide to let it go, forgive him, I must stop monitoring every online comment myself.

A blast of fresh air announces my dirty brown son. Timber is wearing an old batman pajama shirt because clothing wasn't worth a battle. But the miraculous hearing aid is clipped in place and the broken glasses are perched on his face. The unbroken lens is streaked with fingerprints, and there is a small scrape on his finger which he sticks in my face so close to my eyes that I can't focus. If only Vanji were still around! He might have at least allowed his hair to be combed again.

"Celia goed home. But mine finger get pinched in a rock."

An older couple who had been taking their time studying the menu before pre-paying have stepped back to allow this street waif to show me his grievous new wound. Taking Timber's shoulders, I direct him down onto the chair I've been using and I open the cash register. I smile apologetically at the couple while telling him, "Sit here for a second, sweetie, and I'll get you a bandage as soon as I'm done."

"Oh, go ahead and do him first. We can wait."

"Are you sure? I can run this real quick."

"Go on, tend to your little boy."

And I get the required first aid kit from the office and slap on a little sliver of plastic. A kiss and thanks and he is good to go, heading back outside.

"So sweet," says the lady, hoisting a large handbag to her shoulder. "I so love that ragamuffin age! Do you mind my asking, did he have a harelip? My little great nephew, bless his soul, just had surgery number three." She looks to her husband, who intently studies the chalkboard listing of today's soup options.

"Just his lip was cleft. I guess it will always show." Harelip hangs in the air. Another ugly word we've tried to keep from Timber. Truth is we never think about it. The last surgery seems to have happened dozens of years ago. The man is ready to order, and points to the corn chowder, new $3 size mug, not bowl. He must be the quiet type. She talks for both, it seems.

"Oh no, it's just that now we know about it we see them all over. Your child's scar is so tiny and it looks just perfect. I don't think anyone who didn't know something about it would notice."

"Thank you. He has enough trouble without getting teased about appearances. And now, with glasses and a hearing aid..."

"Our little nephew has quite a few other health issues. Weak heart, various organ problems." Her husband has moved to the sliding counter in front of the serving window but he can't get his soup yet without a receipt and she still hasn't ordered.

"Timber doesn't have anything like that. He's very strong and healthy. It's just, I'm starting to learn about neurological things, stuff that has been affecting his learning." I nod at my computer screen, open now to a Fetal Alcohol Syndrome website.

"We all make mistakes, honey," she says quietly.

"Oh, no. I didn't…I mean, Timber is adopted. We think his birth mother probably drank while pregnant."

"What a sweet thing you are doing. What a blessing you are in that boy's life." The husband places his hands on his forehead, leaning against the counter. I nod toward him and she stage whispers that she better order soon. It takes a few minutes longer, as I have to list ingredients to each choice and give my personal opinions and listen to a short discourse on the relative merits of sea salt, but then she is through and I sit back down to the computer.

Yeah. I'm such a great mother that my kid has to throw away valuable stuff to get my attention. What if Timber simply cannot make the connections I keep insisting he make? I don't feel very noble today. I don't feel like such a blessing.

Next Friday is our big appointment at the hospital. A full diagnostic. What will it help? Tell us how to fix problems or maybe just name them? Give us the specifics of a word that fills me with dread: potential.

I have continued to read Celia's gift, off and on. I finished Isaiah (in which I underlined a ton of awesome quotes) and now am reading the parts in red at the back. Jesus' words, I guess. Miracle stories, mostly. I would like a miracle of my own, for my son. Maybe a touch, or a slap of mud or a special bath. Maybe there is something to do, or say or believe, to make his brain develop now the way it should have grown in the womb. Maybe. Or maybe that potential doesn't exist.

Step outside and breathe a little fresh air. Timber has placed his rocks in straight lines, grouped by color and in descending sizes. He is twisting a large granite slice to align better with the wall when he turns at the scratch of the door shutting behind me. He bites his tongue in deep concentration.

"You likes 'em, Mommy? I organize for you!"

"I love them! Good work." My fears for Timber's education are calmed for the moment. He's not a lost cause. Lost causes don't organize!

There is a touch on my shoulder and I jump. Cristian has a call for me, he says. Julie is on the line.

Would I be able to babysit Sally in the morning? Julie wants to go to a mommies group at the church but Sally is registering a slight fever and you aren't supposed to take a sick baby to the nursery, for obvious reasons. Sally isn't sick; she's just teething, but the other babies' moms will get all bent out of shape if Sally shows up with boogers and a temp. Julie hates to ask, but the speaker is giving some talk that she is really interested in hearing. Of course I don't mind. Sally is cuter than a—well, than most cute things. I've done diapers. I can handle an infant.

Chapter Twenty-eight

TIMBER

Timber clipped in his super ear. Check. Fitted laser glasses on his nose. Check. Time to enter the cockpit (and it really truly was a cockpit now, since Timber was allowed to sit big-boy in the front seat like an all-growed person; like an uncle-aunt, like a daddy or mommy). The rocket's flight plan was to the restaurant. The Alpine Soup Line was the very best place in the world. It was Daddy's big chance. The only bad thing? No macaronis. Only the kind in minestrone, which was a soup. Timber loved soup, except for minestrone, even though it did have macaronis in there. It also had some weird thing he hated. So minestrone did not count for macaronis. One day, Timber's father had promised, one day he would invent a runny macaroni cheese soup maybe with potatoes and corn, and then Soup Line would be absolutely perfect.

In the meantime it was still the best place on the planet. And even when Timber was bored and had to Sit Right There Where Someone Could See Him because he forgot to listen once and his mother couldn't find him hiding under the desk and thought he was Stolen by a Passing Car or Run Over Like a Deer the restaurant was still awesome. In Soup Line Timber's daddy moved like a dancer spinning stirring smiling laughing and was happy. His mommy was a little nervous with bit lip under white teeth but laughing and mostly happy too. They were kissing whenever they passed and sending shooting smiles across the dining hall whenever their faces connected. It made Timber feel warm and special, most of all because the smiles flashed to him too so he kept his face pointed in their directions as much as he could, just in case.

Every now and then he'd need a smile but his face wasn't connecting right so he would adjust the glasses and watch to see just where his father or mother was going to turn next and get there and then take off the glasses and use his most deep power to pull the smile to himself. As soon as he felt it coming he'd open his eyes again and put on the glasses to catch it and squeeze it into his Soul, which was the deepest himself part that his daddy told him about when his grandpa died and had to have his old body buried down under the ground in a shiny box with funny pillow-padding all around inside.

Timber couldn't figure out if his mother had any power left over from the sky dancing lights at Safeway. He thought she did, but when a very bad thing happened with his special equipment she didn't know about it until later. He was sure, the whole ride home from the horrible bursting fireworks, that she would suddenly scream and turn and point a finger at Timber. Even the next day she didn't notice, until he said on his own to his favoritest Aunt Vanji that they were accidentally lost. And Mom knew he was lying right off because he had thrown them away and not lost them by accident and they must be still in Como of the fireworks. So probably she did still have some power. But maybe mothers always had the power to detect lies. Was lying part of super power? Jesus said not to lie. Celia said so. She said so when she talked to Timber special in the corner of Soup Line while they sipped on some creamy warm mushroom soup. Lying was a sin she said when he asked but just like a mommy or daddy Jesus would forgive when Timber told him the truth and said sorry. He was sorry, so he did it with Celia listening too and he felt happiness and he got a face connection smile with Celia that maybe came all the way from God hisself.

Babies came from God. But if God was in Heaven, and also babies, and smiles and forgiveness, then what was Grandpa Jim doing up there? He never did smile too much. And Timber couldn't imagine him holding babies like Mr. Thorndove and Sally. What if grandpas turned into babies? And came back down? Timber imagined a grandpa face on Baby Sally's body and giggled. He'd rather have a first-time baby if it was his sister. Better, brother. He wished he had a brother.

LAINEY

"Wah!" I mock the baby. It's funny and she stops crying to stare at this not-my-mommy person. Timber used to stare at me, too, when I'd repeat his baby sounds. I wonder at what point I switched from repeating his sounds to correcting his grammar. I've always meant to help, right? My "fixing" him is for his good, not to ridicule his deficiencies. He's smiling at Sally, tickling her irresistible pudgy toes. He doesn't have to speak perfectly yet, does he? But there's such a long way to go. I resolve to work harder at finding things to praise. Like this.

"Good job, Timber! You are making her happy!"

"But Mommy, she no is smiling."

"She's still too little! Can you believe you have to learn how to smile? Really! That's something you learned especially well, right, buddy?" And he did, and he shows me.

Another diaper change. That's three in less than two hours. Julie had offered to let me use disposables for the morning, so that Sally wouldn't have to be changed after every little tinkle. But it felt like cheating. After all, doesn't Julie change and wash these things all by herself all the time? Well, there is Billy, too, but I can't see burley Billy being very good at it.

Apparently I am not very good at it either. The best thing about cloth, Julie had said, is that the baby gets used to the feeling of dry cotton, and she'll potty train earlier than babies whose tushies have been synthetically sucked dry since birth. And here I thought the sole purpose of cloth was to avoid filling the dump with stuff that takes hundreds of years to decompose.

At least there are no silly frilly pants to deal with. It's warm enough for just a shirt, and that's all she wears. I wonder if Billy has given up some on the doll decorating, or is this just another of Julie's ways of making things easier for me.

After all, I never had to change a newborn.

I snap the sides closed and pick the baby up from the quilt on the floor to walk around a bit, bouncing her as we go. Timber looks up from his position beside the quilt where he has been driving matchbox cars up and down the border. "You know, Timber, Sally is a third the size you were when I first changed your diaper."

"Nah uh."

"Yep. You were just over a year old when you finally got to come home and live with us. And you don't remember, but one year after that, when you were two, we had a huge adoption party, because all the papers were done and final and you became our son forever."

"And you becomed mine mommy!"

"Yes, I became your mommy! Although, I like to think that I always was but we just didn't know it yet."

"And I becomed a Clayson when Gramma becomed American, her said. And then she had'a say all them words of a prayer about a flag from school. And her had'a say tons of questions. VROOM, beep beep."

That's right! Mom had her citizenship hearing that same day. I had completely forgotten. It wasn't a big deal to me, especially not compared to the adoption of my son, but it must have been huge for her. I wonder if she harbors a grudge because we stole her thunder. I can't remember much about the day anyway. Vanji planned most of it and Cristian; Timber and I just sort of moved through the motions of smiling and saying thank you. Timber was just starting to walk and I think I spent most of the time following him around, proud but worried about what he might bump into or trip over.

Mom has always just seemed American to me. Foreign only because she sometimes words things in an odd way. Her food was spicy but so is much of the normal cuisine around here. We weren't the only family watching for the Hatch Chili pickup truck to pass through town. Everyone loves Mexican style and Mexican food, and back when we were in school, they mostly still liked Mexicans, if they knew any. So Mom's pledge of loyalty and full-fledged US citizenship seemed like just a little technicality. A really important one, now that Dad is gone.

What if Dad had died without Mom's citizenship having been established? Would she be deported? Ridiculous! But it's a chilling thought. A woman in her sixties, who has lived nowhere else for forty years, being sent back to the country and language she left as a teen—who would do such a thing? And yet it is done all the time. I've read about it.

"Did America adopted Grandma?" Timber plops beside me, almost on top of Sally's chubby leg. She kicks at him and I smile. Go girl! Defend yourself! I wind an annoying flashing-lights-and-sounds toy and we're regaled by a tinny version of Twinkle, Twinkle.

"It's more like Grandma adopted America, I think. She left Mexico when she was very young and got a job in Los Angeles, California, working at a restaurant, I think…"

"Like us!"

"Yes, kind of like us. Anyway Grandpa Morse liked the milkshakes, he used to say, and then he kept coming back for the salsa!"

"That's silly, Mommy." I smile. It is silly. And as a kid, when Dad would tell this same story, I never got it. As a teen I thought my parents tolerated more than loved each other, but something kept her glued to this little mountain town, to a houseful of messy children, and to a language that was not her first. She has been stoic since the funeral. On the little cleared-off shrine in the hallway she has put only one item: the gold band Daddy wore on his left hand. It was love. I smile.

Sally, whose tummy I have been patting, suddenly gurgles up a clump of cottage cheese-type slime. I grab the burp rag and wipe it.

"Gross, Sally! You are a disgusting little thing, aren't you?"

"Mommy is no nice."

"Not nice, Timber, not 'no nice.'" Oops. Correcting him again! But Timber is not being very helpful. I am still trying to get him to put his wooden blocks back in a container, but Sally just wants to be touched. Look in my eyes and coo, she demands. I am a baby and I will be loved. Now!

I tickle her double chins. "You got a little Angela in you, don't you, Sally?" I ask, in a singsong voice.

"Mom. How come Baby Sally be fat like Aunt Jelly. And where come she from?" Don't do it! Don't correct his mistakes! I can't help it.

"Baby Sally *is* fat, and where *did* she come from."

Timber stares at me like I am the one speaking in unknown tongues. "You not even knowing?"

Is he asking about babies or Angela?

"Angela" (I can't bring myself to bestow the title Aunt just yet, and I refuse to say Jelly) "came from Pueblo. Now finish picking these up before Julie gets here."

"Too late!" Julie laughs in the open door. "Guess you didn't hear me drive up?"

"Nah, with all that…" I pause, so that Julie can hear the whine and whirring of power tools in the distance, "it's hard to hear even semis on the highway these last few days."

Julie scoops up her daughter, who immediately tries to latch onto her buttons. Do I mind? Of course not. Julie has lost her shyness about breast feeding, but she is careful to turn away from Timber while she covers herself with a thin blanket.

"Where are they building now?" she asks.

Where aren't they developing is a better question. But I don't know if Thorndove land is involved and who am I to build Border Fences? I'm half Mexican and I brought in a Louisianan, after all.

"I think the work we hear is coming down the valley from the north. There's a couple of new jobsites near the top of the ridge. You can see them from upstairs."

"It's bad enough to have a roofline on a ridge. Hope they don't paint them orange or something."

"What's worse are those shiny tin roofs that are getting popular again. The silver ones that look like mine shacks. The glare from those things could start a forest fire."

"I actually heard," confides Julie, flipping Sally to the other breast, "that there was at least one rescue call last year because this old guy saw one of those roofs in the distance, and some lodge pole pines were swaying between him and the roof, and he thought he was seeing a lost hiker sending a distress signal!"

The building noises boom to a crescendo.

"I'd like to send a distress signal," I say.

Now that she's fed, Sally is my buddy again. She gurgles and smiles and Timber asks when will she be fun, anyway. Julie tells him that, as soon as Sally is big enough to be fun to play with, he will hate playing with her because she will do it all wrong. She will suck on his toys, and take things she shouldn't, and be an overall pest. That is the job of little kids, she says. Babies only have to eat and sleep and be looked at. Little kids have to learn to bother big kids. What about big kids, wonders Timber.

"Big kids just annoy their mothers," I say.

Timber makes a slapping motion. I have handfuls of gear: porta-crib, diaper bag, weird rubber seat that scared me and an ugly black and white mobile I was supposed to have propped over the baby while she lay on the quilt. Julie has Sally, strapped into a car seat, and we get it all into her car somehow.

Timber yells out the door. "I no annoys you, Mommy. You is always annoy me. Like, pick them blocks and stuff. And all time fix my words."

"Whatever. Bye bye, Sally. Bye Jules!" I watch the brake lights brighten and then go out as she pulls around the corner and out onto the highway.

"Mommy," says Timber, balancing a block on the back of his hand and moving it even farther away from the box it needs to enter, "Does babies all time do that?"

Do what? Drink there. On their mom's boobies. He giggles. He learned the word "boobies" at school, along with "wiener," I suppose. Where's Cristian? Back in our pre-child days I used to say that I would handle embarrassing questions for our daughters, and Cristian could do the sons. Timber says, "When you go have my baby?"

"I'm not having a baby, Timber. I can't. You know. You came from a different birth mother who could have a baby but couldn't be a mommy. It worked perfectly." I move the box under his hand. Just drop the block in, Timber.

"How we go get mine own brother? We adapt him like me?" He throws the block instead of dropping it and I reach across to pick it up and do it myself.

"Adopt, Timber. Adopt is kind of like getting used to."

"We get used him, I promise, Mommy!" This time the block goes in.

"I think we're pretty good with just you, buddy."

"That's because I is stupid. Two boys is too hard because boys is stupid!" He drops two more blocks in, but grabs out a blue one and hurls it across the cabin. It takes a supreme effort not to react to his aggression.

After that display it's tempting to agree, and even more so because Cristian didn't replace the toilet paper roll this morning and Timber left all his clothes and three towels dirty and wet on the bathroom floor. And picking up twenty wooden blocks is an exercise in extreme patience. But I'll play nice.

"Sweetie, boys are great! You are so much fun and I am really glad you are a boy. You'd make a silly looking girl, don't you think?" He crosses the room to get the block he threw, without being told!

"Like Taylor?"

Uh…

"If I have a sister, I want her be fat like Sally. Like—" and he scrunches his cheeks between his hands so that his lips pop out. "Only I would rather want a brother, okay?"

"Timber, there are no more kids. You are it! You get to be the spoiled only child. You're special." I drop in a double handful of blocks. Come on, Timber, just a few more.

"Is not fair! Daddy has got a sister and you has got a gazillian brothers and everybody has got a baby. I wants a baby." Timber is a baby. A six-year-old, perpetual baby. Holding Sally earlier, I have to admit, I thought it would be nice. But the reality is that there is just so much energy in the world. A limited supply allotted to me. And I think I have overspent mine. Blocks are still scattered across the couch. Heavy sigh.

The ringing phone distracts me from the blocks. It is my mother. She wonders, would I like to drop Timber off at her house today? Whoa. I am stunned for a moment. Mom hasn't babysat since Dad's death. And she hardly ever has asked to have Timber on her own volition. Could it be that Angela is behind this? That she might actually want to get to know her nephew? She has spoken to him a few times, but in the way one would talk at a dog whose owner didn't realize you were scared of dogs. I am pretty sure there are no small children in her past.

"I just think," says Mom, "you are working very hard, and Timber must be bored always at the restaurant. Here he can play and explore."

I ask when to bring him and she says as soon as I want. Angela has gone to buy groceries. So Angela is not behind this. And it occurs to me how lonely my mother is, and I am so glad that Michael is a peacemaker and had kept this relationship with our sister going through the years and brought her home now to provide companionship. Timber and I break some kind of record getting a small backpack, filled with toys (including the last of the blocks), and ourselves, into the Tercel. The ride down the highway and up into Harris Park seems to take no time at all.

As we pull into Mom's drive I give Timber a stern lecture about how to behave and what not to do, so that by the time I have parked the car he is almost in tears.

"You always yelling and me no done nothing!"

He is right. He hasn't done anything yet, and when I foresee things he might do, he thinks I am reminding him of things he has once done. Which I am. I stop and apologize and finally, when my mother starts coming out the door to see why we're taking so long, he is pretty much composed.

"Gramma!" he calls. Then he flips his hand up in that stupid mock salute: "How!"

But Grandpa is gone now. And Grandma liked the gesture even less than I did, so she does nothing. Until suddenly we all three begin to cry again. Timber is the first to recover and rather than say the wrong thing he simply hugs my mom and kisses her cheek.

"Timber," she says, straightening herself up. "I have made some play dough. Your uncles, especially Joseph, loved play dough. I made his favorite color, which was orange."

"Who be Joseph?"

"Joe. Uncle Joe, Timber."

Goodbye? But they have gone inside and the door swings shut. I am free today. Julie's baby is gone and my baby is gone and now I am free to work like a grownup. This is a gift. A time to refresh my energy and spirits. Thank you. Thank you.

Chapter Twenty-nine

I park around back of the restaurant. It's only ten after noon so, even though our old Toyota and Chance's beater truck are proof the place isn't deserted, all the doors are locked. I pull out the key for the lock at the front entrance. To think I walked through here with Cristian almost a week ago on our first night in the restaurant! Just as we expected, this thing has swallowed us up. We are no longer a couple. We are "Soup Line": Cristian, the "Soupschef," me, the manager, gopher, or, as Chance insists on calling me, "Boss Ma'am." I smell basil today. Melted butter and fresh bread. Beneath the other scents, that cinnamon that is ground deep into crevices of the kitchen tiles. Wait…fresh bread?

Chance, sweat dripping down his bald head, toils in the kitchen, pulling a long loaf of Italian from the old enamel oven. Across from Chance, leaning casually against the serving counter, Cristian applauds. "This one is perfect. We'll keep her.

"Hey, Lainey!" I position myself just behind Cristian's closest strong shoulder; lean in just enough for a small point of contact. Nice to be noticed. Voice dripping with excitement: "Look at this bread! Have you ever seen anything so perfect? Of course you have, me, and yet…"

In a very low voice I quip, "Now baby, you may be a man of color and all, but let's not go overboard!"

He turns and I kiss his mouth, which tastes of yeasty dough, and I bat my eyelashes. "No Timber! Mom actually called me and offered to keep him this afternoon. After babysitting a newborn I think I earned this break! He's going to sleep over and we can get him tomorrow before his appointment!"

"Appointment..." Wrong reaction. He smiles and then it disappears. He bites his lip. He appears to have forgotten about the neurologist exam at Children's Hospital. Or he didn't think he had to go.

"We both have to do this, Cristian! This is not my little thing. This is about Timber's education and future and..."

Cristian pulls my shoulders in a little embrace. "Calm down. I didn't say anything yet. I was just figuring how to best work it. About closing tomorrow night and the deposit."

Chance has wisely moved to the far end of the kitchen where his large frame is silhouetted in front of the yellow-gold door of the walk-in, supposedly to set the bread down to cool.

"Chance!" Cristian calls. Chance looks up. "Say, would you mind if you had to close up tomorrow night? Just on the off chance we don't make it back up in time? One of the girls, Heidi, I think, will be here to waitress and do the register, but she'll be out by nine and I'd like for you to do a final mop and lock up. You could still be done by 9:30 or so."

"Sure thing, boss." Chance grins. "If you trust me with the cash box?" It's a valid question but one that has already been answered. Our cash box is a small safe, which we've been storing at night beneath Chance's bed. Right now it holds the entire earnings of the restaurant; a week's worth of sales, because of some glitch with the bank account which Cristian says will be fixed as soon as he signs another paper in person, and he will do that tomorrow on our way to Timber's appointment. .

"I'd trust you with my life, man," says Cristian, "you just baked the perfect loaf of bread!"

They laugh and Chance hands me a warm chunk of the second-to-last loaf. It is a little anemic on top and is missing the center cut that helped make the last one so professional. Chance is already sliding two more loaves into the hot oven as I taste the bread's soft interior with a crunchy crust. It is good. And it'll keep costs even lower, unless Chance asks for a raise in the near future. Not even a week in and we've already been toying with the idea of offering him a salary and options. Yesterday I suggested we wait a month before we jump the gun. Make sure this is what Chance really wants as well.

"Boss Ma'am," says Chance, "I have got to congratulate you. You have done a tremendous job on this place. I know that food service is hard business. Lots of 'em fail. But I don't see that here. I think you're going to pull this off in a big way. I'm stoked to play a part in this, I really am."

Cristian speaks over his shoulder while marking up a recipe card. "And we owe a ton to you, Chance. There is absolutely no way we could have pulled this off without your hard work. I mean that. Doing great, Chance!"

Teary eyed, I pour a tiny drink of wine for Cristian and myself. Chance shakes his head and picks up a water bottle.

"Cheers! To Le Soup Line!" And we clink and Chance clunks and we drink.

TIMBER

Grandma made macaronis but she used that gross block of rubber stuff instead of powder cheese from a box and she didn't know about cutting up wieners to add in. Timber ate his whole plate anyway because he loved Grandma and Grandpa was dead underground which made them both sad, even though Timber told her about what his daddy said about Grandpa's spirit was in Heaven dreaming about being dead.

Let's play a game, said Grandma but Timber was nervous about games because they were always too hard and he wasn't sure what to do because he wanted to make her happy. So he said okay but I am too hard for them just so you know and always I am losing. How about Memory? Okay but I am not remembering anything. Dice? Where you roll and pull out the 1s for 100 or 5s for 50? Timber bit his lip while he tried to listen but there were too many numbers and he forgot what the question was. Sorry!? And Timber smiled because he had played that before, kind of, once as Uncle Brad's partner. Stack me, pardner, Uncle Brad had said, which meant flip over the card to see how many squares we get to move.

Sorry! was much more difficult without Uncle Brad, and it took Timber a long time after flipping a card (which he was very good at and quick) to decide what to do next. Grandma would read the number for him, and say, Timber, can you slide your piece six places ahead? He could, and after he looked for a while, finger on the little wooden piece, he would ask How many? and Grandma would say Six and she would help him count, one two three four five—six. Sometimes he kept going and she would say Six, remember? and he would slide it backwards until she nodded slightly. The hardest ones were when there was a choice. You could go forward ten or backwards one. It didn't make any sense. It wasn't supposed to because it was just a game that someone invented but still it was an important decision and Timber wiggled his finger on top of the piece thinking of clicking ten whole spaces or sliding back one. Which would be best? Which was the right answer?

But there wasn't a right answer, either one is fine, it is just that sometimes you are on start and you want to go back toward home or sometimes you are all lined up at home and have to choose back one because there is no option. And Timber didn't know if he had an option and he kept forgetting where was home and he pushed hard on the top of his piece and it flipped completely off the board. Timber forgot about Grandma's sadness because he was mad again. She said, Timber, are you okay? Why I gotta be stupid, Grandma? he asked.

Hmm, said Grandma. Not, you are not stupid, don't say that, which is what Mommy and Daddy always said.

What makes you think you are stupid, Timber? Timber told her that he was stupid because he couldn't do anything. He couldn't decide how to move and he couldn't do anything at school that the other kids did. Do you ask for help? wondered Grandma. Yes all the time and the lady who's not the teacher but some girl's mother says stop asking and you know this already. But he didn't know it, he told his grandma, he really didn't. Why did he have to be this way? It wasn't fair.

Timber's grandmother pushed her chair back from the table and motioned for him to follow her to the saggy couch in the living room. They sat cuddled up tight and she told Timber a story about a boy who couldn't read because something was wrong with the letters. All those little squiggly lines on the page would dance around whenever he looked at them and never hold still. Timber thought that would be fun to see. The thing was, if those lines didn't hold still you couldn't tell what letter it was so you didn't know the sound so you couldn't tell the word. This would make more sense once Timber started reading. Timber could see the lines, he said, he just could never remember which shape meant which letter or what sound the letters had.

Either problem is hard, Grandma admitted. The boy who had the squiggly problem was someone Timber knew. Someone who could read okay now, because some good teachers gave him a lot of help and he worked really hard himself. Timber took a long time thinking of a guess and finally Grandma just said, it was your Uncle Bradley. We were afraid maybe he would never read. It wasn't until middle school that they said he had dyslexia and that was because the coach didn't want him to fail and not be able to play sports. Anyway, once they knew the problem they could help him overcome it.

What was Timber's problem, he wondered. Grandma didn't know. She knew that she had a problem learning to read too, not because the letters wiggled, but because they made different sounds in English and lined up in crazy ways that they would never do in Spanish, which is the language of Mexico where she was born and went to school until she had to leave to come to America. See, Timber, she said, stroking his back, there are lots of people who have a hard time with different things. Do you think that Bradley is stupid? Of course not. Me? And Timber laughed because of what it would sound like to say hey stupid to a grandmother. Neither are you, she said. In Spanish that is a bad word, you know? He did not know. When I hear you say it I feel like you are cursing, Timber. Please try never to use it, okay? And Timber felt ashamed, but also a little better knowing these things. He wiped the lightning bolt side of his glasses and adjusted them on his nose. Anyway, said Grandma, with those glasses you look very intelligent.

Timber smiled, like a smart person, and cuddled back against his grandmother who was so smart she learned to speak and write a whole new language when she was a teenager. Even if she was wrong and he was stupid at least he had the world's smartest grandma.

Chapter Thirty

LAINEY

"I just have to sign one last page," insists Cristian, as he pulls into a front space at the bank. He is right; it only takes a second, and we are off again. Who knows why our account wasn't set up correctly, but anyway it seems to be done now, and either we or Chance will add tonight's cash to the entire week's worth of income in that strong box and we will make the first official deposit first thing tomorrow morning.

Canyon walls pass my window like a background movie on a green screen. Unreal. I still can't believe that we are actually running our own restaurant. It may be smaller and simpler in scale than Cristian had dreamed, but to me that feels safer. For one thing the unused product, handled properly according to the state's cooling and reheating guidelines, is not all lost each night since it never hits the serving floor. For another, being open only for the commuter dinner crowd, which for now looks like 4:30 until 8:30; clean up and night prep done by ten, keeps the hours manageable. Of course, those hours used to be our family hours...

"Cristian, I didn't realize how much things were going to change for us as a family. Timber can't come to work every day after school; they have child labor laws against that kind of thing."

Cristian glances at Timber in the rearview mirror. "What's your deal with child labor laws, Lainey? You still whining about doing too many dishes when you were a little girl? Get over it! Don't worry about our kid. Haven't you seen Timber 'at work?' No danger of this kid working too hard."

Timber is still groggy from being woken up on Grandma's couch. And he's mad that he didn't get to spend all morning there as planned because our appointment was moved up a couple hours. He kicks the seat. We both shout. "Stop it, now."

TIMBER

The doctor man had skin like old paper, white but no wrinkles, stretched tight like skeleton bones. Yes, a skeleton doctor but nice eyes and saying gentle words to Timber. Kind of like Grandma this weekend and making Timber feel like a good boy not stupid. Except that his words weren't true. Timber knew these were tests not games and too hard, always too hard to remember what things you saw in the box even though they were interesting things that he wished he could stop to play with: dark green army man, arm raised in salute with gun long by his tiny side; a pink eraser that wasn't a rectangle but something special with sloping ends and clean, brand new never rubbed on Timber's bad writing before. Also there was a clock like a chicken and who knows, maybe it could lay an egg when the time was up? Bouncy ball like a rainbow, smooth wooden block stained blue, a music thing to blow in that makes you sound like a duck, and even more things Timber had touched and held and thought about, but when the box lid closed and white paper doctor walked to put it on a shelf the treasures disappeared like smoke. He tried hard and made some guesses but it was like waking and trying to grasp a fleeing dream. Still, this man didn't even make a frown or show disappointment but smiled still and talked like it was totally okay to forget things and give answers backwards around and not just what they were supposed to be. He did funny tests too, like walking barefoot across cold tiles and then standing on toes or heels on one foot then the other. He measured Timber's nose and ears and joked about the world's longest booger which made Timber giggle.

Asked about his name and Timber remembered about the baby in a coat and Tall Timber tallest tree in the forest and the doctor said that he must be a very special boy to have such a special story all about himself.

Do you feel happy most of the time? Wondered the doctor out loud and Timber thought awhile but said mostly sad and mad. Because all the time everyone is shouting and not seeing. But sometimes happy too because people who love you are family and that's a good thing because they are the same even if they are not. Timber talking lots but knowing the saying was not going the exact right way. Even so, Paper Doctor nodded and looked, eyes to his own, with an interested turn on the corner of his peely lip. He asked about the restaurant, what was it called and what food did it serve? Then laughed a santa-deep laugh because most certainly Timber's restaurant served soup if it was called Soup Line! Was that a silly question? Timber giggled but the doctor said seriously all questions are good and Timber would learn more and more and more if he also asked lots of questions, maybe be a doctor too one day. Or Questionnaire? Sure. That could be a good profession too. But the doctor, he was partial to restaurants. That meant he thought Timber's family had the best job in the world.

But Timber got quiet. His parents had argued a little on the ride here. Mom thinking about restaurant taking time of family and Timber getting stole on account of he was hiding one day when a redhead boy talked mean and he could have been lost or took away for all she knowed. Dad saying how they were only serving just One Piddly Meal and then laugh-crying when Timber asked which soup was that and how come he didn't get any. It's just suppers is what he meant, the Soup Line doesn't do lunch or breakfast so that everyone together can help Timber go to school and grow up and all. But Timber didn't want to go to school anyway and then they stopped talking because he was yelling again.

He didn't want to tell the doctor all of this but it came out anyway. He was like the boy whose eyes went circles when the sneaky old snake whispered with all S's in the cartoon movie. But the doctor was nice not a snake and didn't say much but helped Timber breath slow and feel good and okay. Guess you can go to the toys out there again, Son, said, but not Timber's father. Send those old people in. Meaning Mommy and Daddy but joking because he was much older than them anyway. Pointed to a treasure box just outside the door. Choose yourself two things. And the choice took until after the grownups were done and shook hands and had to tell him time is up; just take something.

LAINEY

The doctor's office smells of old fashioned Lysol deodorizer. I want to cry. I do cry. Timber plays at a train table in the outer room. The doctor talks quietly with Cristian and me. Early intervention is the best thing they know so far. It is important for Timber to feel the love and support of his parents. Stability is a huge factor in success for people with Alcohol-Related Neurological Defects.

We now have this as our official medical diagnosis. But we will be okay. An intense clarity fills my mind and heart. Timber is okay. His neurological system is damaged, irreparably, but he will survive. My job, my number-one job, is to be his mother. The restaurant is second. I'm kneeling in the rainy parking lot again, feeling the jolt burst through my veins, but my eyes are connected, riveted to Timber's. Love this child. Mother this boy. This is my great calling. I can do it, even if it takes a bolt from the clear blue sky every now and then.

The doctor shakes our hands, holding mine for a second longer. "My pop ran a pizza joint. My toys were cardboard discs and I can't sleep without an open jar of oregano. It was a great childhood."

"Of course, you became a doctor."

He laughs, deep and genuine. "Yes I did," he says, "But I washed a lot of dishes along the way!"

Timber runs ahead down the sterile hallway and spins wildly through the revolving doors. Cristian and I pause to catch the second swing together. It requires a harder pressure than I expect, and I stumble forward when Cristian puts his weight into the push.

"Careful!" he says. Takes my hand and makes eye contact. "Lainey, I do not think that Timber is just your responsibility. I just, I think there are some things that we have to let him do or be. Let go of some of our expectations, maybe." I nod, slightly.

I don't remember where we parked. I slow to let Cristian take the lead. I'm so over being ticked now. I try to smile and grab his hand to prove it. "But he's going to fall so far behind his classmates. And his language skills are terrible. He can't get mad when kids don't understand him and push kids just because they make him mad."

"I know. That's not what I'm talking about. I just want him to learn to beat his own drum. Not to be like everyone else but to become who he is supposed to be." Cristian hasn't even glanced across the lot but walks directly toward our parked car, gently swinging my arm.

"Me too. That's what I want, too," I say.

"Mommy! Mommy! Look at this, look at me!" Perfectly on cue, Timber. As if I have never seen anything as cool as a six-year-old balancing on a cement parking block.

"But still, Lainey. This week has been hard. Incredible, amazing, for us, and obviously difficult for Timber. I mean, look what happened with Rabbit.

"It's almost one o'clock. What if we pick up some burgers and stop at Pine Valley Open Space before we go home? We haven't gone hiking together in a long time. We can still get back in time to help Chance close up, and even if we don't he's already agreed to do it alone." Cristian grins sideways beneath his hat. "Lainey," he says, "Look at my feet."

No boots. Tennis shoes! My man is serious. And he planned ahead.

Chapter Thirty-one

But I'm wearing sandals. Practical strap-ons, not flip flops, but I would have chosen tennies if I had known hiking was on the agenda.

The parking lot is empty at the preserve. It's a weekday. Tomorrow it will be full. Still I'm surprised not to see at least one retired couple with a token dog. Then I remember that another county park has recently opened. Everyone probably wants to experience the "new" wilderness. We haven't been hiking together in…years, I guess. We used to go a lot. Hiking was part of Cristian's Boulder image for a while. We even took Timber when he was little and could ride in a backpack. As I recall, his kicking was one of the reasons we stopped.

"Gimme french fries. Daddy said them for me and I is starving. I no wanna go no walkhike. I is hungry." Today's stress is written in the down-turned corners of Timber's mouth. He kicks the tire of the Liberty while Cristian and I load up a day pack with the fast food and take a starting swig of water.

"Look, Timber. Let's just get up the trail a little bit and then eat. It will be more fun than eating in the parking lot, don't you think?"

"NO!"

So he holds a box of fries as we walk, spilling half. It's obscene, the artificial yellow color of the artificial yellow food falling along a pine needle-strewn path beside a crystal pond. I know that squirrels or birds or other wildlife will soon eat them, but that makes me feel even guiltier. Like the little creatures need this in their bloodstream. Like Timber needs this in his bloodstream.

The trail hits a wall and zigzags suddenly, rapidly gaining altitude with short hairpin turns. We've struggled uphill for about ten minutes, maybe only five, when the complaints begin again.

"I is starving. Leg hurts. Why you make me do stupid walkhike?"

Keep walking. Tune in to the birdsong between Timber's whines. A breeze, cool for July, here beneath the pines, sends a strand of overgrown bangs across my eyes. Unconsciously my fingers reach up to form a hasty braid, to pull it back. I feel Cristian's palm against the small of my back and his breath touches my cheek as he leans in close, matching my stride.

"I haven't seen you do that in a while, Lainey." What? He touches the lumpy braid. It's sexy, he says.

"Sexy?" too loud. Timber turns and I laugh.

"Stop laugh at me," he says, sulking, and stomps quickly ahead. At least it got him moving.

Clearing the evergreens we find ourselves on more or less level ground. Another fifteen minutes of dappled sunlight leads us out into a flowery meadow area. Timber suddenly forgets that he is supposed to be mad at the world and runs toward a clump of boulders, scrambling up as quickly as he can. This was my childhood. My siblings and I with a backpack lunch, splashing in the creek and running up the Rosalie Trail. Watching Timber puff out his chest as he stands on that rock sends me to several summits I've known; Lincoln, Bross and Democrat, Mt. Evans, Yale, Tabeguache...Nothing like the sense of ownership mixed with worthlessness you can only get on the highest point of a Colorado 14er, or even a simple boulder.

Even fast food burgers taste good up here. I'm actually kind of annoyed that Timber dropped so many fries. I would have eaten them! But still we have enough to get some energy; to forge ahead. If we hike an hour in, it should take maybe a half-hour to get back down. We could double the distance we've already come and still be good as far as helping to close at The Soup Line. I collect the burger papers and stuff everything back in the to-go bag, and then into the bottom of the daypack Cristian has brought along. Really. Why didn't he warn me about sandals? But my feet feel fine so far, and they do have decent soles so I'm not complaining out loud.

Timber doesn't complain any more with a full stomach and the flatter, less strenuous path we are now following. Aspens, round-leafed and shaking in all their summer glory, fill me with a kind of music. The soft tamping of our feet plays a cadence for percussion. And then a melody fills the air; real words. It is Cristian, in a soft baritone that I have never heard, singing the words of a song from the church. Cristian sings? My lips open of their own volition and I am singing and even Timber da-dums along, and the words are as true as the aspen shimmering all around. Those that I remember, anyway.

"Then sings my soul…la la la something la!" The Van Trapp Clayson Singers! We join hands as best we can on the narrow trail and swing them as we sing.

And then, even before I note the difference, we have passed through the sunny glory of the aspen grove and are pressed in on both sides by scrub oak and thorny plants. We pick our way down a darker, denser path that drops into a sputtering creek before slanting back up into a thicker forest of pines. Something is wrong, at least, not so right as the sunny world of a moment ago. The hairs on the back of my neck rise slightly.

Once, when Angela and I were small, we decided to climb the granite cliffs we could see from our bedroom window. In reality those rocks are many miles away, and we never got close. But we trekked way down the road, past all the ponds and around the big curve of the closest hill, before darkness fell. Daddy found us in the lights of his four-wheeler. He scooped us up and held us tight for the longest time. Mom did the scolding. In the dankness of this descent I miss my daddy terribly. Cristian hasn't mentioned him in a while, but I think of him a lot. I keep dreaming he is safe at home, that the whole funeral thing was a mistake and he was simply lost for a little while.

I want to explain this to Cristian. How badly I miss my father. How quickly my mood can change, like the landscape; how easily I replace confidence with worry and doubt. How I dwell too much on the wrong things and expect too much from Cristian, Timber; myself. How I want to let go completely, like while we were singing. I want to tell about my recent patches of awareness. The ways I am slowly growing and changing. I want to describe the incredible fear I endured while the lightning coursed through my body.

The breeze near the water of the dark little brook is no longer welcome and cooling. It's cold. Threatening.

"I'm like this trail," I try, but Cristian misinterprets.

"Me too. I really like this, but it's getting chilly. I think it might be time to head back. Where's Timber?"

Where is he? He was ahead on the trail. Wasn't he? Could we have left him behind?

"Timber!" I run the rest of the way to the bottom of the gulley and cross the stones, then on up the other side to check behind a clump of juniper. Cristian says he'll go back a ways to check. We both yell again: Timber! And I think of trees falling, and there is no humor in the thought. Just as I taste real fear a branch cracks and here he is, zipping up his pants and laughing.

"You wants me pee on trail, Mommy?"

Relief and then an odd buzzing. It's the cell phone, stuffed in my jeans pocket and pressing against my thigh. Why doesn't Cristian have this in his backpack?

"Hello?"

"Hey—Mrs. Clayson? Chance. No—" static "—close tonight no problem" and more static and a beeping. I'm trying to see the time and push the Off button and the phone sort of pops up out of my hand and is flying down into the creek and I lunge for it, but my feet are already moving in the other direction, propelling me on, and the trail is slippery, and I am falling.

Slow motion blur of forest, then slam! A big red ball of pain is here almost before I hear the crack of the rock. Or is it my skull? Something gives way. Fight, Lainey.

Cristian is yelling to relax, but I have to get out of this freezing water. It is soaking through my underwear. And I want to get away from that hunk of granite. I don't want to know if I cracked it or it cracked me. Got to get up. Get me out of here! Away from this moment. Out of this reality.

Cristian's hands, firm and warm, grasp mine. He has handed off the backpack to a quiet and serious Timber who is whispering, Sorry, sorry. He helps me pull up out of the creek and step up onto the trail. Almost. One foot makes it, one dissolves. Or splinters. A new explosion of red pain; this one radiates up from my ankle, or toe or foot or something. I can't really differentiate at this point. My head just throbs. My foot is history.

Timber waits for the curse.

"Crap," I gasp.

"Can you walk?" asks Cristian. My nails dig into his arm a little harder than needed. I try again, swinging the problematic appendage toward terra firma. Hell no! Sh—oot. Shoot, shoot, shoot. Something is wrong. Cristian directs Timber to keep climbing. Get out of this cursed little valley and back to the aspen grove where we can check things out. But he looks at my head and winces. Should we go up or maybe he should leave me here and go get help? I don't look like someone who should be moving around. What if my neck is injured?

No way. There is no way I am staying alone under the creaking pines while the sky darkens and wolves and bears come out to play. My neck, at least, is fine. Just help me up to the sunshine, then we can take a break. So we stagger uphill. Me hopping, Cristian puffing. I'm dizzy. I lean on a sappy trunk and touch my temple. My fingers gingerly trace a goose egg already forming, but I know from being a mother that this is better than a dent. Keep the swelling on the outside of my thick skull. My eye hurts a little.

"The phone!" I remember. That's a good sign; short-term memory is intact. Cristian goes back for it with a stern warning to our son to stay put and watch me.

"Yuck, Mommy. Your foot be blood-ing."

"Yep. My foot is bleeding."

The exposed flesh is scratched up and one sandal strap is almost broken, but the whole foot is already fat and red, like a water balloon filled with cherry Kool-Aid. The throbbing in my head is now matched by a throbbing in the foot. And it's good, I think, because anyway it is not the knife-and-scissors cut-it-off pain of the first few seconds. I'm pretty sure the worst damage has to do with a couple of toes. The top stings; that would be the scrapes. However, all efforts to roll my ankle in circles fail. I can't even tell if it is impossible, or just hurts too badly. It simply refuses to move.

Timber presses his cheek to the good side of my face and wiggles his jaw. Cheeky kisses, we used to call them.

"Do it hurt?" He scrunches his eyes and smacks his palms together like an evil genius devising a plan. He is praying. "Make Mommy's foot all good and get her head better. And hope Daddy finds telephone. Amen."

"This phone?" And Cristian shows us what used to be a perfectly good cellular phone. The crazy thing is, he found it right under where I landed, and there's a plastic green smear, matching the missing surface of the phone, down the boulder I hit. Sure looks like the phone broke my fall, slightly cushioning my head as it hit the rock. He looks at my head for confirmation. Sure enough, he insists, there is a slight indentation of the number pad. I am skeptical. So he takes out the camera and takes a close-up. I'm still doubtful.

"Wait 'til I get this picture blown up for you; you'll see. This little puppy just saved your skull."

I would laugh if it didn't hurt so bad. And I know, as I have known since holding Angela's hand on that lonely walk so many years ago, that darkness will fall. It will come as an inky blizzard, soft and silent as this pain, and it will fill the empty spaces of moving matter until I suffocate, if I can't get off this mountain. I hate being alone in the dark. My pulse accelerates. Sweat drips.

Cristian is still wondering. He knows about alligators and black flies and getting caught in storms on a shrimp boat, but he doesn't know whether he should hobble me down or go find a helicopter. He takes his Stetson off and puts it back on. Unsure.

"Baby, now. Either give me a shoulder or step back while I crawl out of here, but I am going now."

We go. It is slow. Three steps, four, and a breath. Cloud shadows pass like seasons in a movie segue. And then the curtain falls. Just as we hit the final stretch, the zig-zagging descent that leads back to the toilets, civilization, and a warm bed at home, blackness overtakes us and with it the cold of night. I can't see anything but flashing red lights and white lightning bolts of pain.

He sends lightning for the rain. I say the words from Isaiah under my breath. Does it mean that peace comes after the violence or is lightning the warning before things get worse? Here in the Rockies, where wildfires threaten, rain is almost always a welcome sight. It's July and dry and I choose to think that my rain is on its way as a gentle refreshing shower. The lightning strike that jumpstarted my heart and these lightning bolts of pain; maybe they are all just a necessary prelude to the change I need. The cleaning and renewing of a nice quick rain shower. One big breath. Ouch. And the lights clear from my eyes for a moment, and the night is very dark, but I am not afraid.

Timber says, "I sees good. Gots Indian eyes and supersonic glasses. I is a hawk. Caw!"

Who told him that? No one. Well, maybe Grandpa Morse. But it is true. Look, it gets really skinny here so go to the side with the rocks and keep touching them until you pass over to where the ground is soft. And our little boy, whose intellectual potential was compromised through no fault of his own, demonstrates an intelligence we have never seen before as he guides us out of danger. I don't ask him to repeat and I don't correct his grammar. I simply dig my fingers deeper into my husband's shoulder and swing one leg forward and then the other. Over and over and over.

TIMBER

The path back down was dark and full of danger. Tall Timber stood back on his heels and surveyed the evil twisting shrub oak and prickling thistles. He smelled something heavy and alive, somewhere within an acre. Stretching his arms he became an eagle and soared up, spirit high, to the sky above the trees. From there he could see the meandering needle-strewn path, straight for a distance then falling down, back and forth, the steep cliff side. Below the cliff waits the family car. I made you for this, breathed a voice, and Tall Timber knew they could do it, together, even with the injured mother. His father could brace her on the hurt side and Timber could pull branches, kick rocks, clear a path before them. She needed him. He could save her, right now, from the beast in the darkness and the fear in their hearts. Tall Timber flew back into his body and shook himself into a boy not a tree and he felt his soul happy deep and loved in the middle of himself and known by God and he took his mommy's other hand and he started walking, shuffle step careful, down the narrow trail.

Chapter Thirty-two

LAINEY

Once the invisible trail hits the hard, flat path at the bottom of the hill, we begin to see a yellowish glow in the midst of the black night, and we approach it like souls slipping from dying bodies. It is a buzzing spotlight at the outhouse door, and it means life and safety. Cristian helps me into a stall and rushes to the car for me to get a pad, which he carries with the tips of two fingers. Even in the stuttering light and through a swollen eye I can see the concern and pain and relief wash over him. When I'm fresh we three hobble to the car and once seated, I smile at my son. "You did it, Timber! You got me down!"

The car heater blasts dust that makes us sneeze while we shiver the cold from our bones. I still can't tell what is actually hurt, because a big bubble of pain envelops the universe. I am a total wreck! Yet somehow whole within this agony. Known. Every molecule screaming my existence. I drift in and out of sleep blinking to headlights on canyon walls, or the painful glare of oncoming traffic. Cristian keeps talking, not wanting me to drift off but to give him an appropriate Uh huh or Really? every so often. As it turns out, I will live.

I am so thankful for these drugstore clinics. Fifty bucks tells me what would have taken a night in a hospital ER to find out. Two of my toes are most likely broken. But you can't cast a broken toe, and since the ankle is also either sprained or torn, I am instructed to simply stay off the foot. After a week, if things are not beginning to improve I must return or see another doctor. My brothers have several old crutches in Mom's garage leftover from various impact sports injuries, so I decline the offer of a rental. I have a bruised face and a very slight concussion. My heart rate is within a normal range, though higher than usual for me. I'm lucky it isn't worse. The thing is, it feels worse. This is just about as bad as I've ever hurt, anyway.

It's 11:30 at night by the time we reach our driveway. Home. Cristian glances at me and I wonder if he is thinking about swinging by the restaurant. Painkillers have me a little loopy and Timber snores in the backseat.

Family wins over career. Cristian pulls the Liberty to a stop with a crunching of gravel as the headlights go off and we are in the dark once again. But this is a safe dark. This is home.

Warmth spreads across my cheek. An itch. I scratch and gasp from the shock. Ouch. Touch it again, gingerly, and remember the bump. The bumps. Folding back the bedclothes uncovers a colorful foot with a purple line straight across the biggest three toes, as though they simply folded in half. Which is more or less what they did, I suppose. The house is silent. The clock on Cristian's side of the bed says 9:02. A jay pecks for bugs somewhere on the opposite wall. I smell antiseptic.

Cristian probably took Timber over to get the deposit from Chance. He was pretty excited about the size of the deposit and will be relieved to get it safely into the bank. By taking Timber he is allowing me to sleep and recuperate. My reflection in the little mirror over my dresser is satisfyingly grotesque. I'd hate to have made all that fuss and have nothing to show for it. The lump on my forehead is almost flat already. The skin is irritated but not scratched deeply, and the bruising is beginning to show a purplish blue. My face is tender but doesn't throb. As soon as I put my foot down I see why they told me to keep all weight off of it. It does throb. I will obey!

I need to use the bathroom. There are about three steps from the edge of the bed to the top of the ladder. Ladder! How am I going to get down a ladder? How did I get up here? I have no memory. I remember the driveway and the overwhelming relief of survival. I must have been practically unconscious on painkillers and Cristian must have been Superman to get me up here. Now what? I grab the smooth aspen trunk of the bulky footboard and hobble two awkward jump-steps until I'm slung up against the railing. My breath comes ragged from the exertion. Breathe deeper, breathe. The ladder stretches below, an Indiana Jones-sized hurdle.

I hear a spray of gravel in the drive. The front door opens and I see Cristian's ashen face turned up to me.

"Lainey," he chokes. He staggers to sit down.

They went to the restaurant. They went to the bank. There has been no deposit. There is no cash box.

Chance is gone.

Chapter Thirty-three

TIMBER

Timber was scared. A Really Bad Thing was happening; had happened, and he hadn't been able to stop it. He didn't even know such a thing could happen, so he wasn't prepared. Had let his guard down and now his family and his world were crashing down around him. A good guy was a bad guy, maybe, said his father, on the phone. Saying nothing to Timber and not noticing his presence silent beside him in the restaurant, in the car, while he spoke frantic and scared and confused. What do we do now? Asked more than once. When they got home to the cabin Timber lagged behind, shutting the car door slowly and looking straight up into open, pure sky and wondering.

He stretched to his toes and felt himself grow bigger. Taller. Finally Tall Timber looked down on the little cabin and across the valley over the ridge to the restaurant and wondered where Chance had gone and why he would take the money. Grownups knew that taking things was stealing and Chance was not a Bad Guy. Therefore he did not steal the money. Tall Timber wondered who did. Looking through his lightning bolt cracked glasses through the forest to the cave where bad guys hide out. If he knew where that place was he could maybe find the money.

But then Tall Timber was being called inside and he was again a child and they were telling him something happy which was the completely unexpected and shocking news that he would get to spend the night (and maybe two!!) with Uncle Brad in Uncle Brad's very own exclusive apartment with a community swimming pool and pool table that had nothing to do with water or swimming but was called pool table on account of it was like a box. Timber wasn't sure about leaving, though. What if he were needed to protect his parents from other bad things? There was his poor old mother, crying and gasping while his red-eyed father helped her down that ladder. Saying some of those Never Say That Timber words on the way on account of how bad it hurt her broke-up foot and everything. Saying no way she wasn't going back up and would sleep in front of the fireplace instead for a while. But she said go on Timber and have a really good time and be careful—but Timber's father said to her relax it will be okay. Would it?

Before he jumped back into the Liberty to go to town with Dad and stay at Uncle Brad's house Timber looked back up again at the on-and-on-forever blue sky. Then he screwed his eyes tight like Miss Celia and asked that boy named Jesus to please, please, if he wasn't too busy, fix everything good for his broke-up mom and sad scared dad.

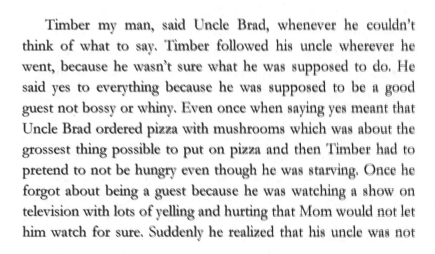

Timber my man, said Uncle Brad, whenever he couldn't think of what to say. Timber followed his uncle wherever he went, because he wasn't sure what he was supposed to do. He said yes to everything because he was supposed to be a good guest not bossy or whiny. Even once when saying yes meant that Uncle Brad ordered pizza with mushrooms which was about the grossest thing possible to put on pizza and then Timber had to pretend to not be hungry even though he was starving. Once he forgot about being a guest because he was watching a show on television with lots of yelling and hurting that Mom would not let him watch for sure. Suddenly he realized that his uncle was not beside him on the scratchy couch so he got up to find out where he went and heard him whispering into a telephone. Gotta go, sweetheart, he said and hung up looking at Timber with his hands out. What? What do you want now? And then laughing, everything okay and Timber wondered about the sweetheart was that a girlfriend? Oh sure, said Uncle Brad, one of many. One of many.

And Timber wondered about having many girlfriends and was that a good thing? I think so, said Brad, but I don't think they would think so if they each knew about the others! You're gonna be a lady-killer, too, some day. And Timber was scared but Uncle Brad figured out that Timber was thinking what he said but not what he meant and he explained that what he meant was that Timber would have many girlfriends too and make them all jealous of each other. But he stopped and said, you know, maybe that's not such a good thing. Look at your ma and your Uncle Mike and maybe finding the one true love of your life is better. But the phone rang and it was another girl and Brad got smiley and covered the mouthpiece and whispered, Nah! and went into another room and shut the door.

Timber wandered alone back to the hurting show and was nervous about the blood and went instead to the kitchen and looked and looked at that pizza, smelling warm still but with slimy mushrooms touching all over, and he took a piece and carefully pulled the fungus and it slid right off and he thought maybe that was true that If You Don't Like It, Just Take It Off! like his mother always said and he didn't believe. He tried a bite. It worked! His uncle didn't come back until he'd eaten four whole pieces and was yawning, head on arm on the counter and didn't argue when he heard, Come on, Little Man, let's get that couch made up for you. Sleeping in the Man Cave with his uncle nearby. Warm and full of pizza and deciding that he'd never want a girlfriend anyway.

Chapter Thirty-four

LAINEY

"Baby, that is ugly." I am wiggling my toes, which I can do now without causing lightning streaks of pain to shoot up my leg. The bruise line looks like a toe tattoo.

"I know, right?" I say, looking up. But he isn't looking at my toes; he's staring at my face.

"Thanks a lot!" I protest.

"The bruise, Lainey. Look at the TV."

I haven't even thought about pain in my face all morning. So I am shocked at my image reflected in the gray box.

"Hey, that's my first shiner! I always wanted one. Take a picture to prove this to the boys!"

Sunday and Monday are over and I can't pull any real memory of either day. I have a dream sequence of blankets and pills and a fingerprinted glass of water and that's about it. Cristian has been watching me closely. He says he's withholding all drugs from now on except the anti-inflammatory. Doesn't want to have to go to detox later. I haven't seen Timber this whole time.

"This is the longest we've been away from our son!" I stretch my shoulders back and raise my arms as I say it, and the effort is like scratching a bug bite. It feels at once cool, satisfying, and agonizing. No wonder it's such a big deal when older people take a fall. Bodies twist and muscles you never use are suddenly ripped awake. Cristian winces as he watches me.

"Yeah. Speaking of drug rehabilitation centers, I wonder what vices we're gonna have to rehabilitate Timber from once he's back from your brother's influence."

"Pop, for one."

"Heavy metal music. Chicks in bikinis in his condo's pool."

"Ugh. Don't even say that, Cristian. He's only six."

My husband's hands on the back of my neck are gentle and the massage helps loosen my back. I reach my hand and he pulls me to my good foot and I balance a crutch under my arm. Cristian folds the blankets and sleeping bags we've been using and dumps the pile on the corner of the couch. He's already dressed and helps me slide into a loose tee. It can no longer be called wine-colored and definitely defies a description of form-fitting, but putting it on doesn't hurt and I don't ask him to go find another. He kisses me goodbye and leaves to buy groceries for Soup Line. He'll be busy prepping the next few hours and will eat his sandwich there while I eat mine here.

He's promised to get me this afternoon just before opening. Hopefully my face won't scare off too many customers. In the meantime he's made me a little breakfast and borrowed a couple of chick flicks from Julie. I am to do light stretches and try my hardest to wait until noon before taking another ibuprofen, and nothing stronger if I can at all manage.

It's a pain, for sure. But my heart, Celia would be glad to know, is good.

Chapter Thirty-five

We still have people at the tables at 9:30. Some are on their third bowl; many are friends who have eaten and now merely sip coffee and enjoy conversation. The restaurant smells strongly of sweet basil tonight except for the area closest to the coffee counter. It's a warm night and an aspen-whispering breeze enters through an open window. Celia brought me over this evening rather than Cristian, as he was knee-deep in a potato soup emergency, and I was still dozing until well after opening. I guess she had just walked in when I called to say I was up, and hearing his half of our conversation, she jumped in with the offer to get me. A side benefit of nosiness, she explained, is the ability to offer a helping hand now and then. She's lent a hand in the kitchen, as well, and is still here all these hours later.

Julie Thorndove has tucked her sleeping cherub under a blanket in a carrier and continues to sit in the midst of an animated discussion with a small group of teens I don't recognize. She waves me over and they make a space and help me slide down into it. Conversation resumes. Within the past week there has been another death of a local kid. He was dared to kill himself by his best friends. How can the church help? Julie asks. What is the biggest need of these kids? What drives someone to join a weird gang, wear offensive clothing and adopt a creed of nihilism and despair? The kids say boredom. Mostly they are bored, and lonely, and everyone just wants to have fun and have friends. Parents? Who even sees them? They don't have a clue...

I feel old. I am no longer the kid but the parent. I'm the one without a clue. My teenage self would have rolled her eyes at my thirty-year-old self. Thirty? Can I really be turning thirty next month?

And even so I haven't gotten any of those magic grown-up answers. What if my son is the lonely teen with no friends? How do I keep him safe?

"Hey, Mrs. Clayson," says one of the teens, and I realize this is our normal waitress, Heidi, come on her day off to eat. Only I think she is spelled Haydi or something. I wish she would call me Lainey, because the Mrs. Clayson bit doesn't make me feel any younger.

"When I grow up I want to open a coffee shop, like for teenagers. So they can hang out, you know, and stuff. It would be epic, but, would that be okay? I mean, I wouldn't serve food, so people would still eat here. Mine would just be like a cool hangout, you know? That wouldn't bother you and Mr. Clayson, would it?"

"I think that would be neat, Haydi."

"It would be like ten years, Mrs. Clayson. Do you think you'll be retired yet?"

"Wow. I'll be like 40. I don't know..." And Julie busts out laughing, and Celia, too, and tells the girls to guess her age. They guess our ages, too, and are surprised to hear that we graduated together and have been friends since elementary school.

"Were we ever this young?" Julie asks me. And we were, and we remember. We remember the day we grew up. All of us, during our own class tragedy. Only one person died and it was just an accident, but we all lost our innocence on that end-of-the-year hill climb. We mostly ran away to college as soon as we could. But Julie stayed. And I came back. The girl in our class who died was not a close friend of either of us. She was a younger member of Angela's crowd. A good friend of my sister. And for the first time ever I realize that maybe Angela hasn't been hiding from her family. She may have even been there that day; I don't remember. Maybe she was up at the top. In the group that was going to "boulder surf" all the way down to the ball fields. Maybe she helped push.

It was one of those senseless random things. A stupid high school prank that left a handful of kids with blood on their hands.

Julie says quietly, "Remember, Lainey?" and I nod.

"Wait a minute—if you graduated then—wasn't that the year that girl got killed on the hill? Were you guys there?" Haydi asks, hushed. "Were you guys students when…you know, the boulder crushed that girl?" We were. We don't tell them much. We can't, anyway. You can't ever explain what it was like. A horrible rumble and crash. A small blot of red high on the hill. And then the screams. Never-ending screams.

"They say," Haydi begins but I cut her off.

"If you are ever in a group, and people want to do something stupid, you can stop it. Try yelling and if no one listens, leave. At least you will be far away." I am speaking more harshly than I intended. The teens are shocked into silence.

And how will I protect my fragile son from this world? How can I keep a girl or a bully or a teacher or his own mistakes from driving him to despair or stupidity? I am surprised to realize that I'm asking these things out loud.

Because you love him. Get involved at school. Let him have a lot of freedom. No, set lots of limits. Don't have weapons at your house. Teach him how to use one. Watch out for girls who are users. Careful about parties. No weed and no booze. The teens have a lot of advice, and I wonder if they'd say the same to their own parents. It gets quiet.

"You cannot," states Celia firmly. Her wandering eye turns out toward the darkened window. "You just can't protect Timber from the world. Terrible things happen even to kids whose parents have completely cut them off from the world; maybe even more so. You can't control his emotions. He can't even control his emotions. There is only one thing you can do. Well, two. Trust and pray."

"But…"

"Lainey, if there is a plan for you (and there obviously is or you wouldn't be sitting here alive!), there certainly are plans for the rest of us. Including your son. I'm not saying to roll over and give up. I'm saying to trust, every day giving up everything, and I mean everything. Like these precious kids," she says, stopping her eye from wandering by squeezing it shut. She begins to pray for the teens around us. By the time she's done she's also covered this restaurant, Chance, her friend's little grandson with medical issues, as well as everyone driving down the highway to get home tonight. Covered us all with loving thoughts and hopeful prayers. Sniffling but peaceful teens walk out into the cool night air, and I lock the door behind them.

Someone clears his throat in the black space between our now-dark restaurant and the safety of our car. An icy wind brushes the back of my neck. Cristian stiffens beside me and moves his body between me and the sound.

"Who is it? How can I help you?" he asks, feigning calm.

The throat is cleared again, and then we hear a familiar drawl.

"Uh, hey. Look, do ya'll have a minute?" The voice is Travis' but it lacks his usual bravado. It's late and my foot hurts, but Cristian tells him sure, we have a minute, and we go back inside. Cristian flips on more lights than necessary. He sits and points to the bench beside him, and I fall back into the upholstered chair we brought from home for my recovery, but Travis remains standing.

"Look. I heard what happened. The guy who stole your cash box. Mrs. Vanderbrandt, well, yesterday I saw her at the gas pumps and she told me it was another unfair blow. And that I was the first unfair blow. My firing you. I hadn't thought about how much that might have hurt ya'll. I didn't think about it at all at the time. I was pissed about losing you and the words just came out, you know?"

Cristian sits quietly, head bent. Travis glances toward me but looks quickly down at his pointy cowboy boots. I wonder, oddly, if he has also taken on these boots as a part of an image, like Cristian. Maybe he grew up in some Austin suburb and living here, in the Rocky Mountain West, is part of a fantasy he wants to make real.

Travis raises his eyes imploringly as he tells about his family. How his wife left him for a richer man, taking his son and leaving him just enough to pull together the Crow Barre. But it wasn't enough. What he really wanted, needed, was to be a father to his child.

"You probably didn't know, but he's come to live with me a couple of months now. I didn't hardly know him at all. Didn't know my own kid! He's a handful, and it ain't been easy, but we're doing okay."

Travis says that he started doing counseling with this guy, the pastor of the Baptist church, who has been working with him now, on forgiveness, better choices, that sort of thing, for a bit. Anyway after Celia confronted him last night he had come to realize that he'd done Cristian a great wrong by firing him. He was here to offer his regret and apology and a job, if we were interested.

"So I didn't know if you were going to have to close down now or what, but uh," he speaks fast, as though to finish before he changes his mind. "Anyway I could probably put you back on rotation, some, you know, mornings especially…this new cook I got, she can't fry an egg. Maybe. Maybe even if you keep going here, maybe some morning hours would help. I could keep you on the payroll and you could get off whenever you need, to, uh, do your own thing here."

Cristian stretches his fingers together and touches his lips. It's his think gesture. He bounces them a couple times. This exchange is not normal Travis. Something has happened. People are destroying my preconceptions all over the place!

"You know, Travis," he says, "we really aren't in direct competition with you. We are only doing supper, and so far only soups and breads. You do breakfast and lunch. We do supper. You didn't need to hit us with that slam campaign."

Travis' cheeks flame. "Cristian," he says, "I got to tell you, that internet crap was all my son. Wade's good with that computer geek stuff and he thought he would help me out. It's the first time he's ever done something for me, and I do know it was wrong, but I admit I was kind of proud of him anyway, for knowing how to do that, I'm sorry to say."

"It hurt our reputation, just like you firing me in public, telling people lies about my work, hurt me."

Travis turns to the door.

"I'm sorry. I meant disrespect and I meant harm, and I did wrong. I'll just get on out of here now."

"Wait." Travis freezes, and I freeze, halfway off my chair. Cristian rises and holds the door open to the black night for his former boss.

"I forgive you, Travis, and your son Wade, too, and I may take you up on the offer to cook mornings. Maybe once a week during the school year or something. I need to check all this over with my family first. I appreciate the offer and I'll let you know within the week."

Travis is taller, but he bows a little before the bigger man. We all step out, and the key turns all the way until the lock clicks tight.

Chapter Thirty-six

I awaken to a ringing phone. Cristian rises next to me on our make-shift bed on the living room floor, rubbing sleep from his own eyes. It turns out to be Brad, calling to say he's bringing Timber home later this morning, but he's got something for Mom and wonders if Cristian and I can meet them at her house. I try hard not to be annoyed. After all, my single brother just kept my six-year-old for two nights. Talk about cramping his style! I owe him big time. So I don't want to be picky or selfish, it's just that Brad has to pass here to drive the fifteen minutes farther to get out to our parents'—I mean our mother's—place. Which means I would waste a half hour with getting there and back plus whatever time it takes to greet and then un-greet our mother. And Angela.

I keep forgetting the chunky prodigal sister. The chunky de-pressed prodigal sister. If Timber can't help the way his brain pro-cesses information and emotions, maybe Angela's can't either. Remembering other details from that bad day at the high school, I am almost certain now that she was up there right when it happened. Is witnessing something horrible like that enough to break your brain? Make you crazy? Cristian hands me the phone. Forget Angela. What is Brad playing at?

Brad mumbles around a little in explanation. The thing is that, well, uh, oh yeah, the thing is kind of—heavy. He needs help with setting it up. It's a, uh, bookshelf thing. I have a bum foot! Of course, but that's why Cristian needs to come too. Okay, I'll just send Cristian. No! Because, Timber is really homesick. Needs his mommy. By now I can hear Timber in the background protesting that he is not homesick. So whatever is up is a surprise, and I can easily push Brad into giving it all up or I can just play along. At least my son sounds okay. Maybe it's a girl he wants to introduce to the family. Nah, with Brad it's a matter of which girl. Which girl this week.

"Fine, Brad. You are full of something, and it stinks, but we will come. When?" Roll my eyes at Cristian. "Fine. See you in a couple of hours, then."

Cristian is annoyed as well. He was planning on making up some trial batches of bread to try and replicate Chance's French loaf. And we were supposed to call the State Patrol this morning; see if anything has turned up since Chance cut out. They have his truck description and have certainly taken his plates from the registration.

"Let's check your foot, gimpy," Cristian says. I carefully roll down a stretchy chenille slipper sock. The colors are brilliant and beautiful, but the swelling has come down so much that the injured foot now matches its pair, size-wise. I think I can probably even put weight on it now, at least on my heel, but Cristian warns me not to attempt it. He promises to personally smash the other one if I try.

"Think Misery, Lainey, as in Kathy Bates, Stephen King," he threatens, while moving into the kitchen to start breakfast preparations. My face is still ugly. But I am not worried about permanent scarring just yet.

While we wait on Brad and Timber we eat fresh waffles with tangy blueberry syrup. It's a perfect match for Cristian's strong black coffee. He tells me I can have the cream either on my waffle or in the drink but not both. Always trust the chef. It's perfect.

While struggling into a pair of Julie's maternity jeans (a ridiculous idea that I give up in favor of my own dated wide-legs), I bring up the doctor's visit before the Fall. Thinking words I don't dare let fall from my lips: Timber has fetal alcohol syndrome.

School starts in a couple of weeks, and we need to be ready, I say. We have to understand as much as we can so when opinions start to fly we have some kind of base. After hearing those teenagers last night I'm not so much worried about his academic future as his social one. How can we possibly navigate these waters? Pants on now, I crutch my way back to the kitchen stool.

I know Cristian isn't thrilled about my line of "discussion," but he doesn't shut me down. Earlier someone must have brought in the folder of papers and the information the doctor gave us at the review at Children's and dumped it on the counter. I move the butter tub from on top and pick up the folder, brushing crumbs away. It's heavy, this stack of bad prognosis.

Fetal exposure to alcohol causes problems as diverse as small head size, various birth defects, failure to reach milestones on time, trouble verbalizing, and reduced memory. As these FAS kids grow up, things can get even scarier. Many suffer problems with relationships, problems with employers, problems with the law. Without early intervention the outlook is bleak. My eyes are overflowing now, and I put my head on my arm. I want Cristian to wipe my eyes and tell me not to worry. He pulls up the stool next to me and flips to the next brochure. His voice is soft and sure.

"We are intervening, Lainey! Since Timber was scooped off those fire station steps he has had continuous 'interventions' of one kind or another. Speech and physical therapies, reconstructive surgeries. We took him to Head Start preschool and now he'll be starting special education classes, too."

The next pamphlet recounts an age-by-age description of what FAS can look like at its worst. I read out loud, but as hyperactivity telescopes into alcohol and substance abuse I stop. I can't take it. I can't see my little boy, difficult as he may be, in the descriptions before me. I won't.

"We need a miracle," I choke. Cristian has been shaking his head as I read. Willing the words away. He takes my hand and shuts the folder. "It doesn't go away if we ignore it, Cristian. There is no cure. We can't fix him. He will never grow out of the damage that was done. We need a miracle."

Cristian tips my chin up. Do I remember that day when we first met our son? Remember the rain? Remember how sad the world was because of a shooting at the Academy? Another Colorado tragedy had hit the news that morning. We had turned off the car, silencing the radio with a sense of doom. And then, as we were entering the flagstone county building, we heard a beautiful birdsong coming from a little brown dot up under the roofline. We stopped to listen, and Cristian said that the world isn't all shootings and crashes and death. He said sometimes it's babies and lovers and birds singing, even in the rain.

"Timber is the miracle, Lainey. He is our miracle baby. He was our answer. He made us a family. We knew he was going to have problems. We knew he wouldn't be ordinary."

"So we just go on? Just keep trying?"

"It's worked so far, hasn't it?" And he is right. It has worked so far. One intervention is probably all Timber really needs, and that intervention began the instant the first fireman gazed into his eyes. No, I have to believe it happened when his birth mother did the same. They loved him. The foster family loved him. Everyone who meets him seems to automatically love Timber. And Cristian and I, exponentially more than any of these, love this boy.

And yet I know how desperately my parents loved Angela. And all the parents of all the kids who keep taking their lives for no reason, or harming each other as a diversion, or screwing things up in one way or another, love their kids too, and I am still unsure. Cristian stands to brush my hair, overly gently and parted to the wrong side.

"Did you hear Celia last night?" Yes I did.

"There is no promise that life will be easy. Not for you; not for our son. She said that the promise is that we are not alone in the difficulties. I would have said that wasn't enough, if we hadn't just come through this thing with Chance. When Timber and I pulled up at Soup Line on Saturday morning I got this bad feeling even before we went inside. But as I began to search for the cash box and the reality of what was happening sank in, I felt a presence, Lainey. I knew that God was right there with me, and that's what kept me from panicking. Timber held my hand, even though he didn't know what was going on, and told me not to worry."

"Oh, Cristian…"

"And you know, my fears have only increased since then, but I haven't exactly worried. I've been almost detached, you know. Watching, I guess."

"I understand, but I wish I knew what we were watching for!"

"Yeah. But," and he indicates the stack of papers, "partly it is this stuff. We're watching to see if Timber is okay. And he isn't. And he is. He's not without a moral compass, Lainey. He messes up, but he knows that he has done wrong. Like with Taylor. Like all those pictures and the 'I'm sorries' and the 'I still wanna be your friend, do you wanna be my friend' cards. That's sweet, but it's also proof that he knows right and wrong, feels remorse, and wants to do better."

Cristian holds my hands and closes his eyes. Whatever he says, it is not to me, but his silence moves me. I open wet eyes and feel again that rain. I am refreshed and renewed. The world is drizzling all around us, but we are safe inside. That baby who was an answer to our prayers is on his way home. And it is time to go get him.

TIMBER

Timber and Brad flew up the mountain highway like crop dusters with a storm trooper on their tail. Timber took off his glasses and let the lights do the spinning thing from the front part of the movie Dad liked. Light speed, said Brad. I wonder when your mom will let me give you a ride on the Yamaha. I can see the love of speed on your face, dude.

Timber asked, How come love you so many girlfriends? Uncle Brad, choking a little, said, Out of the blue, dude, but that's how you work, huh, kid? Told Timber that he didn't actually love any of them. He liked them all a lot. Just like Timber liked his friends. Some are guys and some are girls, that's all.

Timber asked, You go on kissing all the time your friends? Which accidentally said that he had seen Brad at the door with Trisha and heard that gooey phone stuff.

Look, Timber, let me redeem myself or my sister will kill me! And don't tell her any of this. See, love is special. Like your mom and dad. They have a real love. And Mike and Vanji. Whispered, almost, but Timber sat right up straight, glasses back on his nose. It's why we're heading up there now, dude. Your uncle and your aunt fell in love and they want to tell everyone! They have been seeing each other down in town and stuff. It's what happens when you are in love, you want to see each other all the time. Timber asked, What about Uncle Mike's other girlfriends? He doesn't have any. When you find the right one there is only one.

Timber making engine sounds. Beeps. Uncle Mike no can marry Aunt Vanji, Timber said quietly. Aunt Vanji love me. She Timber's girlfriend, no Uncle Mike's. Brad laughed but it was friendly and Timber thought he understood that his aunt would always love him most but in a different way and it sounded okay to him. Anyway by now he was thirsty and hungry and bored with all the talk of love and kisses.

Had to make a stop at the bus station. Pick up Uncle Joe, who would go on up to Bailey with Timber and Brad. Joe was annoyed about the trip because of missing something important—a special practice, but family is important, too, Uncle Joe said, leaning up from the back seat and swatting Timber's head in a gentle way.

Getting hungry, dude? asked Brad, you look a little grouchy-faced, while reaching beside him into a duffle for a bottle of water and an energy bar. Here you go, Little Man. Fortify yourself! Timber was okay. Wanting his mother's arm around his shoulder, warm cheek on his in a cheeky kiss, but not too sad. Not since he had man deodorant to match his uncles, sticky neck since he shaved with a backwards razor last night. Loved his aunt Vanji the most but loved his uncles, too. Looking sideways now at Brad, readjusting his body to mirror, hand casual on an invisible steering wheel.

Brad noticing, gearing down though unnecessary and making a grind. "I love you, man."

Timber grinned. "I love you too!"

Chapter Thirty-seven

"We should have waited until we were sure Brad had already passed before we left. Made him honk or something." Cristian sulks. As it is we've been sitting here in Mom's dark paneled living room for half an hour. Mom is making tea but she doesn't seem to be doing things in the proper order. Alzheimer's? I have just entered the ranks of the "sandwich generation." How can I talk this woman into a neurological check-up? She's as bad as my father, and we saw how that worked out. I guess Angela's coming fell at a good time. Having her here may be of more help than we realized when she first showed up at Dad's funeral.

Except that it is 10:00 a.m., and my big sister is still in bed. Thirty minutes is plenty of time for the woman to come and have a get-to-know-you conversation with her brother-in-law, but she stays in "her" room with the door shut.

"Oh, hey," she says, finally, blinking in surprise to see Cristian perched on our sagging old couch, me sprawled comfortably across his lap with the bad foot up as he caresses stringy bangs away from the bruising around my forehead and eye.

"Hey," I mutter.

"Sorry. I didn't know you were here. I was just…doing this stretching regimen thing. Gets my day going, you know." Angela begins to squeeze her wide bottom into the old rocker across from us but then she hears some clinking in the kitchen.

"Mama," she calls. "Everything okay in there?"

"Yes, Jim. The tea I am making. Be a moment longer, please." And we all look at each other. How long has this been going on? But

Mom comes through the doorway, with a tray set up, chuckling daintily.

"Oh, listen to me. I get confused sometimes. I meant Angela. Only I thought you were not awake?" Quietly, touching Angela's arm, "Feel better today?"

Angela has taken the tray, and I sit up enough to balance a cup with my leg still extended. Cristian takes one too, despite the fact he hates tea.

"Shall I check the stove, Ida?" He asks. "Make sure it's all the way off?"

Angela is already taking the tray back to the kitchen and yells over her shoulder that everything is fine.

"Some sugar spilled. I tried to clean it, but it is in all the cracks," admits Mom. We can hear Angela wetting a rag and probably wiping it up. No problem, everything is under control.

Angela comes back and sprawls in the rocker, beside our tiny mother who perches on the stiff wooden chair she has always favored. They look like they have been roommates for years. It is scary. I wait for Angela to begin a conversation. Tell us about her depression. Learn something about my husband. Ask about Timber. Soup Line. Anything.

Nothing.

Cristian clears his throat. "Ida, what is it that Brad is bringing you?"

"Bringing me? Nothing! Brad is bringing Timber. I guess we're having some time here together because Elena asked for it."

"What?!" I did not! What is this boy trying to pull? And spinning tires give the indication we will soon find out. No one gets up. We'll just let Bradley Isaiah explain himself.

But it is Joe who walks in the door. Joe? He looks at us in surprise. He sticks his head back out the door and yells.

"Why did you drag me up here, Brad? You are a geek! You don't need my help if you already have Cristian. And Angela." Joe says to me on his way back in, "not that you couldn't normally split faster than me, but I know you are sidelined right now, Lainey. By the way, ya look awful!"

And then Timber runs in, followed closely by a sheepish Brad.

While I hug and kiss on Timber several voices join in an attack: what's going on? What's he playing at here? We all have places to be on a Monday morning, for crying out loud. Mom has a whole stack of firewood split already. Firewood? Wasn't this about a bookshelf or something?

Brad holds up his hands. "It isn't me. It's them!" And another engine dies and car doors slam and seconds later, with a burst of fresh air, Mike and Vanji squeeze into the living room, hand in hand.

The newly presented couple remains standing by the door, and a sudden shaft of light glimmers off a certain interlocked finger.

"Oh my goodness!" I am screaming, and crying, and no one else knows why.

Vanji's chameleon skin deepens and for once it's not by her design.

"You are blushing! Sister! This is totally WHAT?!, but congratulations!" And I hobble over and we are blubbering on each other and slowly an understanding breaks out among the gathered family members. Cristian's mouth hangs open. He has still been trying to get his mind around the two of them dating.

Timber shouts: "Auntie Vanji and Uncle Mike is going marry—but is a secret!" And he slams his hand across his mouth.

"You have got to be kidding!" Joe moans. Brad actually giggles. Of all the brothers to trust with a secret I can't believe Mikey chose Brad. Angela doesn't quite get it. She probably doesn't even know that Vanji is Cristian's sister. But then I'm not even sure Angela is clear on which of our little brothers is Brad and which is Joe. She doesn't exactly whoop for joy, but there is an almost-smile on her saggy face. She says, "Sister-brother; brother-sister. How sweet. Your kids will be double-cousins."

"I wants a cousin!"

"I want a cousin, Timber." I correct. Stop correcting!

"Later, Timbo," says Mike. "MUCH later!"

Our mother remains seated, serenely watching the scene from her hard little chair, shoulders back and chin up. This is the elegant woman who raised me. This is the mother who has been missing since she fell into sorrow. What is going on in your mind, Mama?

"La segunda boda de mis bebes," she says, and we freeze again. Mom never speaks Spanish, except for maybe the names of things. Like Tajin or chiliquiles. None of us even took Spanish in school. Dad didn't know a word, that's for sure. But the fact is that a foreign language just popped out of her mouth, pure and melodic, as though she spoke it always. And maybe she always did, in her dreams.

"What did you say?" asks Mike. His arm has tightened on Vanji's shoulder, protectively. As if maybe our mother was cursing his bride-to-be in Spanish.

Mom blinks. She turns to Angela. Angela says that Mom said something about another wedding for her babies. Mom smiles. That was correct. Angela dated a guy, she begins, but we cut her off. Has our mother forgotten English? May I offer the newly engaged a cup of tea? To our great relief, she answers in English.

"Yes, of course. I forgot. Tea. But when is the wedding?"

And there is Cristian, mouth still open, eyes glazed in shock.

"Actually," says Mike nervously. "I uh, need to do something first." He steps away from Vanji, who moves closer to where I balance upright with the help of my crutch. She whispers sorry for keeping a secret and I whisper wait until later you traitorous fool. Mike moves awkwardly to where I had been, beside Cristian. He clears his throat, but it makes an almost squeaky sound and probably constricts his voice more than it helps.

"Cristian," like a little soprano choir boy. He tries again, deep from his chest: "Cristian. I would like to ask your permission for the hand of your sister." Whoosh. A big breath to fill his burning lungs. It's not funny; pain is etched into his features. I laugh.

If Cristian's pupils weren't the same color as his irises we would see them zooming in and out, trying to focus. He turns toward Vanji and me, smiling our heads off, and slowly to Mike, whose body has tensed in fear of the panther beside him.

"You want to marry Vanji?" He's quick, that man of mine.

"Y-yes sir," answers Mike and it's all we can take. The room fills with hoots and hollers, the thin old floor creaking beneath the stomping, and no one except Mike and I see Cristian's lips form the word "Yes." Our mother sits primly. Angela pushes herself to her feet and goes to get the heated water. Vanji whispers to Timber, who runs out and comes back in with a box of specially iced cupcakes. They are gold and silver and all together in the box spell out: SUR-PRISE! I SAID YES!

Cristian recovers finally and moves to lean against me. He accuses me of knowing and keeping a secret from my own spouse. What kind of example is that? He shakes his head while I explain I only knew they were dating, had no idea of the nuptial plans.

"Isn't this kind of sudden? Or have you two been sneaking out of every family gathering and we never noticed?" asks Joe, taking a swig from a Solo cup and smacking it down on the little table beside him, actually hitting a coaster in the process.

Cristian and I have known each other for twelve years. We will have been married for nine this Thanksgiving. They probably met then, at our wedding. But Mikey was such a kid. Boys taking longer to mature and all. When did they fall in love?

"For me," answers Vanji, "It's been about five months."

"Five years!"

"No, honey, that was just your hormones." She pokes his shoulder muscle which he flexes.

"She's right, dude, we all had a crush on her…" Brad turns crimson and clamps his mouth.

"Too much information, dolt," says Joe. Mike is moving into rooster mode. Vanji kisses his neck and smooths his feathers. She takes a cup of tea from Angela and keeps her thin beautiful pinkie stuck out so that Mike can remain wrapped around it, maybe.

"A few months ago I had this singing gig where I needed a male backup, and I show up and here was Michael. Like the rest of you, I thought he was just teaching painting and still coaching so I was totally unprepared when I heard his sound. You are so good, Baby Boy," she coos, tickling his in-need-of-a-shave chin.

"It was the most amazing duet I've ever done. It was a love song, and I was like, Oh shit, how am I gonna pull this off with Lainey's brother, and afterward I was like, Oh shit, how am I going to live without this man?"

Timber jumps up and down. Oh joy, he's heard a cuss word. Brad grabs him and mock wrestles him to the ground so that Vanji can continue. She looks at me. "That's when I started stalking his Facebook page and found this song and sent it to him. It wasn't real hard to get him interested!"

But Mike says, "That was it. We've been seeing each other every second we can since then, and even if we've only been dating a few months, and sort of secretly as far as you all are concerned, I know I can't live without this woman. We're going to be married at Christmas, and we're touring as a couple. It's building already. We have an agent..."

"You sing?" asks Mom. "For us, will you sing?"

Mike rises and shuts the front door behind himself and Vanji starts in, low, and after a few lines Mike's part starts and I don't think I've ever heard anything so amazing. Or as sappy, as their doe-eyes melt into each other, but that is okay. I like sappy.

They finish. There is a pause after the applause, and Timber breaks it.

"Can I have a other pup cake?"

Cristian really does need to get working, and Joe, Brad, and Vanji have all taken the morning off to come to this big false emergency that Brad helped concoct. So the party ends, tears are wiped, and I actually hear Angela say congratulations to my sister-in-law. Soon to be hers too, I realize.

I'm still kind of annoyed about being out of the engagement loop. I mean, I saw the kiss and knew something was going on, but marriage? After these few months? Okay, technically years, but come on. Car doors are opening and shutting all around and the sky is as blue as truth. With the sun shining warm on the tops of our heads, I kiss my bestest goodbye and promise all my love and all my best wishes for her and Mikey. They are my second favorite two people in the whole world, after all.

Chapter Thirty-eight

Timber sits quietly in the car behind Cristian and me, and we praise his good behavior at Grandma's. I thank him for the terrific report Brad gave, too, although I am worried about the movies he may have seen. Are Aunt Vanji and Uncle Mike going to have a cousin for him at Christmas? No, they are just getting married. Maybe sometime they will have kids who will be extra special cousins but who knows when. But they are already married, right, because they are Uncle and Aunt. Someone in Timber's class told him once that uncles and aunts are married. It's too complicated. Quiet game? No? Let's count power poles.

The plan is to stop by Soup Line to drop Cristian off, and then Timber and I will head home for a while. Let him decompress in familiar surroundings while I do some laundry and check the books. I reach to turn the radio down while Cristian spins the wheel to cross the highway. As we enter the drive we can see that something is going on around the back side of the restaurant. There are a couple of vehicles in the lot and through my open window I smell freshly turned earth. Billy is here, canvas-gloved and mud-spattered, un-rolling chain link fencing. There's a recently scraped dirt square inside a row of aluminum fence poles, and the small tractor that apparently did the leveling is parked beside it. A pile of lumber; mostly telephone poles, from the looks of it, lies balanced along one edge.

"Howdy, Claysons!" yells Billy. He's wearing his typical plaid rags, and I realize the last few times I've seen him has been at church when he's all cleaned up. He seems more relaxed today with a wide dirty streak across his tanned cheekbone. Cristian flips the stick to park, brows furrowed in confusion. Timber's out first, of course, but I follow at a pretty quick clip for someone on crutches.

"Julie and I and the folks been thinking," Billy calls as we walk up, "that we forgot one big improvement we should have seen to before you got going. There's bound to be a lot of little tykes, and of course big guys, like especially Timber here, who would benefit from a safe play area. We had all this playground stuff already, and we're putting it in fast as we can. May take two or three days, so I hope it doesn't bother you too much. We're not in the parking lot here," and he gestures to show that business can go on as usual.

Timber trembles with excitement. We adults all know that Billy is full of crap. If they really already had this equipment ready, it was because they were going to build it at their house or something. On the other hand, we know what a relief it will be for Timber to have a safe fenced-in area to play in during the hours between school and bedtime. We can't speak.

Timber grabs Billy. He loves it! Dirt is great! And Billy explains that there will be gravel on top of the dirt, and a slide and climbing thing and swings. And Timber will be the Official Safety Playground Guard, making sure that all the little kids are safe and happy, and ringing a doorbell thing that will sound off in the office kitchen if anything is wrong. Timber's chest puffs out just like Uncle Mike's this morning. He promises never ever ever to push anyone off of anything on his playground.

"Oh, Billy! I love you!" Cristian isn't the least bit jealous while I plant one on my old friend's cheek. But when we step inside for a minute before Timber and I leave to go home, Cristian breaks down. What is Billy doing? We don't even know if we can keep going! I know. But here it is.

I leave Cristian to work on bread baking and the night's new soups and take Timber home to clean up—two days' worth of change-into clothes are all still folded in the backpack, along with a suspiciously dry and clean toothbrush. Brad never was much into rules.

While Timber showers I lay down on the couch. I can't fill the washer while he's showering anyway or he will have no pressure. A lifetime has passed in these last few days. My head itches beneath the yellow-green bruises, again, a reminder of the stupid fall. I hear the drone of construction equipment up on the ridge between our home and the restaurant. I think of this new playground, and the Thorndoves' investment, and Chance's deceit. Everything was going so well. Yet despite the mess I have an overriding peace. Life is still fine. Timber is rash and hyper but also loving and kind. Angela threw her youth away, but she is now in the perfect position to help our mother. These teenage kids keep mourning friends, but they develop a wisdom and a love that transforms their own families. Maybe. Or is it all just chance? Chance. The man who seemed so genuine but couldn't be trusted. Is faith like that? It is not. I hope that it is not.

"Mommy, I all done. Can we go Soup Line? I wanna help." And the stupidity of having this kid shower before playing in the mud hits me. What was I thinking? Still. He had a noxious smell of Axe about him, and I would rather smell the dirt. I warn that there will be another shower tonight, and he says he doesn't care. Promises not to argue. But anyway he showered NOW! And immediately begins a category three meltdown.

TIMBER

Was a playground, what Mister Billy was building Timber Clayson, for himself at his family's own restaurant so that he could be a big brother to all the kids who come with their moms and dads to eat soup. Mister Billy was nice, so nice and maybe the dirtiest grownup ever on account of the mud on his clothes and skin. But Mommy and Daddy didn't even say thank you; they cried! And went off together like they didn't even like the best gift ever while Timber stayed close by to the tractor, smelling diesel and grease and man stuff. Mister Billy, who was Baby Sally's daddy now that she was born and all, didn't tell Timber don't climb, but asked if he wanted to see and showed about levers and things. It was like Uncle Brad's car and Timber thought that one day he would be old enough to drive.

Mommy still wet-eyed like she didn't like the playground when they came home. Grabbing Timber's shoulder to make sure he didn't walk into the house with the mud-stuck shoes before he even had a chance to take them off. He was going to, he really was!

She was opening his backpack then, outside too because who knew what might fall out, she said. Making tchtcht sounds about his unused toothbrush which he'd told Uncle Brad he forgot. And Uncle Brad had unwrapped a new one that was made for grownups with no animal feet bottom to stand on like his own. Timber kind of liked the way the big bristle head filled his whole mouth so he was brushing all his teeth at the same time when he chewed on it. And Uncle Brad let him put it in a special bottom of the cabinet drawer with the comb he gave him because he also thought he had forgotten one. But Timber's mother just got frowny and pulled out stacks of folded clothes and sighed like they had done something wrong by packing back up nice and neat and for no reason at all she was mad at him.

When he got out of the shower she tcht'd even more as she followed behind picking up his dirty clothes and throwing them into the laundry basket. Talking to herself about what was she thinking because it would be even worse tonight after playing in that muddy mess at the restaurant and then Timber couldn't help it.

Me new playground going to be the nicest thing and you are always yelling when I no do nothing! And you are not saying thank you to mine uncle and mine mister friend and you always telling me say sorry and say thank you. Slamming the bathroom door and then seeing Mom's foot there, too close to that door and so it got hit. That little pain noise and there she was, sitting on the closed toilet seat and holding onto the leg up above her foot, saying it's okay it's not too bad but looking so sadly at Timber that all his anger left and he was only sorry. Sorry, sorry, so sorry. He didn't mean it, really. And she, touching his shoulder that was closest, telling him neither did she.

Chapter Thirty-nine

LAINEY

Last night was low. Way too low. We had thirteen customers. Even the number is unlucky. We stare at our coffee to avoid looking each other in the eye. We had set a goal: Twenty. If we got twenty patrons we would keep the doors open. That was the sign. Twenty. We didn't actually say that we would fold if we got fewer, but...

Cristian swivels the kitchen barstool like his son. Eyes down. A woodpecker mocks from somewhere beyond the back window.

"I could go back to the Crow Barre full time."

"Billy is building a playground. This is our whole life right now."

"I know!" he snaps. "I know," quieter.

My coffee is cold and black. Cristian didn't offer real cream. We can't afford real cream now. I hear echoes of my Business 101 professor: Initial Loss, Unforeseen... wait, we have charts for this. And I reach across our sticky countertop for the file folders and search and find the various plans for Worst Case Scenarios and hand them to Cristian. We aren't at bottom yet. The well goes down a little deeper.

"We can still do this," I say.

"But we're failing."

"No, not yet. We are struggling, but it isn't over. Work for Travis. Two days a week. Three if you want. Help him out. But no more. You have your own restaurant to run. Be a cook there. Be an owner/chef here. If our siblings can make it as musicians, we can make it with Soup Line."

"Maybe."

I am surprised to hear myself say, "But maybe it's too small. Too narrow. Maybe to grow we have to expand a little." A dusty sunray hits my eyes.

"It's what I keep thinking, Lainey. Kids want chicken fingers, at the least. But not now, not with the losses…"

I know. The losses. There's a gurgling sound from the lump on Timber's bed and then it moves and a little brown hand reaches up, fingers outstretched. A second hand follows and then he sits, rubbing sleepy eyes. The microwave beeps and I remove my mug and sip hot java.

The phone rings. Cristian pushes it toward me and I press talk and hear an official-sounding woman's voice. The sheriff's department has had a call from Utah State Patrol. There was an APB on Chance's truck, and they located it. Stopped one Chauncey Sherman Grant, just before he crossed the state line, headed back this way. The voice sounds like it is coming through a police radio. It is so loud we both hear easily. He has a story, says the officer. Would we like to hear it?

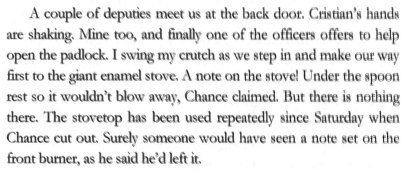

A couple of deputies meet us at the back door. Cristian's hands are shaking. Mine too, and finally one of the officers offers to help open the padlock. I swing my crutch as we step in and make our way first to the giant enamel stove. A note on the stove! Under the spoon rest so it wouldn't blow away, Chance claimed. But there is nothing there. The stovetop has been used repeatedly since Saturday when Chance cut out. Surely someone would have seen a note set on the front burner, as he said he'd left it.

"Anyway," says Cristian, "that spoon holder has been missing." One of the officers hands Cristian a flashlight and he shines it between the stove wall and the side of the nearest cupboard. Wait.

Something is here. Yes, it's the spoon rest. But no note. He opens the oven.

"This hasn't been used because we haven't made bread in several days, without Chance. We have been purchasing bakery rolls from the supermarket." There is a hole in the center of the bottom panel, where the pilot flame burns blue. Cristian hooks the panel and lifts it carefully. Nothing. But if the spoon rest fell sideways, and if the note slipped into the space of the burner... Cristian shuts the oven and lifts the top of the stove. These burners get used a lot and no one has cleaned here yet. I am glad these guys are from the sheriff's office rather than county health inspectors. Over-boiled cheese soup, potato foam, and a chunk of raw bacon. And yes! Here beside the front left burner is the curled burned corner of a piece of yellow notepaper. There is nothing left to read. Only a small strip remains, but we don't need it. This simply verifies that Chance is telling the truth. He left a note.

Now we move quickly to the walk-in cooler, where he said we should pull out the two large buckets of lard. Cold stale air fills my nostrils as we kneel on the wooden planks before steel shelving. Just as he said, the buckets were concealing an empty potato sack folded carefully around the gray metal box full of extremely cold, hard, cash.

This changes everything! Success is ours again! Cristian squeezes way too tight and kisses me hard on the wrong side of my face. The stars take a few minutes to clear. But I am not angry. Who should we call? Billy! But he is here, brushing dirt off his hands and coming inside to see what the screaming is about. The cops being here already had his interest piqued.

"Hallelujah!" he exclaims and pulls out his phone to tell Julie.

Cristian calls Joe, who as part owner should know, and then I call Mom. Celia gives a little hallelujah, too, when Mom drops the phone to share the news. Cristian is finishing inventory of the box's contents with the police, when the question smacks us both. Why? Where did Chance run off to and why?

Because of the APB, Chance gets to spend a night in the clinker, as he calls it. He says he doesn't mind, and anyway the bed is softer than the cot in the bunkhouse. In fact, there is a brand new twin mattress in the back of his truck, which he had been bringing as a replacement. If he still has a job, that is. He'll be up by midday Friday, God-willing.

TIMBER

Timber's friend Chance was not a thief but had to go to jail. Which everyone knew jail was for bad guys. Timber's Uncle Brad drank beer which was a bad thing, but Brad was definitely a good guy. Aunt Vanji cussed sometimes which was always funny but not right, Mom and Dad always said, but who was better than Aunt Vanji?

Timber watched the leaf change color while he spun its stem between his palms. One side light green, one side darker.

Himself. Timber was good sometimes, like now, helping Billy by watching him quiet and nice, but sometimes bad, like really bad when he pushed Taylor. Could he be good and bad at the same time or was he one or the other? Was being bad like having super powers? Being good? He reached to his ear and turned the little dial a tiny bit, and suddenly heard wind in the aspens, crow wings cutting blue sky, murmurs and laughter inside in the restaurant. What if he could turn on good like that? Good filling him up. Good spilling out all over.

Sammy truck on the highway, brakes too loud. Timber touched his ear again. Adjusting, lowering. Timber in control. More help or less help; up to Timber himself to choose alone. He liked that.

Chapter Forty

"Let's hear the story, and then we'll decide about the job, Chance," says Cristian, but his eyes are twinkling, and he has already moved beyond forgiveness to curiosity. My leg is stretched out on the bench to my right while I lean sideways against Cristian. Chance leans heavily on the long table from the other side, and Joe paces nervously. Dust motes float in the rays cutting across the dining hall.

Chance has been staring at my eye. He wants to know what happened.

"Cristian beat me because I told him to trust you, Chance. This is your fault."

But Chance doesn't smile. So we explain about our hike, and how I slipped into the stream and smacked my head and cracked my toes. It really was Chance's fault, I tell him, because I was answering that cryptic phone call when it happened.

"I certainly didn't mean for that to happen! I didn't think the call was going through," says Chance, "I couldn't hear anything on my end. Just trying to let you know that I was still okay to close up. Later on, when I knew I had to leave, I called but couldn't get you to pick up. So I left a message on your voicemail. And then, for good measure, I wrote the note. I still don't know how that all fell apart."

"Lainey cracked the phone between her head and a boulder," says Cristian. "It didn't have a prayer!" Ha, ha.

"Anyway it's broken. We haven't gotten a replacement yet, so we can't get to voicemail."

Chance looks wounded. "So ya'll just assumed I stole the wad and lit out. If it were the other way around, I would have tried harder before I'd believed that of you," he says, quietly. We are all quiet for a moment. Thinking. Do you ever really get a second chance? Or do your former sins follow you forever? If Chance were clean-cut and dressed in a suit, would we have thought harder before involving the police? And the phone message thing, why didn't we think of working with the cellular company to make sure there was no other message? I have no answer, except for my state of incapacitation those first couple of days.

Cristian touches Chance on the arm. "We had a hard time believing, Chance, we really did. But you know, we haven't known you for that long, and lots of people can put on a pretty good act."

He understands. He really is sorry. Should have called back again, to be sure everything was okay. Could have called someone else to get a message to us. It just didn't occur to him either. But the burden lies with him, not us, and could someone get a tissue for Lainey?

Skip the long apology, Chance! "Are you going to tell us what happened or what?"

Chance grins. "Long as you forgive me in the end, Mrs. Clayson. And only if I can get a cup'a joe while I'm talking."

Joe pours the cup. He's taken a four-hour lunch break to come up and hear this story. After Monday's engagement announcement, I can't believe he'd take more time off. He really must be valuable in his mysterious company.

"Better be good," he says. He looks at his phone. "And it better be fast. You got twenty minutes, man." We all lean over the smooth beams of the table, alternately looking into one another's eyes and blotting our own with our napkins. Haydi works prep in the kitchen, and the sound of a knife chopping vegetables punctuates Chance's speech.

"I have a daughter," starts Chance, taking a fortifying sip of our bitter brew. "Her mother took her when she left me, a few months before I entered Shackles Free. The first time." He coughs. "I was a first-time failure. Lasted less than a month and was back on the street. But a few years later God got a'hold a me; I watched a man die. Old Red they called him. Just a homeless elderly guy, probably suffering dementia. Cart full of tin cans he called gold; pretty typical street man. Anyway, it was a cold night, and Old Red was freezing. He tried to get in some swinging doors to an old factory that'd been converted into one of those LoDo upscale loft things, and someone kicked him out. Hard. He sort of slid across the sidewalk, and the bouncer-slash-doorman pulled him by the boots around the corner to the alley. Probably broke a rib and punctured his lung because Old Red just wheezed and spat blood and then stopped." Chance stops to cough himself. Shudder. Sun glints in through the big window and we glance at each other, but now no one makes eye contact. Fingers absently trace knotholes covered by a half inch layer of polyurethane. Chance continues.

"Right next to me. I was so drunk I couldn't hardly move to lift his head or anything. Anyway I went back to Shackles Free the next day and begged and pleaded and they let me back in. I did each part of the program twice that time, for good measure. Wanted to be sure it took, you know? I've been hiding at the mission ever since. Afraid to step back onto the grid, until now."

Joe silently pours more coffee from a dented carafe into each of our mugs.

Chance shakes his head slightly. "Anyway, all that to say it has been close on to six years since my wife left with my daughter. I saw my girl only once in all those years, soon after I quit the program the first time, just a few months after they were gone. I had heard from a buddy about this apartment they were living in and I went to see. It was Shanae's thirteenth birthday and she had girlfriends over, you know, doing nails and all that, and I banged on her window, drunk, and she told me she'd call the cops if I didn't disappear. There was already another man there with my wife." Chance stops to wipe the corner of his eye.

"What a chump. And I thought I was this great dad, wishing her happy birthday; remembering the day, for crying out loud. Anyway, I have written Shanae every month for years. I send them to my ex's grandmother who sends them on for me. I don't know what they think I'd do—pop in drunk again, I suppose, so we play this secret agent game and I don't complain. Got no right to complain.

"Over the years I got two letters from Shanae. One telling me to get lost and never write again, and one, a few months ago, telling me she was going to have a baby but her mother didn't know yet. Somehow that last one, even though my girl was only 18 and pregnant, gave me my first real hope. I've been writing a lot lately, trying to encourage her, you know? I wrote her recently, telling about this job. Thought maybe she was ashamed of me still in the program and would be less embarrassed to know I am out in the world again. Sent her my cell number and begged her to call someday.

"So late Saturday afternoon the girls are waiting tables, the soup is selling like nobody's business, I'm trying to call you to say don't worry about closing up and the phone starts beeping with a call. I was trying to rush and couldn't hear you at all. Ended up pushing the wrong button and losing the incoming call, too. Half hour later, same number. Turns out it's Shanae, calling again. It's my baby's voice! I haven't heard her in almost six years, and she's crying and saying she needs me. 'Daddy' she says, which just about kills me."

Chance stops to blow his nose, loudly, on an actual handkerchief. I didn't know anyone still used those things. Joe is nodding along. Oh, yeah, the old long-lost daughter story. Hears it all the time. Right. Joe is my curly-haired baby brother and we've spent our lives protecting him from this kind of story. He thought Angela left to go to college, for goodness sake. But maybe I'm a little mistaken about his naiveté. Joe is a pretty savvy entrepreneur, and of all the family, he's the one who had money to invest with us.

I watch Joe watch Chance as he continues his story, telling about this frantic phone call and his decision to rush to his daughter's aid.

"So," says Chance, "I've agreed to go help her. And all along I am thinking she still lives in the Denver area somewhere. I mean, I have looked twice at every black-haired teenage girl I've seen in the last six years, you know? 'Where are you, Shanae?' I ask. And she is like: 'Fresno, of course.' I say 'Fresno, California?!' and she laughs. 'Is there some other Fresno, Daddy?'

"And that second 'Daddy' just did me in. The waitresses were gone already so I finished the night's work, hid the money, and started driving. Left a real detailed message on your voicemail, put the note under the spoon rest, and so on. Got to the hospital just in time. There was my little girl."

Chance starts to sniffle. Shakes his head as if a mosquito is bothering him.

"My little Shanae. Brown skin shining, big black eyes batting back tears, and this basketball sticking out of her belly. She looked about twelve and I swear if I had seen the fellow who knocked her up I would have knocked him out. 'Course he's AWOL. And Shanae's mother, my ex—trying tough love, I guess, but a little too late. Kicked her out. Didn't even know she was in labor. Maybe for the first time in her life, my baby needed me. Her daddy. So I held her hand in the delivery room, and I did whatever the doctor told me to do, and I got my baby through it."

Chance stops to look at me. He swipes at a fly buzzing the back of his neck.

"This was Sunday morning through about Monday noon. If I had any idea what I was putting you through here…"

"Forget about it. Tell us about Shanae."

"She was a champion. She got 'er done. Birthed a bouncy baby boy!"

The room erupts in congratulations. Chance beams.

Cristian says, "Forgive me, but—your daughter is African American?"

"Her momma's from the Dominican Republic, town real close to Haiti, I guess. For her faults the woman is a real beauty. Anyway the whole time through labor I'm telling my Shanae these stories about Bailey, and about you people and this here Soup Line. I tell her about Timber being adopted and what a great mom you are, Lainey. And Cristian, she nearly punched me (well, actually she did punch me) about six in the evening when I started to describe your jambalaya. Guess she was getting kinda hungry. Anyway she wants to come. Wants to meet the legends, she says. And taste the soup."

"So?" asks Cristian. "Where is she?"

Chance coughs again. "She's still in the hospital. It was kinda hard on her, the whole having-a-baby thing. I was hoping to, uh, gather up some clothes—I didn't pack enough, I was so excited, I guess—and go out there to stay until she's doing better. She's so little, you know. It was an eight-pound baby. They say she'll be fine."

"She's not in real danger, is she?" I ask.

Chance's eyes are moist but clear. "No, I don't think so. They told me not. The baby, he's a strong little bugger, but they got him on this lamp thing every now and again to perk up his color a little." He nods out the window at Timber, who is making faces and smearing the glass. "Babies change, you know. My Shanae, she was almost white when she was born. Took a while to brown her up nice. I don't know nothing about Shanae's—about the baby's father."

"What did she name him?"

Chance grins. "Well, you know, I told her she could name him after her deadbeat dad: Chauncey Sherman Grant II. She says, 'You don't know nothing if you think I'd saddle a kid with a name like 'Second Chance!'"

"I don't know why, or where it comes from, but she called him 'Chase.' Says it's a nickname of an old friend, Charles. I have this secret hope that it's on account of being real close to 'Chance,' no matter what she says. Don't know what's up with names these days, but there was a baby in there named 'Dawg,' I kid you not. Anyway, 'Chase' seems to suit him."

Chance pauses, chokes. "If someone don't change it, that is."

He hides his tears behind the handkerchief and breathes in deep until they stop. "She can't do it, she's so young and she don't have no help." Cristian walks around the table to put a hand on Chance's shoulder.

"She's got to give it up. My little grandson…but it's good, right? He'll get a family like you folks and he'll be loved, like Timber there and, oh my God, I wish I was younger and could just take him myself, but what business do I have trying to raise another kid when I let my Shanae grow up without me? And I'm fifty-eight, man. Almost sixty. I got no business being Shanae's dad, to tell you the truth."

Chance coughs and rubs his hands from his forehead back over his shaved head. He looks over his shoulder and then leans in close and drops his voice a notch. "Time to 'fess up. I didn't really need to get more clothes. I just didn't want to ask this over the phone. Although, in retrospect, it might have saved me a night in the slammer!"

He blows his nose. Again, loudly, on that handkerchief. He looks up straight across the table and into my eyes and through my arteries and capillaries and into my innermost soul and whispers, "Don't you want another baby boy, Mrs. Clayson?"

Chapter Forty-one

TIMBER

Timber heard every word. Grownups never thought kids were listening, but they were. The stinky green stuff his father liked to add on top of potato soup was tickling Timber's nostril because that girl in the kitchen was a-chopping it up teensy tiny. He wiped the back of his hand across his upper lip, over the trace of surgery scar. Standing quiet and still for all those long moments, long talking times of Chance, things he didn't understand, waiting for this moment. The words he had been expecting. His very own prayer with its very own answer, made especially for Tall Timber James Clayson: baby boy. Baby brother. Tall Timber's supersonic ear was turned up loud as he stood at the kitchen entrance across the room from his mother. CHOP CHOP CHOP the knife in the kitchen. His mother's super powers might have dried up, but Timber's were just beginning. His secret wish was working. His brother was coming.

LAINEY

Getting struck by a thunderbolt was less of a shock. Cristian and I drive away from the restaurant in relative silence. Relative because Timber doesn't believe in total silence. He's driving a toy car across the back of my head rest. Vroom, vroom. And those sputtery spitty bad muffler noises he loves so much. My fingers spread across the fading bruise on my cheekbone, protecting and investigating a lingering tenderness. Wondering.

Cristian's eyes are fixed on the road ahead. We've passed our home and curve our way to Aspen Park. His usual casual one-handed steering has been replaced with a driving instructor's dream of a tight three-and-nine o'clock position. His knuckles glow white.

"All of it," he is whispering, "all of it."

Huh? Nothing. He didn't say anything.

I pat the cashbox on the seat between us. We are making the day's deposit. Chance and the two girls are working meanwhile. Chance will stay through closing tonight and drive back to his Shanae in the early hours of the morning. Wait until they release her, and try to bring her with him. Get her back on her feet. Maybe she could waitress a little in the meantime. But the baby...

So she stays there, if her mother will let her back home. Choosing an agency. Choosing a family. Meeting them; passing off the baby. It's that, or she signs a blank check and the baby hits a receiving home in Fresno and somewhere down the road a family comes along. Little Chase becomes a ward of the State of California. Hopefully gets adopted by somebody. Anybody? It's an option Chance doesn't want to think about. Me and Cristian taking the infant, that's an option he does like. For that matter, he had said, he'd rather see the baby enter the system here—call it a Coloradoan's prejudice, he said, but he'd just feel safer about Chase's chances.

We told Chance to just go and see his daughter. Probably holding a baby makes it too hard. Maybe trying to nurse him these first few hours makes an unbreakable bond. By now she probably wants to keep him herself. Could be that Shanae's mother has shown up. Wants to be a grandma-mom. Just because she and Shanae's current stepdad have small children of their own doesn't necessarily mean they have no place for another baby. We really aren't in the picture yet, even if we'd had time to digest the offer, which we haven't. The taste of it, however, is on my tongue.

Cristian slides the gear stick into park and it strikes me that Timber has been getting himself in and out of the car alone lately, snapping his seatbelt without being told. Progress seems so slow, but the boy really is growing. Learning. Getting older. What would it be like to suddenly throw a baby in the mix? A real baby; the infant kind that can do nothing to meet its own basic needs? The kind that doesn't sleep at night?

And a deep pressure radiates outward from my nipples. The physicality of the sensation shocks me. What does this body know of having babies? And yet it's almost a pregnancy feeling I sense, I think. Some part of me wants another child. How deep is that part? How strong is the desire? Cristian puts his right hand in the small of my back, helping me hobble, while he balances the cash box. I've given up on the pinching crutches and already can use my heel without pain. Those toes are what mostly still hurt.

"Here, Timber. Take this. Hold the door for me and Mom, okay?" He leans in to whisper. "You would be good. With another one."

"You mean a baby? The baby?" But we are in the bank now so I get quiet. What is going on with Timber and Chance and now Cristian? Take a baby. Get a dog! You don't just wake up one day, and learn that your employee who stole everything actually didn't but wants to give you his grandson like some sort of birthday present.

Chance was adamant about one thing. Shanae swears she hasn't had a drop to drink. Ever. She saw her dad, the drunk, and decided to play her own cards differently.

One less thing to worry about. One huge elephant of a thing not to worry about.

The bank teller, who saw Cristian at church last week while I was at home hopped up on painkillers, knows about the restaurant problem and is delighted to hear a condensed version of what has been happening since the non-theft. I still can't believe this has all happened in less than a week.

"Mister Chance maked mine baby brother," states Timber, to the teller's shock. How did he even hear that? Wasn't he safely playing outside by the new fence?

"Now, honey. Long story," and we spin our son away from the counter and take our leave quickly, stupid smiles pasted on our faces.

A second deposit is made! Tonight I might actually enjoy doing the books again. I haven't caught them up since the Big One was found and Cristian ran it down, still cold, to the bank. It will be great to punch the numbers and see the losses flip back on themselves.

Skin tingles. The harder I focus on something else, the more my mind goes back to two words: a baby. A baby. A baby. A baby. I am furious with myself for getting carried away. For even daring to harbor a thought. The odds that this girl will go through with an adoption are slim enough. Let alone choose complete strangers unless she just goes through the system, and that would be easier to do there, in California. We just started a restaurant, for crying out loud. Timber has a basketful of issues and disabilities. I'm no good at stress.

"Let's not talk about it," pleads Cristian, before I open my mouth. "Let's just…not talk about it. Yet."

Chapter Forty-two

We don't talk about it. Friday rolls agonizingly into Saturday. We are on shift for dinner when Chance's old pickup comes into view in Soup Line's side window. Chance? Already? What can it mean? I bump a waiter, causing her to splash a little soup on the floor. By the time I get to the mop closet, Chance is holding the front door open for a pretty young girl. His daughter. She doesn't have a baby as she makes her way, head tucked down, in a beeline for the bathroom. Chance lets the door shut and turns slowly. He holds the baby.

"Cristian," I gasp. "Chance is here."

And he turns, sees the girl running for the toilet and his eyes focus farther back. He smiles at Chance and then he sees the baby, too. Wipes his hands on a towel and hangs his apron. Walks out of the kitchen, touches me, and moves toward Chance. Calm. Collected.

Tiny sprigs of black hair pop up all over the baby's head like a garden just sprouting. He is tiny and delicate and perfect. I blink and inhale quickly. Something important. And I know what it is. This baby looks exactly like Cristian's only baby picture. His sculpted lips open and his eyes close.

"So," croaks Cristian. "She is keeping him, huh?"

"Oh, no," whispers Chance. "She wanted to meet you. She wanted to see Timber. And if you say no, she said she'd still rather give him up to the Colorado foster system than California's. I'm trying to get her to nurse him some. For immunity and all, but she doesn't like it and he's mostly doing these bottles." And Chance balances the baby in the crook of his arm while tipping a bottle high. It makes his sleeve go up, revealing a dragon tattoo I hadn't seen yet. The milk is spilling.

"Doggone it. I don't know what I am doing here," he complains. Cristian reaches over, takes the baby, sits in the upholstered chair stuffed in the corner, and expertly gives the baby the bottle.

"Name still Chase?" He asks.

"Yup. You make me look bad, man. I don't think I ever gave Shanae a bottle. I was the worst father. Too macho for bottles and diapers. No wonder my wife took off when she could. I've been propping those things up next to him while we drive. Shanae said she don't think he needs to drink all the time, but she doesn't have any more idea than me. He needs a home, fast."

I am staring again at a tiny perfect face. Cliché rosebud lips grasp the nipple and tiny fingers with nails too long curl around Cristian's fingers. Insanely long lashes surround his eyes, still slightly blue, open and focusing in and out. Timber slams open the main door and runs to my side.

"Aww! Cute! Teeny weeny baby, Mommy! Him look like baby Daddy!"

Timber looks to me for permission, before gingerly touching his fuzzy hair. The curl is tightest close to his scalp.

"It gots black Africa hair like Daddy. I got Mom hairs and my brother gots Dad's."

I open my mouth to correct his grammar and his false assertions, but Cristian shakes his head. He smooths a drip from the baby's cheek. He looks at the window and I know what he's looking for. We hear it on the roof, first. Ping, ping. It's the first few drops of a nice late summer rain.

TIMBER

The first day Timber held his baby brother Chase it was raining. The baby was still breakable so the grownups wouldn't let Timber walk to the window to show Chase what rain was even though he wanted to because since Chase was new to earth he'd wonder about water falling from the sky. Might even think his big brother was squirting him with a turkey baster or bath-toy whale like when Timber and Daddy played water war when Mom was gone. But the baby was so new he'd never seen those things so maybe he wouldn't think that after all.

Timber sat in the fancy chair they brought for Mom because of falling in the creek and breaking her toes and his arm rested up on the chair's arm and the little tiny curly black head laid right there inside his elbow and felt warm and soft like a puppy. Its eyes were soft like a dog's too but not seeing very good, Timber thought. This baby brother person was the best thing Timber had ever held. He would have given a thousand Happy Rabbits to have this brother. Mother whispering we don't know yet, Timber. Don't call him Brother yet, but Timber knew different. Knew it deeper than he knew anything.

Tall Timber closed his eyes and grew large and filled then exploded the room around lifting face up to the sun and smiling broad enough to swallow the mountain. All this for to say THANK YOU to the boy on the tree who knew Timber deepest and said he would be good, could be a great big brother.

Shrunk back to boy size Timber rocked the baby. He saw the girl who was blackish like Daddy leaning against the window and watching hummingbirds feed under the eaves while the rain fell softly behind them. She was Timber's brother's mother somehow, even though she was just a girl. Maybe she was Timber's mother too but he asked and Mommy who was sitting beside him, arm around both Timber and the baby, said no. Whispering. Even though they didn't know who was the woman with the Tall Timber jacket? No, because Shanae never had another baby and anyway she was just a little girl when Timber was born.

Was Timber's mother as pretty as Shanae? Well, Timber was handsome so she must have been very pretty, as well. And Timber saw that the girl Shanae did not want to hold his brother and she did not like to look at him much but she cried a little when she looked away. He also saw that his own mom and dad only wanted to look at the baby and smiled not cried when they did and they loved him already like Timber even though they didn't know him yet and weren't the ones praying secret prayers and he knew that all the stories were true, that Mommy and Daddy loved him most of everyone in the whole world and he was glad that he was theirs and that his brother, too, could be theirs.

Did they know it yet? Did everyone know that this was all forever?

LAINEY

Of course we don't want Shanae and the baby sleeping in that draughty, dusty bunkhouse of Chance's, so we bring them home with us. Timber is too hyper to sleep, so we let him roll around in bed with his favorite toy cars, crashing and squealing brakes as quietly as he knows how. He stage whispers a monologue about how he's driving one and his brother has borrowed the other one from him, because he is rich and has a gazillion anyway.

Brother. His brother.

Shanae is tired, wounded. She's a beautiful girl, it is true. But she keeps her eyes mostly averted and her cheeks seem inflamed. I don't know if it's from giving birth or shyness around strangers. It's neither. It's guilt.

"You must think I'm the worst person in the world," she finally whispers, leaning over the arm of the couch as far away from the baby as she can get and still be in our living room area. He's still in the car seat in which Cristian carried him. Sleeping. Soft pops from those rose bud lips as he breathes out. I want to take him out. I want to undress him and look at every millimeter of his tiny body. Bathe him, feed him, touch him! I wait.

We shake our heads, slightly, but don't verbalize an answer.

"I know my dad wants you to do this."

"Shanae. This is your decision. It's not about your dad or us—"

"Sorry. I don't want to interrupt. But. I want you to know everything. Before you, you know, get attached." Her eyes rise for a brief moment and her irises are overflowing with a depth of grief I've never seen before. They flit almost imperceptibly to the car seat and then back to the hands she wrings in her lap.

"He looks like a good baby. I think he is. I think he is going to be okay. I, I named him 'Chase' because my boyfriend was a really good guy. His name was 'Charles' and he treated me nice. I thought, maybe the baby could be like him if I gave him that name. He once said his mother never let him have a nickname, but that's what he wanted to be called." It's hard to make out everything she's saying, as Shanae talks about this guy, past tense. His accomplishments in music and sports, his tenderness and care. A real jerk, I think. He must have dumped her after he knocked her up.

"Charles died last April in a car crash," she cries, shutting down my internal criticism. Oh.

"Did he know about his son?" asks Cristian, gently.

Shanae turns a tortured face toward the baby for the first time. Gets up, walks up to the carrier with tears streaming down her face. Her arms are wrapped tight against her body, fingers digging into her arms while she holds herself together. Is she straining under a desire to pick him up or kick him?

"This is not his son," she states. "If it were, I might, I might be able to do it. Or even if he were still alive maybe. But I can't. I know it's not the baby's fault…but I can't." Shanae turns away and walks woodenly to the kitchen counter. Timber's noises have died out, and I see with relief that he's fast asleep. I should go to her. Rub her shoulders. This young girl is hurting. But she'd just throw her baby to us? Because it was from a lover other than the preferred dead one? Or what? I struggle to understand. Wrap my head around her. Then she cries out, a loud, wrenching groan and I do go, hopping without the crutch, to stand awkwardly beside her.

"We never did it!" she chokes. Composes. Almost like a shadow descends over her face. She's talking about someone else now, survival-mode.

"Charles wasn't like that; we wanted to wait. It was an…older man… he pushed me into his car…"

The horror hits me and I almost fall but for Cristian, who some-how holds us both up, and we get back to the couch and I'm saying, "Sorry, sorry," and petting her pretty hands. She should be crying. Rivers of tears should wash down her cheeks. Shanae's stoicism scares me more than her confession. How could any girl survive this with her heart intact?

"Don't tell my dad, please! Or anyone! You have to promise or I can't give him to you. I just, I just couldn't let you take the baby without knowing. I know it isn't his fault. He's just a baby. He de-serves to be nursed and loved and all that, but. But he isn't Charles's son. If only he were Charles's son, I would have something."

At the sound of Shanae's pleading voice Chase has awoken. His huge eyes blink slowly, face twists into an impassioned cry. I have to take him up and I do. He quiets immediately and nestles against me, rooting about with open mouth. Cristian puts the bottle in my hand and I sit, rocking and nursing, while Cristian speaks softly with our baby's mother. And I know it as a truth. He is our baby. Despite an evil father. Genetics aside, there is not a trace of hatred in this small body, this tiny new being who has been dropped in my lap. I'm locked on these milky orbs, drowning in them. Such pain! Could something this beautiful really be the result of the awful crime of a horrible man?

"I don't know," Cristian mumbles. "Shouldn't we tell? The guy should be behind bars! What if he does it again?" Chase is done mouthing the bottle and Cristian reaches to take him from me.

Shanae pleads and we waver and finally she tells more. We sit, stunned at her story. She knows the guy, and her mother knows too. Her mother has forbidden the truth. Promised to disown and disavow. Denial.

Cristian's mind is making the same circles mine is, I think, because he says, "Shanae. My father was just as bad to my mother as this child's. We're more than genetics, we humans.

"I feel," looking at me, wide-eyed, for confirmation, "we feel, that this baby is an amazing gift. Like we just won the lottery for the second time. Like we were chosen by God, and I want to be faithful to the task."

"Just please don't tell my dad, please, no," rocking now, almost, and I think she should have a blanket and so I wrap her up.

"What should we say," said gently.

"Just pretend he was Charles's. I don't want to ruin his reputation, since he was so good and wouldn't do this, but my dad never met him or anything. He would have understood. Just, just say it was Charles's baby and it will be okay. I'm going to So Cal in a couple of weeks. Nothing's changed, right? I can still go on with my life, I did the right thing, right? I didn't ever even think about you know, killing it. I even tried to nurse a little 'cause Dad said I should. But I can't...I just don't want to hold it again. Please. After tonight can I stay with my dad until I leave? I'll sign anything. Do whatever, but...it's easier, right?"

A second baby, dropped from the sky by a nervous stork. Into our cabin, into our laps. Too good to be true? Sure. Maybe most blessings are. Quietly we slip up the ladder, Cristian cradling the bundled baby and then me handing up the carrier with diapers and bottles and then myself, one step at a time, weight placed carefully on the rungs. Foot healing, getting stronger.

A gray camp robber jay has chased off all the anonymous fat brown birds and is strutting his stuff. Someone must have had cold feet last night because there is a faint smell of chimney smoke drifting up the valley. The boys are asleep still, just as Vanji had been before I woke her up to tell about Chance's grandson. My timing sucked. Vanji's reaction sucked. I feel a weight in my gut. A golden aspen leaf, my first of the new autumn, skitters across the porch and the phone rings.

"You hung up on me! You've never hung up on me!" She's right. When I told her about Chase she made an ugly comment about how our kids' names would sound like an expensive housing development. I was pissed, so I hung up.

"Must have gotten disconnected." I pick up the golden leaf and twirl it as she speaks.

"You are a lying sack of...potato flakes. Nasty freeze-dried plastic-tasting potato flakes. And, Lainey, I am a jerk. Or worse. I shouldn't have made fun of the baby's name. I am just like totally shocked and unprepared to think of you adopting again. We had like a year when you saw Timber on the news and then did all those classes and all that work before you finally got him."

"How do you think we feel, Vanj?! We're totally swept off our feet by this thing."

"Do you think—now don't get mad again—that he'll have problems, too? Like from her drinking or drugs or something?"

"No."

"Well, that's a relief, huh?"

"Yeah. I don't want to get into it now, but his dad is, well, a major jerk. Criminal, even." My voice stays low to keep this conversation private, even from the birds. They have continued singing so I must be doing okay.

"Lainey, Cristian believes his own father raped our mother. Can't be any worse than that, can it?" I suck in my breath, and she has her answer. "Oh, honey, I'm sorry. Sorry for that girl, too. But you know, could you find a better example of something evil being turned to good? Like that sermon at your church, remember?" I don't, but she's been more affected by the preacher than I have. My divine inspiration seems to come from the mouth of Celia or my son Timber. My sons, Timber and Chase. Saying it to myself makes me feel full, like hot air is expanding inside me and I'm growing bigger. Pregnant with possibility. Like I'm a rich woman with an immense inheritance. The Timber Chase Ranch. Maybe we should post a sign in the driveway.

"Hey Vanj, I better get moving, I guess. And let you get back to sleep maybe."

"Sure. Now that I'm totally conscious. It's too early. I wasn't anywhere close to awake when you called first, Lainey. I'm so sorry. I mean, a baby. Damn. That is huge. It is huge and wonderful. Will you forgive me?"

"Vanji, it's just so out of the blue, you know. We seriously talked about other kids a couple years ago, but Timber is so hands-on. I couldn't see us juggling two. Maybe I still can't. Maybe it's still just an idea, that's all."

"Lainey. If there is a baby sleeping in your house, this is more than just an idea. And didn't you say Chance's daughter is there?"

She's right. There is a baby sleeping in my house. I momentarily forgot. We put the baby in his car seat beside our bed and took turns last night. At least, I guess we did. I only had one turn; changed a diaper and gave a bottle at about one in the morning. It's going on seven now, I see from the phone. Shoot! I did call Vanji early.

"Are you sure she'll really give him up? Not change her mind once you get attached?"

"Shanae doesn't want to see him anymore; she just wants to sign him away. She's supposed to go start college in a few days! She took care of herself and had this baby, but now she just wants to move on, she says."

"Harsh! Then again, if the father…"

"Maybe. Maybe realistic. But in the meantime." In the meantime, it's too late.

"I just have to get used to the idea, Lainey. I mean, hell, a baby?! Timber is so great, but energy times twenty. I can't even imagine having my own kid 24/7, let alone two!"

If I can mother one, why not two? "We are already in love, Van-ji. He looks just like your brother. It's like Cristian and I produced him ourselves. He's so quiet." But he isn't quiet now. Newborn cries reach me all the way out here, but that's because our upstairs vent window is still cracked.

"Gotta go, double-sis," I say. "I am sorry and I forgive you, now go back to sleep."

Cristian has already done the diaper duty when I pull myself up the ladder. Timber and Shanae are still asleep. Cristian is apologetic. He was supposed to take turns, too. But there were no other awake times. A few days old and this kid slept almost six hours in a row. God knows we need our sleep! I am loving this baby. Chase works the bottle and blinks up at me with these huge wise eyes, twisting his fingers around mine. He needs these nails cut, and a bath thanks to Chance's bottle propping and a day's worth of spilled formula.

"It'll be hardest for you," Cristian says. "You wouldn't be as much a part of Soup Line as we wanted. We'll always have to have Chance, or someone like him, to help me run the place. You'll be stuck going home early to put the boys to bed and stuff."

"I already decided to put motherhood first, remember? We'd just have to stop thinking of me as a viable worker anymore, at least not until they're both in school. I mean, I would still hang out at Soup Line as much as possible, but I'd have to put the kids first. Do the books and stuff here."

Will it be awkward with Chance? A constant reminder of his missing daughter? But they have a relationship now. She is no longer his little lost sheep, and he has graduated from deadbeat dad. He already loves Timber, and says he wouldn't play favorites.

I sigh. "We'll be going to special conferences at school forever. And we will have to borrow somehow to build on that extra room. We have to have an extra room."

"And maybe this calm right now is a total fake out and he is going to be a wild child."

"Maybe he will be wilder than Timber. Or difficult in some other way...violent?"

Cristian traces a curlicue above Chase's ear. "A wuss? A nerd who gets picked on all the time? An evil genius...?"

"Oh no! Maybe he'll be a chef like you."

Chase's attention shifts from my eyes to Cristian's. His fingers curl and uncurl as he suckles the bottle. He is so perfect; this tiny human boy. Like Timber, like me, even, he is full of potential. An amazing gift. He followed me home. Can I keep him?

There is a sneeze downstairs. I slide off of the bed and look over the banister. Shanae stretches to her toes, hands on hips, yawning up at me. She stands in silhouette in front of the living room window. Around her head a halo of springy curls. Inside that shape of girl, though, is something more. A good but broken heart. Behind her I see a clear, blue sky with one puffy cloud.

Sometimes we find an energy we never knew existed. Lightning sometimes does strike twice. Here I am. Wake up. Look around. Maybe you really do have super powers, Lainey Clayson.

"Good morning, Mrs. Clayson," says Shanae. "Are you going to keep the baby?"

"Shanae," I answer, "I think your baby has decided to keep us."

TIMBER

And the story might have come to an end, if someone had said happy forever after and the pictures stopped and the music got loud. But Timber looked at Chase whose big eyes only opened bigger when he saw his brother and the door shut because the brother's mother went outside to live somewhere else. Be something else not Chase's mommy, because Timber's mommy would be Chase's mommy now. And Timber knew that something small or maybe big broke inside that baby because the girl was gone and the world had different sounds now, voice of a brother playing cars too loud, jaybirds squawking in the pine trees. Scents of those trees, too, and all the crumbly plants the baby's new dad liked to put into the things he cooked. Taste of milk in a bottle not booby-juice like Sally drank on account of having her birth mother keep her for her own. Would that be a different thing as well? Timber expected so. Feeling that little break or tear in the tiny heart, Timber leaned in close to tell him a secret. This is a better story, he said. This is a different story but it's better because it's ours.

This story was getting another beginning. Timber's family chose itself bigger and nothing would ever be the same.

-end-

About the Author

Joy has spent time in several countries. She and her husband of 26 years, Cliff, have two daughters by birth and one son by adoption. She's a graduate of Goshen College, and winner of the 2012 Fiction Award from the San Miguel de Allende Writers Conference. "Raising Timber" draws from her family's experience with Fetal Alcohol Exposure. Joy wrote and edited this novel at the dinette table of her '59 canned ham trailer while living in Oaxaca, Mexico. Now that they reside in the Colorado mountains, she misses riding her motorcycle on the cobblestone streets.

Learn more at joymccalister@wordpress.com and connect with Joy on Facebook.

If you like this book

Please spread the word. Leave a reader review and tell your friends about it.

CPSIA information can be obtained
at www.ICGtesting.com
Printed in the USA
LVHW04s1511120918
589921LV00011B/746/P